GOOD MORNING AFGHANISTAN

BASED ON A TRUE STORY

WASEEM MAHMOOD OBE

Dear Murad
hope you enjoy
reading about
my adventures

eye books

Challenging
the way
we see things

Published by
Eye Books Ltd
29 Barrow Street
Much Wenlock
Shropshire
TF13 6EN

www.eye-books.com

First published in Great Britain in 2007
Reprinted 2008
First Eye Classics edition in 2016
Copyright c Waseem Mahmood

British Library Cataloguing in Publication Data
A catalogue record for this book is available from the
British Library

Printed by CPI Group (UK) Ltd, Croydon CR0 4YY
ISBN: 978-1785630248

DEDICATION

For Khurrum and Khaiyyam,
Believe in the power of your dreams.
For Farah and John,
Who believed in the power of mine.

For Charles, Barry, Ramin, Bent, Ralph, Colleen, Rachel,
and all the rest of the 'Good Morning Afghanistan' team
who shared the adventure.

And for my father,
I do not think of you as gone;
You are with me still
In each and every new dawn

PROLOGUE

DUBAI 2016

Initially, I was to have been writing this update for the new edition of *Good Morning Afghanistan* in Kabul. The idea was that I was going back to work there again after ten years and would be able to offer a fresh personal perspective on how the situation had changed in the intervening years and where Afghanistan was as a country after the withdrawal of Allied forces. I would see how the country had moved on and where the Good Morning Afghanistan project and people were now.

Alas on 20th January a vehicle carrying staff from the media organisation I was to have been working with was attacked and seven colleagues were killed. All expats working for the organisation were evacuated and it was deemed too much of a security risk for me to go back. Ironically the fact that I sit in Dubai writing this update says virtually all there is to say about the current situation in Kabul. Never in the five years that I worked on various projects in Afghanistan was it ever seen as too much of a security risk for me to physically visit the country. I was able to go into Afghanistan easily and move around pretty freely without that many restrictions. Movement for the expat community in Kabul now is severely restricted due to major security concerns in the city with many confined to their compounds and offices as I would have been if I had managed to get there. Also in the time I was in Kabul never were media outlets or media personnel seen as targets for the insurgents. Both these points say a lot about where the Afghanistan is as a country fifteen years after the Taliban were driven out. On the plus side, several international airlines now offer flights to Kabul airport including a daily Emirates flight making Afghanistan a lot more accessible to a lot more people. The country is doing its best to present a semblance of normality. The media company I work for recently ran a national campaign in Afghanistan for the energy drink, Red Bull. A recent party invite in Kabul included the following line: "Please note that a cloakroom will be available for your coats and bulletproof vests", which in my opinion best sums up today's Afghanistan.

The European Commission funded the Good Morning Afghanistan project for a further two years after I left. After that Manocher and Jamshed continued to produce GMA subsidising its production from other communication projects that they managed to get from the donor community. The political clout that GMA had garnered was worth cultivating even as a loss leader for the Manocher and Jamshed. GMA provided them with a brand that was recognisable both with the public at large and within the political fraternity whom the programme was now beginning to hold accountable. GMA remained on air for nearly ten years till 2012 when financial sustainability became untenable. Both Manocher and Jamshed have subsequently dissolved their business partnership and gone their separate ways. Manocher to pursue politics and civil society activity and Jamshed keen to study abroad.

Others in the team have gone on join other media in Afghanistan which has flourished since we started GMA. Karim the young boy is studying in London and Shakeela in Turkey both grown up and wanting to work in Afghanistan once they complete their studies.

Waseem Mahmood

PART 1

'Only a few more days, my love, a few days more.
Here in the shadows of oppression condemned to breathe,
Still for a while we must suffer, and weep, and endure
What our forefathers, not our faults bequeath.'
Faiz Ahmed Faiz

'We consider this our duty – to defend humanity against
the scourge of intolerance, violence, and fanaticism.'
Ahmed Shah Massoud

NORTH AFGHANISTAN – SEPTEMBER 9TH 2001

The Shamal, a mystical wind that inhabits the stark arid landscapes of Afghanistan, had begun to blow, whipping up plumes of dry sun-baked dust as it started its annual, almost regal, sojourn across the much divided country. Many Afghans believe to this day that the Shamal holds magical powers, and across the land poets and romantics venerate it with an almost religious passion. For the poet, the wind rustling the leaves on the trees is the true voice of God Himself, communicating with mankind in a language that we lesser mortals cannot yet understand. To young Afghan lovers, the Shamal is the whisper of stolen early morning kisses before they disappear separately into the hazy abyss of the impending dawn.

For most Afghans, however, the Shamal holds a far more mundane significance: the breeze brings them blessed relief from the sweltering heat that for most of the year turns the country into a large clay oven, where all who dare to be out in the open get well and truly roasted.

This year, the Shamal, possibly the only certainty remaining in Afghan life and usually as punctual as the Swiss Railway system, had deceived the Afghans by arriving several weeks earlier than usual. Some Afghans were surprised, some took it as a sign of yet more impending doom for their already battered nation, but in reality, the truth be told, the majority of Afghans just didn't care.

Unlike tornados, which can spiral upwards several hundred feet, the Shamal remains firmly at ground level, resembling the dust thrown up by the hooves of a galloping horse. Rising out of nowhere as if by magic in the dust plains of Northern Afghanistan, when it reaches a size approximating that of an army of several thousand horsemen, it begins a relentless charge across the country. And like any advancing force, the Shamal marches forward during the day only, using the nights to rest. This invisible cavalry force can take several weeks to complete its journey, and then it vanishes as quickly and mysteriously as it arrived. The pious amongst the Afghans swear that the Shamal is a militia of benevolent angel horsemen galloping across Afghanistan to survey the battlefields before some final heavenly vengeance.

The Commander looked every inch the international statesman that he had grudgingly been forced into becoming. Even dressed in well-worn battle fatigues and standing in a mud hut in the middle of a small village in the inhospitable mountainous North of Afghanistan, he exuded the unmistakeable aura of a born leader. Massoud Ahmad Shah was the charismatic chief of the Northern Alliance, likened by many in the West to a latter-day Che Guevara. His presence and stature alone demanded respect. By any standards he was a good-looking man, with sharp features, and he spoke eloquently. His face, both resolute and yet somehow dreamy at the same time, represented the dichotomy that had begun to epitomise Massoud. Journalists who interviewed him found it impossible not to be captivated by the 'Massoud charm' when he spoke, even though they did not understand a word of what he said.

The story of how the son of a Police Commander from Jangalak in the Panjsher Valley had forged an almost unbeatable army from a small band of fugitives living on wild mulberries was already the stuff of legends. The heavy losses that his crudely equipped troops, armed with just ten Kalashnikov AK47 machine guns and two rocket launchers, had inflicted on the invincible Red Army had earned him a standing as one of the greatest guerrilla commanders ever.

But now, after two decades of almost continuous conflict, the Commander was showing signs of fatigue. He was feeling less the sly, belligerent predator and more and more the cornered prey. His once sharp brown eyes looked weary, and strands of grey now speckled his thick black hair. This man who went to college to become an architect and create beautiful buildings had inadvertently ended up as his country's last hope of salvation, and the heavy burden was now starting to show.

Standing at the window crudely hewn in the mud brick wall, Massoud looked out at the nomadic village that stretched down into the rocky gorge below his hut. The heavy hemp cloth hastily pressed into service as a curtain flapped in the light breeze. The village, Khawaja Bahauddin, looked like the rest of Afghanistan: downtrodden and soiled, beaten by almost two decades of successive conflicts into submissive oblivion. The dilapidated buildings resembled rotting teeth in the receding gums of streets littered with war debris. Each wall left standing in the village was blemished with pockmarks representing virtually every calibre of ammunition known to man. Windows barely hanging from frames clattered in the wind. Ceilings were propped up on floors and pools of undeterminable slime covered the ground. The roads were strewn with the paraphernalia of war; rotting Russian tanks sat outside the perimeter of the village, soldiers patrolled the streets in a concoction of cannibalised vehicles with an equally cannibalised arsenal of weapons, Kalashnikovs and RPGs cradled in their arms, young faces smiling nervously. Hastily-constructed gun ramparts housing field artillery and anti-aircraft munitions haphazardly dotted the village. And everything was coated in a thin layer of brown dirt.

Down by the riverbank several young fighters sat cleaning their rifles, while others nearby were loading up an abandoned Soviet truck with crates of ammunition. All were wearing snow parkas with blankets thrown over their shoulders, some had old Soviet army pants, and several were without shoes. Above them vapour trails of Taliban MiG jets criss-crossed the clear blue skies. In the distance, the dull thuds of artillery exchanges provided a stark reminder that Afghanistan's problems were far from over, for fighting had once again enveloped Afghanistan and with it had come all the ingredients of Afghan warfare: brutality, greed, starvation, and poverty. To Afghans, this was nothing new; the cycle of invasion, war, bribery, liberation and subjugation had been a part of Afghan history for centuries – only the cast of players kept changing. The Greeks, the Romans, Alexander the Great, Genghis Khan, the Moguls – all at one time or another had laid waste vast areas of Afghanistan, killing countless people in the process.

Khawaja Bahauddin was a strange place, by any stretch of the imagination. For almost a year now it had been the unlikely capital of Afghanistan. As they had settled in for the long haul, Massoud's Mujahideen had begun to commandeer the ramshackle huts in the village and to rename them – Ministry of the Interior, Ministry of Education, Ministry of Foreign affairs, each with its own Minister, accompanying bureaucracy and assorted hangers-on. Villagers who had been simple farmers until a year ago had now become 'government officials', full of self-importance and an assumed air of arrogance that they felt a necessary prerequisite for the positions they now held. Some of the buildings supported satellite dishes pointing up somewhat expectantly at the western skies hoping perhaps to catch some good news. There wasn't any, and more often than not neither was there any electricity.

With the Taliban regime in Kabul not officially recognised by the rest of the world, Massoud and his rag-tag entourage had become, in the eyes of the West, the legitimate government of Afghanistan. Thus the village attracted various foreign diplomats and dignitaries intent on meeting with the 'Afghan Government'.

Massoud closed his eyes and began to drink in the hot wind. 'The Shamal, Khalili. The winds of freedom begin to blow. I wonder, will they bring peace to our land this year?'

'If Allah wills it then it will be so, Commander.'

Massoud Khalili was the Commander's most trusted and loyal friend. Having known each other from childhood, they had fought side by side and thus had that rare bond that could only have been forged on the battlefield. Like Massoud, Khalili was in his forties, smart, cheerful, and ready-witted. Both sported beards, not unruly like the Taliban dictated, but stylishly trimmed. Khalili sat on the gaily-coloured sofa, his green and brown fatigues clashing with the multicoloured soft furnishings.

Both had arrived back in Khawaja Bahauddin by helicopter the previous evening. Massoud had uncharacteristically summoned Khalili, the Northern Alliance's Ambassador to India, back to Afghanistan and had flown across the border into friendly Tajikistan to receive his old comrade.

'Just listen to the wind, Khalili. Trust me, God has sent the Shamal early this year to sweep our land clean...'

Khalili nodded pensively. Of the two he was the pragmatist, and this, when combined with Massoud's philosophical outlook and growing political savoir-faire, made them a formidable team.

'This is a sign, my friend. I see a new dawn for our country. No more divisions.' Massoud continued looking out over the valley, surveying the frantic military activity taking place outside. 'I see a future where we will all be Afghans first – not Tajiks, Pashtoons, Sunnis, Shias,.' He turned to face Khalili. 'What we have started will end only in one way – the destruction of the Taliban – and we will do that with or without the West. It may take us a month or it may take a year, even longer. But ultimately, mark my words, we shall prevail.'

What had set Massoud apart from the other Mujahideen leaders and proved much more deadly than the limited archaic firepower available to him was his use of revolutionary tactics which he unashamedly borrowed from successful twentieth-century people's uprisings: the ideas of Mao, Tito, Lenin, Castro and Ho Chi Minh formed the cornerstone of his strategy. And the intellectual arsenal had proved to be deadly. Massoud had carefully adapted predominately Communist tactics and ideas that would appeal to the rigid Islamic-based Afghan mindset to rally the rural peasants to revolt. So successful was he, that in less than two decades he had played a major role in the ousting of both the Afghan dictator, Muhammad Daoud, as well as the powerful Red Army of the Soviet Union. And now he had set his sights set on ridding his country of the biggest scourge of all, the Taliban.

The two Moroccan journalists sat on the edge of the *charpai*, a wooden bed strung with course string, and watched as the Shamal blew around them like a whirling

Sufi dervish, kicking up intricate swirls of dust in some feverish dance. After a long, mind-numbing week in the dusty village of Khawaja Bahauddin, they sat riveted by this, the most humdrum yet compelling of spectacles.

They made a strange couple to onlookers. Karim Touzani, the journalist, was a big, bespectacled, serious-looking guy who was often lost in his own world, paying no attention to anything going on around him. Kassim Bakkali, his cameraman, was an ex-boxing champion who, even to the uninitiated villagers, looked very ill at ease handling the television camera. He was often seen fiddling with the equipment whilst consulting the instruction manual.

Touzani and Bakkali behaved nothing like the numerous other film crews and reporters who frequently made the trip to the village. They had spent several tortuous days travelling by road through Taliban-held Afghanistan, crossing the front line on foot. Though not many voiced their opinion, this had struck people in the village as odd. Why risk life and limb crossing a battlefield where ferocious fighting was still taking place, when it would have been much safer and easier to take the special United Nations flight into the region as all other journalists who visited Khawaja Bahauddin had done. And whereas other crews with tight budgets and even tighter deadlines would have been long gone, the two Africans just sat there waiting, day in day out, for the opportunity to interview Massoud. They were unperturbed when Massoud, who was not keen on the interview, kept repeatedly cancelling appointments arranged for him by his aides.

The austere building of the European Parliament in Strasbourg appeared to physically reverberate with the thunderous standing ovation afforded to the Mujahideen leader.

'We consider this our duty – to defend humanity against the scourge of intolerance, violence and fanaticism. We will build a democratic Islam in which the rights of all citizens,

men and women, are protected and in which all are free to determine their political leadership by ballots, not bullets.'

There was more rapturous applause and another standing ovation that lasted several more minutes. Massoud struggled to make himself heard above the uproar.

'The international community must support us in our struggle. If the West does not help us eliminate al-Qaeda, if they do not help us rid our land of those terrorists who have invaded it, there will be a tragedy, a horror visited on you that is beyond comprehension or endurance. Help us, and in doing that, help yourselves.'

Ahmed Shah Massoud, the fearless warrior, had one all-consuming passion, his love of Persian poetry. Even in the thick of battle he tried to read poetry every day. Love of poetry is not something that one usually expects from an Afghan Mujahideen leader but then Commander Massoud was not an archetypical Mujahideen. He had extensive libraries both at his home and in his office. Massoud tried hard to understand the Western mind instead of condemning it like the Taliban. His vision of Afghanistan was one that would fuse the best of the West with the ancient traditions of Afghan life, an inconceivable thought for the ruling Taliban regime which was intent on purging the country of anything remotely connected with the West.

The previous evening, as the sun had sunk behind the mountains leaving the landscape bathed in a deep hue of red as if all the blood shed by a million dead Afghans was spilling from the skies at that very instant, Massoud had settled down with Khalili to discuss their favourite subject, poetry. The stars had ventured out one by one in the clear crisp night, and the only sound was of dogs baying in the distance. The skirmishes that spasmodically erupted around the valley had temporarily abated, and a strange silence hung over the village.

As the night drew on, the friends moved on to the ancient Persian poetry of Hafiz. The writings of Hafiz are particularly revered by readers who look for *faals*, or hidden messages, in the texts. It is said that if you open a book at a random page, the first verse you see answers the question in your heart. Hafiz had always been a particular favourite of Massoud's.

That night Massoud chose a page at random. He did not say to what question he was seeking an answer. He just handed the book to Khalili and asked him to read the words out loud.

> *'The two of you must cherish this night*
> *Cherish the words you share*
> *Cherish the time you spend together…'*

Khalili became unsure about the words he was reading. He began to stutter and his voice tailed off. Massoud encouraged him to continue. 'Read, my friend. Never be afraid of the truth.'

Khalili reluctantly nodded, recharged his glass with more tea from the thermos flask and turned back to the page.

> *'As many nights, many days, many months,*
> *And many years will pass*
> *When you will not see each other…'*

Both men sat still, silently reflecting. In the distance, occasional artillery exchanges punctuated the otherwise still night. The clicking of crickets in the courtyard suddenly seemed to dominate the room. Finally Massoud spoke. 'What fate has written, we cannot change – so we might as well be happy, my friend.' He stood up, and without looking at his friend or acknowledging him, left the room and retired to his sleeping chamber.

In a fatalistic society such as Afghanistan, there is no escape from what destiny has written. One might be able to defeat mighty armies on the battlefield, but there is no fighting the words of the *faal* spoken by Hafiz.

The following morning, business for the Commander had continued as normal, and on the face of it the *faal* seemed all but forgotten. At the Ministry for Foreign Affairs, a young aide reminded Massoud of the two African journalists who had now been waiting nine days to interview him. Aware that he could not avoid them much longer, he capitulated.

'I will see them around eleven or twelve and they can have quarter of an hour, no more,' Massoud shouted to the aide as he went to find Khalili whom he had not seen since the previous night. Khalili was sitting alone by the bank of the river throwing pebbles into the water when his friend found him

Massoud called out, 'Come with me, I have to meet some African journalists. Then, after lunch, we will go to the new house. It has a library and the view is magnificent. Okay?'

'Yes, if you like,' Khalili replied, trying hard to ignore the sense of foreboding that was increasingly overwhelming him.

They headed to the visitors' pavilion in the Foreign Ministry hut where the interview was to take place. The Moroccans were already there setting up when Massoud and Khalili arrived. They exchanged pleasantries with the two journalists and took their seats. Something was askew, nobody knew what was wrong, but something just didn't seem right. The universe was out of alignment somehow. Khalili felt as if he was experiencing some out-of-body sensation, as if he was an observer of some surreal tableau unfolding before him. The world had taken on a weird cinematic quality. A cold chill went up his spine and he shuddered, trying to shake himself back into the reality that was before him.

As soon as the Commander had sat down, both Moroccans had asked to leave to go to the washroom. An Afghan journalist friend of Massoud's, who was making his own film about the Commander, was present, and he chuckled when the journalists left the room. 'I guess that they're too excited to finally be meeting the Lion of the Panjsher. I have seen you make enemy soldiers nervous, Commander, but never journalists.' Massoud and Khalili both managed to raise a wry smile.

When they returned, the Africans seemed preoccupied. Touzani sat down in front of Massoud while Bakkali continued to set up the camera. His clumsy antics continued to amuse all those in the room. Touzani seemed embarrassed as Massoud's producer friend stepped forward to help the bumbling Bakkali.

Massoud, sensing Touzani's unease, turned to him and asked, 'Who do you work for?'

The Moroccan replied that they worked for Arabic News International, a London-based organisation with offices in Paris.

As Khalili translated, he wondered why his friend was wasting his time with these clowns. It was obvious that these two were nothing more than amateurs. Bakkali, the cameraman, was totally incapable of using the camera and would never have managed to set it up without the help of the Afghan producer, and Touzani, the journalist, was no better. He appeared to have no clue whatsoever about the editorial content of the interview. All fifteen of his questions dwelt solely on Massoud's 'relationship' with Osama Bin Laden and had nothing at all to do with the Commander's ongoing struggle with the Taliban or even his recent meeting with Western leaders, about which one would have expected questions from any sensible journalist.

Khalili leaned in towards Massoud and whispered in his ear, 'Is he here to make a film about you or Bin Laden?'

The Commander smiled and said, 'Okay, let's get this over with – start recording. I do not have much time.' He then asked his bodyguard to go out and close the door behind him.

The Afghan journalist, who was recording the interview for his own film, switched his camera on. Touzani turned to Bakkali and nodded. Bakkali switched the camera on.

The explosion was heard several miles away.

In the eerie silence some tumbleweed blew by. The Shamal had begun to blow again, whipping itself up into a frenzy before heading west. Many witnesses would later swear that they saw four ghostly horsemen galloping away from the village, also heading west.

Part 2

The evil that men do lives on after,
the good is oft interred with their bones...
William Shakespeare

It is a man's own mind, not his enemy or foe, that lures
him to evil ways.
Buddha

September 11th 2001

Stratford upon Avon – 08.00 hours

It is the smell that stays with you. The sweet sickly smell of
death alternating with the putrid gut-wrenching stench of
rotting human flesh somehow managed to get right under
my skin, assaulting a refined nasal palate more in tune with
discerning between the vintages of various French châteaux
than having to cope with the damning evidence of atrocities
that man has inflicted on his fellow mortals.

The trip to the village of Racak in Kosovo six months
earlier to document the discovery of mass graves had
haunted me since, the events and smells a continuous loop
that replayed endlessly in my mind the moment I closed my
eyes and attempted to sleep. Until then, I wasn't aware that
smell was a sensation that one could experience so strongly
in nightmares – but now I know.

That bright September morning I was fighting yet again the spirits of Racak; the smell, the sights, and the piercing, high-pitched wailing of mothers, sisters, daughters and wives who had come to find news of their loved ones had made my body tense, and I was sweating heavily, tossing and turning, violently lashing out at the multitude of demons inhabiting my every space. But there was no respite, no hiding; every single night, four hundred residents of Racak taunted my suburban complacency from beyond the grave, condemning my nights to a perpetual state of purgatory in that strange world that exists between sleep and waking.

Then the cat whose space I had dared to encroach upon in the bed, which it obviously saw as its personal territory, jumped onto my chest hissing and spitting loudly. In response to this unprovoked attack, I immediately sat up. Having spent so much time working in war-zones over the last few years, my body reacted instinctively to the threat, while my consciousness lagged several minutes behind. As my mind walked the long narrow tightrope from the killing fields of Racak back to the real world, Farah, my wife, walked through from the shower room into the bedroom. She was wrapped in a towel, drying her hair.

'You've been annoying Simba again, I see,' she said.

Slowly my brain registered the fact that I was at home and not in some theatre of war. Farah, though petite in stature, exuded an air of regal authority which she used with consummate ease to bully me incessantly. An open wallet and a sympathetic bank manager, I had learnt over the years, were always good weapons to counter most of these offensives. I was often tempted to believe her story that she was related to the Iranian royal family and had had to flee Tehran with the march of the Ayatollahs. Farah was without any doubt the embodiment of the Dorian Grey legend, except that in my wife's case her youthful looks were connected to my rapid decent into middle age and not some wretched portrait. Though only seven years apart in age, on more than one occasion in the past six months I had been asked by people we were meeting for the first time if I was her father, much to the amusement of our children. Visiting the gym every evening and living on a diet of fresh air and lettuce obviously paid dividends.

I watched my serene Iranian Princess get dressed and ready to go to work with a strange fascination. Her morning ritual has remained the same since the day we married; first she applies foundation to her face, some gunk made of stale seaweed and crushed diamonds that my accountant would testify costs the same as the GNP of some minor South American State. Then she examines her body in the mirror for non-existent fat and cellulite. She seeks affirmation from me that she is still in good shape. When I offer it, she disagrees with me saying that I am only saying so to make her happy and that she is, in fact, fat. She then puts half her clothes on and completes her make up. She dries her fashionably bobbed hair and finishes dressing. At the end of this routine, the outfit is always deemed not suitable and two or three changes of designer wear ensue. For her, designer clothes have never been a luxury but an essential part of the equipment, to be used in her work very much the same as others would use computers or, for that matter, chairs or desks.

While all this is going on, Farah, the super-mummy, is also fielding questions from the two teenage monsters that we have bred who are up and getting ready for school.

It seems to me that boys must be genetically programmed not to be able to remember where they left their sports equipment or assorted pieces of school uniform when they got back from school. They also possess some innate inability to prepare for school the night before, always leaving it to the last minute and having to shout to mother to help find whatever may be missing. For every Ying there is a Yang. This is the reason, I believe, that all mothers of teenage boys have evolved some advanced radar system by which they can magically pinpoint in which pile of heaped clothing the lost items can be found.

I dragged myself out of bed and got ready. In comparison with a woman's routine which can last up to two hours, mine, like most men's, takes less than a minute and four tops if I decide to shave.

On first sight when my colleague Alex and I had arrived at Racak, all we could see from the jeep were what seemed like hundreds of small neat bundles of clothes laid out on the side of a long trench. It was only when we got down and started walking along the line of jumble that we began to see traces of human anatomy. An arm here and a leg there still didn't register, the bundles looked more like misshapen mannequins than the former repositories of living human flesh. Then I saw the faces: eyes staring into oblivion, the expressions blank and frightened of people who barely had time to realise their fate before a single gunshot to the head had sent them into the trench. A little further on I saw a child, no more than a few months old, clasped in the arms of its mother who had tried to save it from the fate that the misfortune of being born into the wrong religion and wrong ethnicity had bestowed upon it. Even in death it looked like a small Cabbage Patch doll, big black eyes and chubby limbs, a symbol of flawless innocence spoilt only by a single bullet hole right in the middle of its forehead. The hole was obscenely clean, almost too neat to have snatched away a life before it had really begun. I tried to understand the amount of hatred that could have driven any sane human being to fire that particular bullet. I couldn't. I heaved and emptied my stomach of the remains of my breakfast and lunch. A few feet away, Alex did the same. That morning 'Genocide' became more than just a seven letter word, more than some abstract notion liberally bandied about by politicians and Pulitzer Prize-winning journalists. 'Genocide' became such a small insignificant word...

A crisis was underway by the time I reached the breakfast table. My younger son, who, in the few weeks that I had been travelling, had miraculously transformed into a skateboarder, wearing jeans so baggy that I worried that a small gust of wind would launch him into the stratosphere, and with an attitude to match and speaking a new language that needed subtitles, was debating with his mother why he could not dye his hair red and paint his nails black. He had joined a rock band called Decapitated Dolls, and apparently some kid called Josh who was the lead singer had been allowed by his parents not only to have two tribal markings tattooed on his body, but also to have the most revered sign of adolescent rebellion – a pierced lip.

Mummy was putting up a good fight, in between feeding the cat and sipping cups of herbal tea which this morning smelt of apples and cinnamon. However, our son was not buying the argument that red hair and black nail polish were not part of the prescribed uniform for Stratford High School.

Less than six weeks previously I had been in Africa dealing with the problems of child combatants. Kids the same age as my own children were being trained to go and fight wars. Did red hair and black nail varnish really matter?

He continued the frontal assault on Mummy. 'Baba would let me! Wouldn't you?'

Three pairs of human eyes and one set of bright blue feline eyes all turned to me.

'Come on guys – time to go,' I said, avoiding the issue totally.

My wife shot me a look as if to say, 'Leave the diplomatic crap for your work.'

'See, he didn't say no,' said my son.

Thankfully the post dropped through the letter box, giving me a valid reason to retreat towards the front door.

Fade up. Wide shot – Albanian Muslim youths surround a Serbian farmhouse in Mitrovica. Flash frame. Cut to Medium Close Up – gang drags Serb man out of house. Sound on film. 'Keep the fucking camera on, you British scum.' Cut to Close Up. Grinning youth puts gun to temple of Serb. Sound FX single gunshot. Zip Pan across to house. Youths light Molotov cocktails, look to camera, grin. Flash frame. Zoom in as youths hurl petrol bombs and set house on fire. Flash frame. Close up of flames. Flash frame. Wide shot. Building ablaze. Cut away – reaction shot of youths cheering. Mix to freeze frame – young child's face at window staring helplessly.

Slowly, as flames engulfed the window, the image drifted downwards as camera and cameraman dropped to the ground.

I knew that something was wrong the moment Alex arrived back at the TV station we were setting up in Kosovo. He was bright red, drunk out of his brains, hyper-ventilating and physically shaking. When I viewed the day's rushes, I knew exactly what had happened.

'No way am I running the story,' I said.

Alex stared at me, incredulous at my decision. 'But why? Doesn't the world have a right to know what is going on – don't tell me those innocent bastards died in vain, or doesn't that matter to you any more?'

'I run this tonight and then tomorrow Serb gangs will go out and kill twenty Muslims... is that what you want? No, I refuse to run it in the interests of maintaining this fragile fucking peace that all of us are pretending that we have here...'

'My point exactly... let's show this pretence that the Yanks and the UN wankers call 'peace' for what it really is.' Alex was getting redder by the minute and I could see that he was having difficulty remaining coherent. Standing upright was also proving to be a challenge.

'No Alex... I cannot allow you to run it.'

'So, you are going to let those fucked-up murderers get away with it?' Alex turned away from me and punched the sound-proofed walls hard with his left fist, drawing blood from the knuckles. 'Screw the UN, screw the Americans and screw you, Waseem!'

'Alex... please... please, try and understand that by putting that tape out on air you are giving those bastards what they want... this is a serious mind-fuck... they know that the media is where the wars are won or lost... this is a fight for the hearts and minds... do you really think that they would have done what they did if you had not been there with a camera?'

I knew before I had even finished the sentence that I had said the wrong thing. Alex had been looking for absolution from his role in the killings and I had bloodied his conscience. We both knew that his presence with a camera was the catalyst that had provoked the atrocity, but he didn't need it shoved in his face.

Alex snatched the tape back from me and stormed out of the edit suite before I was able to finish the sentence. Three days later a trainee sound recordist found him in a bar, passed out on the floor.

The rest of the family joined me in the hallway. The kids were putting on their shoes and straightening their ties, at least for the duration of morning assembly – by break time I knew that one tie would be in a pocket and the other serving as a bandana. Farah checked her make up one last time before facing the world, straightened her skirt, and we all headed to the car.

Whenever I was in town, I made a point of driving Farah to work and the kids to school. When you spend as much time away from home as I do, the simplest things in life give you such immense pleasure. The drive gave me the chance to 'James Bond' with the boys, as Khi used to call it when he was younger and as we still insisted on referring to it, just to annoy him. During the drive, after dropping Mummy at the office where between looking good and indulging in the gossip, she allegedly worked as some customer care manager, I took the opportunity to catch up on all the boy stuff: new gadgets, new phones, cars and computer games – all the cool stuff that matters to us – in a mummy-free environment.

'Baba, you know that you are heavy, fat and you're really bad!' Khuza, the older one commented, as he left the car. Translated from teenage-speak into English, I believe it was meant as a compliment, not a comment about my growing waistline. God, I'd been gone so long, the English language was changing to such an extent that I now needed an interpreter to communicate with my own children.

KABUL – 12.30 HOURS

At that instant, 5,000 miles away in Kabul, Manocher Izzatyaar, a twenty-two-year-old field officer with ICRC (International Committee of the Red Cross) was offering *Zohr*, the lunchtime prayers, with his faithful colleague and friend, Jamshed.

The beard and turban strictly enforced by the Taliban hid the handsome looks that Manocher had been so proud of many moons ago. Jamshed sported a similar look. 'Taliban chic', as they jokingly referred to it, made them look like twins. But then again, they looked like every other man in Kabul. By edict of the Ministry of Promotion of Virtue and Prevention of Vice, anyone without the prescribed beard length would be thrown in jail until the beard was deemed to have grown to an acceptable size. The beard was the male equivalent of the *chadari* or *burka*, the all-encompassing covering that all women were forced to wear. Both were means by which the Taliban shackled the people. Appearances had become the least concern of any Afghan since the Taliban had seized power five years earlier.

Manocher and Jamshed had spent the morning in the baking streets of Kabul distributing what little food aid there was to widows. For the recipients, these meagre handouts had become their only means of survival after the Taliban administration had forbidden any woman to even leave the house, let alone work.

They had walked the short distance from the office to the Shaira-e-Naw mosque to offer prayers, not out of a sense of deep religious conviction, but out of fear that if they did not go to the mosque, some one might report them to the *Munkrat*, the feared religious police of the Taliban. Religious zealots, dressed in black from head to toe, they patrolled the streets brandishing long sticks and whips, randomly lashing out for the most minor of transgressions; smiling in the bazaar or wearing a brightly coloured scarf could guarantee a couple of lashes for the perpetrator.

The *Munkrat* were also charged with the responsibility of making sure every male in Taliban-held-Afghanistan offered prayers five times a day. Neglecting to do so resulted in severe beatings, prison sentences or, as the tree of hands in the centre of Kabul testified, a fate far worse.

Having spent a couple of nights in a Kabul prison recently for missing prayers, Manocher and Jamshed were determined not to waste any more time enjoying Taliban hospitality, so five times a day every day they dropped whatever they were doing and went through the motions of offering *Namaz*. Taliban spies were everywhere now; no one could be trusted anymore, not even the children begging in the streets.

The mosque was teeming with worshippers, so much so that extra prayer mats had been laid out in the courtyard to accommodate the overflow. Though the people were there in body, nobody seemed to be there in mind or spirit. All wore the stark blank expressions that had typified the Afghan people since the Taliban had come to power.

After prayers, the congregation was made to sit in the suffocating heat for another quarter of an hour listening to the *Khutba*, the sermon which, instead of reflecting on religious teachings of Islam as was the custom elsewhere, had become a tirade against America and its allies. Prayers were offered for the destruction of the West and, particularly, the death of George Bush, 'the great Satan'.

Amidst rousing chants of 'Allah-o-Akbar', God is great, led enthusiastically by the Taliban cheerleaders and echoed meekly by the gathering, the prayer meeting drew to a close, the gates were unlocked and the people crowded out through the doors quickly and silently.

Five-year-old Manocher was not very impressed with the streets of Kabul as he was driven through them for the very first time. While the myriad of bazaars he could see through the bus window offered numerous temptations – tantalizing grottos of sights, sounds and smells – he longed to be back home in Badakshan, running wild in the foothills of the Hindu-Kush where the wide open spaces, fast-flowing rivers and snow-capped mountains had formed an idyllic world. He was intrigued by the kites he could see dancing in the sky above the city and the children playing on the streets, but nothing could adequately compensate for the carefree life that he had left behind. The gruelling four-day bus drive across the mountains and dust plains from his former home to Kabul had done nothing to endear this mystical place to the youngster. Manocher hated the smelly crowded city and no amount of cajoling or bribery on the part of his family would change his mind. A normally placid child, he cried incessantly for weeks after his father, Abdul Majeed, was transferred to Kabul, the family's fourth move in as many years.

Abdul Majeed Izzatyaar did not care much for the politics that his country had become embroiled in. All that mattered to him was to be able to provide for his large family, to lead a righteous life and above all to be able to indulge in his one passion, poetry. Over the years he had begun to be recognised as one of the foremost Dari language poets of his generation with a burgeoning number of published collections to his name. People who visited him for official business at the Department of Water and Power would sit for hours drinking tea and discussing poetry once they found out who he was. At times his office resembled a Mushahira, a traditional gathering of poets, rather than a civil servant's office.

It had been some time since Abdul Majeed had been to Kabul and he saw that under the rule of the Russians the city had perceptibly changed; it had begun to resemble a suburb of Moscow. Public buildings had an austere look that would not have been out of place in downtown Kiev. Identikit mass-housing schemes of a type which littered the communist bloc countries were springing up around the city. Russian-made Lada and Volga cars had all but replaced the German and Japanese models which had been so favoured by Afghans before the Soviet take-over. Western fashions had disappeared, to be replaced by drab Soviet garments. The Soviets had also brought with them to Kabul the mistrust and suspicion endemic to the communist political system. Spies were everywhere, in the workplace, in schools, on buses, on the streets and even within families. With execution the penalty for dissent, it was no wonder that most family gatherings dared discuss nothing more controversial than the weather, and even that they did in hushed tones.

Manocher and Jamshed made their way along the once-affluent streets of the Shaira-e-Naw district back to the office. They made a small detour to pick up some lunch on the way. Every building they passed bore the scars of countless battles. Those which had not been reduced to rubble had gaping holes caused by indiscriminate missile launches and were riddled with bullet holes. With sanctions forcing most shops out of business, what little trade remained had moved on to the streets. Bartering had taken over as the main form of commerce in an economy where money had become a scarce commodity. The traders, the numerous beggars and the potholes had turned the streets of Kabul into a formidable obstacle course for those trying to negotiate them on foot.

The trees that lined the wide boulevards of Kabul were burnt and dying. The city, once so proud of its open green spaces and parks, had been turned into a scorched dust bowl by the drought that had accompanied its capture by the Taliban. Though this was a coincidence, the people of Kabul did not see it like that and blamed it on the Taliban. International aid had all but vanished in protest at the Taliban's harsh regime, and now it seemed that even God had given up on Afghanistan.

The Taliban had turned the once thriving metropolis into a dull sullen place where few dared venture out. Those who had to go out went about their work with heads bowed, hardly uttering a word to anyone. Children no longer played in the streets; they were discouraged from doing so by the Taliban. Birds no longer sang, as if in deference to the Taliban's ban on singing and music. With few vehicles on the streets, an eerie silence enveloped the city. The population of Kabul didn't live any more – it just existed. And women didn't even really exist. They had been replaced by a legion of ghostly blue shrouds. With an edict from the Taliban that women's shoes were not allowed to make a sound in public for fear of corrupting male minds, when blue apparitions were occasionally spotted in the street, they seemed to glide along as if by magic.

Kabul had a surreal post-apocalyptic feel.

Young Manocher's anger at having to move from Badakshan had not abated in the six months that the family had lived in the Khair Khana district of Kabul and he would show his displeasure by throwing a tantrum at every given opportunity. One such morning was the twenty-seventh day of Ramadan.

His father was getting ready to go to work. Abdul Majeed had spent all the previous night awake praying for Lilatul Qadr, one of the most auspicious nights in the Moslem calendar, the night the Prophet is said to have ascended to the heavens on a winged horse. Prayers offered on that night have a special significance for believers and, it is said, have a better chance of being answered by God.

Manocher was pacing the small courtyard of the house swinging a stick, frustrated at being caged in such a confined space. A scrawny, mangy cat sat high on the mud wall, mocking his imprisonment. Birds flew around in the clear blue sky revelling in their freedom. His father came out of the small mud brick room at the far end of the yard that served as a bathroom for the family. He was towelling his hair dry after having had a bath and he made his way to the veranda to comb his hair in front of the ornate mirror attached to the wall. Manocher's mother was clearing the remnants of the food that they had eaten before the sun had risen, as Ramadan custom dictates. His eldest sister was helping to wash the dishes in the courtyard under the hand pump that was the family's only source of water. All the other siblings were preparing to go to their respective schools and colleges. Manocher's elder brother, Ehsan, entered the bathroom just vacated by their father, infuriating his younger sister Faiza whose vehement protestations that she had been next in the queue went unheeded.

Manocher called to his father and asked him to come and help him dig holes in the yard with his bright red plastic shovel. In the hubbub of domesticity, or simply because he was tired after the sleepless night he had spent praying, Abdul Majeed failed to hear and continued combing his hair. Manocher, indignant at his father's seeming indifference, skipped over to him and with all the might that his four-year-old body could muster, whacked him over the head with the shovel.

Stunned silence descended upon the household. Abdul Majeed turned to face the culprit, rubbing his head as he did so. His wife picked up a slipper that was lying nearby and made her way towards the miscreant, yelling a multitude of names at him. The other children watched, fearing the worst for their brother. Abdul Majeed had a terrible temper and did not tolerate any sort of misbehaviour from his children. He put up a hand motioning to his wife to quieten down, stopping her in her tracks, while he just stood there looking into his son's eyes. Manocher's eyes met his father's. Tears welled up in the child's eyes and began to roll down his reddening cheeks. Abdul Majeed moved towards his young son, and to everyone's astonishment, not least Manocher's, just ruffled his son's hair and went inside the house to pick up his things for work. He emerged a few minutes later carrying his battered leather briefcase, a copy of the Koran wrapped in his prayer-mat under his arm. He crossed the courtyard and, without acknowledging anyone, went out of the door into the street where his driver was waiting for him.

Almost immediately, a loud popping sound was heard, almost like a balloon bursting. Manocher who was closest *to the door rushed out in time to see his father fall to the ground clutching at his chest. Why was his father lying in the middle of the road? What a funny man. His brother Ehsan, still in his underwear, came running out into the street and Manocher giggled at the sight – surely he would get into trouble with his father for coming out in that state. His mother followed, and Manocher watched in fascination the red-coloured stain spreading on her pristine white pyjamas as she cradled her husband's head. Why was everybody screaming and crying – wouldn't all the noise wake his father up?*

Manocher and Jamshed arrived back at the room in the corner of the warehouse which served as their office. Ignoring the rickety chairs and the lopsided table which acted as a desk, they sat on the floor to eat.

As Manocher broke off a piece of bread to dip into the bowl of fresh curds, he looked around to make sure no one else was in earshot. He whispered to Jamshed that the reports of Commander Massoud's assassination being broadcast on Radio Shariat were true. Jamshed almost choked on his food. 'But the Northern Alliance has already dismissed those claims as Taliban propaganda. The Commander survived the attack and is recovering in a hospital in Tajikistan,' he muttered.

The electricity supply that had been coming and going all morning finally gave up, and the fan, the young men's only relief from the sweltering heat, spluttered to a halt. Jamshed and Manocher hardly noticed.

'No, he is dead. Believe me. I saw a confidential telex to my boss this morning. It arrived a couple of days ago from the ICRC office in Tajikistan. The Northern Alliance is trying to keep it quiet to prevent panic among the people.'

The thought that Commander Massoud, the Lion of Panjsher, could be dead, beggared belief. For many, Massoud had represented Afghanistan's last hope of deliverance from the Taliban. During the past few years, Afghans had been treading water, bearing all the excesses the Taliban subjected them to only because they knew their saviour would come to the rescue. He had promised that he would not let his people down. And his people had believed him. With Massoud gone, the future looked bleak; an eternity of Taliban rule was an inconceivable concept.

Somebody walked past outside. The two young men waited until the person was gone before they continued.

'Are you sure?'

'Yes. I am telling you. The telex is from someone in the hospital who has seen the Commander's body. Let's face it, it is finished.'

'What now?' Jamshed lost his appetite, stopped eating and leaned back. As he did so, his shoulder parted the curtain, allowing the sun to stream in. Since the electricity had gone, they had been sitting in virtual darkness. Suddenly the room was bathed in bright light. Manocher rubbed his eyes as he adjusted to the sunlight. He looked at the room as if for the first time and saw it for what it was, a dusty storeroom with broken furniture masquerading as an office.

'I tell you, Jamshed, I cannot stay in Afghanistan now. Believe me, I have made too many enemies in the Taliban, it is not safe for me to stay here anymore. It is only a matter of time before the bastards catch up with me.'

A wry smile appeared on Jamshed's face as he replayed in his mind some of the escapades that Manocher had got up to over the past year. The more draconian the Taliban edicts had become, the more pleasure it seemed that Manocher derived from flaunting them. Less than a week ago, Manocher had organised a clandestine music party in a friend's basement. The penalty, if caught, would have been death.

'I am getting out. My uncle has spoken to an agent and arranged for me to be smuggled to London. We pay some money here and the rest I can pay off working for them when I get there. The agent's people will provide me with a job and somewhere to stay. When I am settled, I will call my family to join me.'

Jamshed let out a deep sigh. 'Can you trust these people?'

Having finished eating, Manocher started cleaning up. 'This agent was recommended by my cousin in London. He is an official in the Interior Ministry and he has sent many people abroad. Anyway, I do not see that I have a choice. I will go with my uncle this afternoon to finalise the details.'

The fan jerked back to life as the electricity came on.

'So this is it − the end? Soon you too will be gone.' Jamshed was close to tears.

'*Inshallah*, this time next month I shall be sitting in some London café, sipping coffee with some English *memsahib*,' joked Manocher as he put his arm around his friend in a feeble attempt to placate him. 'Maybe I will find a mem for you as well!'

Jamshed did not laugh.

PESHAWAR − 13.00 HOURS

Across the border in Pakistan, Farida Karim, Manocher's cousin, was sitting at her desk at the Danish NGO where she worked. Even though they were 4,000 miles from home, the Danes had managed to create a little bit of Denmark in Peshawar. The office ambiance and décor resembled a page out of an IKEA catalogue. The walls were decorated with posters of Copenhagen and photographs of the various projects that the organisation was involved in. Even the magazines and papers on the coffee table in the waiting room were Danish. The smell of freshly brewed coffee was everywhere.

Farida worked as the principal information officer for the organisation, making sure that its work in Afghanistan and with Afghan refugees was highlighted in the right circles. The same age as Manocher, Farida had moved to Pakistan with her family a year earlier to take up the job and escape the Taliban.

Sitting in her air-conditioned cubicle, Farida was trying to digest the news of Massoud's death. She, like her cousin, was concerned about the possible fallout of Massoud's assassination if the news from the Taliban was to be believed. With access to the internet, she was frantically searching the web for any scrap of information about what had really happened in Khawaja Bahauddin. Blessed with a sixth sense and the power of premonition, her instinct told her that something was not right. Massoud had perished in the attack, of that much she was sure, but something was amiss. Something else was going on, something that Farida just could not quite put her finger on. She searched for hours, trawling through every news website and every website about Afghanistan that she could find, for clues.

Farida's elfin looks belied the immense responsibilities and burdens she carried on her shoulders. The fact that she was the sole breadwinner in the family was not such a big deal to her. That much she had in common with almost every other Afghan refugee family living in exile in Pakistan – although, working for a European organisation, she was in a far better position than many fellow Afghan refugees. What worried her more than anything else was well hidden in a secret compartment in her briefcase. A seemingly innocuous floppy disc, it contained the real reason why Farida had left Afghanistan.

Kabul at the beginning of 1978 was the most 'happening' place on the face of the Earth. The guarantee of cheap hash and painless enlightenment had made it a Mecca for all the hippies who were travelling the overland route to find nirvana in the ashrams of India. An essential stopover for these travellers, Kabul had become 'the flower power capital of the world' – instant-cut-price-karma for those saffron-clad devotees who did not travel on to India.

Taking a clear lead from the neighbouring Shah of Iran, it seemed clear to Afghanistan's ruling elite that development in their country had not only to be a steady progression towards availability of education and health services, but also, like Iran, there had to be a gradual embracing of Western secular ideals. Thus, in a cultural dichotomy which summed up Afghan society in the late seventies, young women wearing fashionable mini skirts on the streets of Kabul were as numerous as those wearing burkas.

For the well-heeled young of Kabul, café culture flourished. Life in Kabul society circles was about seeing and being seen in the right spots in town.

The new houses being built in the Wazir Akbar Khan area with their neat concrete walls and plain boxlike modernism made the neighbourhood look more like some suburb of California than Kabul. Children were picked up in yellow school buses for the short journey to the American International School and spent their weekends playing Little League baseball games on a baseball field specially constructed in the park opposite the American Embassy. For the chosen few, it was entirely possible to lead a lifestyle in Kabul that was closer to a suburban American existence than an Afghan one.

Everything in Kabul in the seventies had become an approximation of a life lived elsewhere. However, this did not matter to Abdul Karim who had just bought one of the reproduction Californian houses in the Khushal Khan district of the city. A direct descendant of the Persian ruler Nadir Shah, this young rising star of Kabul was definitely one of the chosen ones. The rapid progress he had made in the government-run National Cement factory, rising from administrator to director in less than four years, was seen as unprecedented. Many had already earmarked Abdul Karim as a potential minister in the Daoud regime within a few years. With a successful arranged marriage to a cousin and a child imminent, Abdul was sure that Allah was smiling down on him, and into this prosperous young household Farida Karim was born in the spring of 1978.

Farida was of a generation that had never known peace. For all her twenty-two years Afghanistan had been held to ransom by some conflict or other. First it was the guerrilla war against the Soviets, then the bloody factional fighting among the Mujahideen themselves, and finally the Taliban. She had become part of an underground women's movement trying to educate Afghan girls through a network of clandestine schools. The movement wanted their country's freedom from the Taliban and believed that this could only be achieved with foreign involvement. The West had let Afghanistan down before – once the threat of the Soviet Union had vanished, the plight of the Afghan people had been quickly forgotten. Farida's main responsibility was to assist the movement in bringing the sufferings of the Afghan people, and in particular those of Afghan women, to the attention of the West.

On the floppy disc was a complete dossier evidencing the extremes of the Taliban regime which Farida and her group had been meticulously compiling over the past two years, complete with photographic evidence and documentation. Also on the disc was a letter that she had started writing to Bill Clinton a couple of years before, and which was now addressed to George Bush, imploring him to intervene and save what remained of Afghanistan. The letter warned Bush that if America did not do something soon to help her country, American citizens would themselves experience anguish and suffering no less painful than that of her own people.

She urged the President not to underestimate the Taliban and their allies.

Having nearly been caught twice with the information during random raids and searches at her home, Farida knew she had to leave Kabul. If the Taliban had discovered the disc and its contents, not only Farida, but every single living relative of hers, together with those of the rest of the movement, would have been executed. To even think such thoughts under Taliban rule was an offence punishable by death. To write them down and plan to send them to a foreigner was tantamount to high treason, grand larceny and mass murder all rolled into one.

If she had stayed in Kabul, Farida would also have faced the very practical problem of how to get a letter to The White House. Even after a year in Pakistan, the solution to this problem still eluded her. With this thought in her mind, Farida logged off the internet and went back to working on the press release she had been trying to write since the morning.

She knew that even though he was gone, Massoud was still going to save his nation... she knew that he would not let them down.

Farida's shawe-shash, the traditional celebration held by Afghan families on the sixth day after the birth of a new baby, took place with the pomp and ceremony usually reserved for weddings in Afghanistan. Numerous sheep, goats and chickens were slaughtered to celebrate the arrival of Abdul Karim's first born, even though Farida was not the son he had secretly been hoping for. Cooks had been put to work immediately after the birth of the baby to ensure that the food was up to the exacting standard demanded by Farida's father. Many rare delicacies were bought from around the country. Two buses were hired to bring relatives and friends from the family's home province of Ghazni to

Kabul. In a society where celebrations like this were used to establish a person's social standing in the community, no expense was spared by Abdul Karim to ensure that his daughter's ritual welcome into the world would be the talk of the town.

The date 27 April 1978 would be remembered for a long time to come – of that much Abdul Karim was assured – the moment just after lunch when Russian tanks began to roll into Kabul and MiG fighters flew over the city.

STRATFORD UPON AVON – 10.00 HOURS

I was sitting at home watching some woman called Ricki Lake refereeing a verbal wrestling match between a husband and wife. The wife who was approaching forty-five was insisting on going clubbing every night wearing clothes that would embarrass Christina Aguilera. Even on the show, she was wearing a pink crop top made from spandex and a skirt that seemed more like a belt. The husband was insinuating that the clothes and the night clubbing were only the tip of the iceberg.

I had left the study to get a cup of coffee, and found myself getting hooked on this 'discussion' as I walked through the lounge to the kitchen. I always left the television on in the background when I worked; it was a habit from when I worked at the BBC where televisions were on all the time in every part of the building.

Suffering the banality of daytime television that morning had been forced upon me. I was supposed to be in America in the early part of September for meetings at the UN in New York and the World Bank in Washington, and then I was going on to meet some old friends in LA, but a kebab eaten in Nepal had put paid to all that. I had ended up out of action for nearly three weeks. It is amazing what a bit of char-grilled goat can do to a grown man. The knock-on effect of this assault on my body was that I had not only become a good few pounds lighter but was also now having to play catch-up with outstanding reports and other administrative tasks. To think I could have been strolling along the streets of Beverly Hills that very day instead of wondering what this man was going to do about his night-clubbing wife...

I decided to leave the couple's problem in the capable hands of Ms Lake and answer a few emails. The first mail was from John Murray, not only my closest friend from college days but also now a colleague.

Less than a year earlier he had been appointed head of training at the international media development organisation where I worked. We travelled to forsaken places around the world extolling the virtues of a free media – in essence we gave the voiceless a voice. It was so good to have him working alongside me. He was Robin to my Batman, Starsky to my Hutch, and Mark Anthony to my Julius Caesar – a solid rock for me both in my personal and my professional life. We had even begun to look alike, both balding and both now buying clothes from the XL section of Marks and Spencer.

When John and I first met over twenty years ago at college, it seemed we'd be lucky if our acquaintance made it to the first break, never mind to a life beyond college. John was the very antithesis of everything I was; he was from a large, working-class, Catholic family from Castle Vale, one of the rougher housing estates in Birmingham, and had spent the last five years at a comprehensive school, whereas I was an grammar school boy from a small, white-collar, Pakistani family living in the quiet Birmingham suburb of Edgbaston. On the face of it we had nothing in common.

Fate had thrown us together at Sutton Coldfield College of Further Education's brand new, state-of-the-art, drama facility where the College played host to the only pilot 'A' level drama course in the country; that was the reason we were both there.

The drama studio was truly stunning for any budding thespian. Even the smell of the studio was inspiring as I filled my nostrils with it and took in every last detail of the place that was destined to be my home for the next two years.

Unfortunately, my immediate reaction to the 'A' level group was a little less enthusiastic than to the environs in which the course was to be held. There were about fifteen students in all, and the only pleasing aspect of the group seemed to be the fact that the girls outnumbered the boys by a ratio of five to one. They were all a little lacklustre, and not one of them seemed to possess the fire and ambition that one stereotypically associated with drama students, particularly after the release of Alan Parker's movie "Fame". I could not imagine any of them getting up in the college refectory to do an impromptu song and dance.

If I was looking for a Leroy Johnson type of talented misfit rebel, the black street dancer who was one of the most enduring characters in that film, then I got him in great abundance in the form of John Murray – except that he wasn't black and didn't look as if he could dance to save his life. He arrived at the drama studio in a great commotion. The class had already started the registration procedures when the door burst open and in strode John followed by the Deputy Head of the Drama Department, Millicent Turner-Browne.

'Another one of our flock, Ernest. Poor soul was wandering aimlessly around the college. I thought I should personally bring him down to you for the class.'

She surveyed the rest of us seated in a semi-circle of chairs listening to Ernest Smythe-Bottomley, the Head of Drama. He was regaling us about his career treading the boards and in particular about the time just after the war when he had understudied for John Gielgud in a repertory production of

'The importance of being Ernest', the closest it seems that our drama tutor's acting career actually came to becoming a reality.

'My, my, what a wonderful group of young people. I will so much look forward to teaching you this year.'

With that Millicent Turner-Browne turned on her heel and flounced out of the studio. I knew that this woman in her early thirties, dressed from head to toe in tweed, was to teach us some element of drama but that short performance was remarkably demoralising. Where was the stunning dance teacher, Debbie Allen, where were the leg warmers, and where was the 'Fame costs – and here's where you start paying' speech? The movie Fame had a lot to answer for.

As Millicent left, John Murray stood there, eyeing us all up. A childish grin came over his face when he realised that there were at least twelve girls and only three boys. I know that it is wrong to use first impressions to stereotype a person, but to me, short of sporting a skinhead and having a Nazi swastika tattooed onto his forehead, John had 'racist lout' written all over him. He was about the same height as me and unshaven – it was unclear whether this was because he was attempting to grow a beard or had just been too lazy to shave that morning. In addition to the facial hair, his face was covered with the last remnants of teenage acne. His hair was fashionably long, just touching the tops of his shoulder. He was wearing a blue checked lumberjack shirt and baggy jeans ripped at the knee – long before ripped jeans became a fashion statement. He wore Doc Marten boots, much to the distress of Ernest who strictly enforced a no shoes policy in his precious drama studio, and draped over his shoulder was a blue rucksack, the decoration of which professed a dying allegiance to Aston Villa football club. John's eyes met mine for an instant as he made his way to his seat which was directly behind mine. That single look confirmed my worst fears: John Murray was a racist bigot.

From: John Murray
Date: 11th September 2001. 11.00 +1.00
To: Waseem Mahmood
Subject: Back in civilisation.

Yo Big Man,

Just a quick note to let you know that I am safe. I got into Tallinn this morning after a gruelling 36 hour journey from the Nepalese jungle. Annapurna sends her love and wants to know how you are now. Do send her mail if you can. In fact, all the staff were quite concerned about your illness and dramatic evacuation. Told you you should have stuck to the chicken curry!

The flight out of the jungle was cancelled because of the bad weather, so in the end I had to be taken to the nearest road on an elephant, and caught a taxi to Kathmandu…

The course went well, will need to do follow up but will brief you fully when we speak.

Got you that Pashmina shawl you wanted… though I don't think baby pink is your colour. ☺

Am jetlagged… not slept in two days so don't even try to call me…

Catch you soon.

Best

JM

P.S. Love to Farah and the boys.

P.P.S When do you leave for LA?

When I had had my encounter with the kebab, John had been wonderful, a real star. He had organised getting me back home from the middle of nowhere and had then taken on my workload as well as his own heavy schedule.

I had been a little concerned that I had not heard from him for the past few days – but even though I had made allowances, knowing that the state of telecommunications was somewhat dodgy in the jungle, the mail was a welcome relief.

I smiled, fired off an acknowledgement, closed down the email programme and turned my attention to the pile of travel expenses I had been putting off all morning. Would the donor pay for an elephant?

KABUL – 15.30 HOURS

Manocher and his uncle were in the office of a minor official in the Taliban government waiting to be granted an audience to meet the man himself. Working in the Ministry of Interior, this was the person who was going to be Manocher's ticket out of Kabul, out of Afghanistan and out of reach of the Taliban.

The outer office was as spartan as Manocher's own. At one end, behind a desk, sat the official's official PA. He was a studious looking, bespectacled Talib, who was almost hidden from view by a stack of manila files piled high on his desk and an ancient typewriter strategically placed in the centre. Each file was bound with a variety of different coloured ribbons, Manocher noticed as he sat there waiting. The use of these coloured ribbons had obviously escaped the attention of the Taliban, but it would surely only be a matter of time before such frivolous use of coloured ribbons would be banned.

The typewriter, which had not seen much use since the letters A and S had stopped working a few months earlier, took pride of place on the official's desk. It was there only to reaffirm the importance of the person occupying the office. In a country where illiteracy was rife, having a machine that wrote in the '*Angrezi*' language was a status symbol.

The furniture consisted of a number of garishly upholstered sofas and armchairs, none of which matched any other, creating a psychedelic battering of the vision as soon as one entered the room. The chairs had seen better days; they were all ripped or broken and should have been condemned to the rubbish tip. The armchair on which Manocher's uncle was seated was propped up by a brick on one side and what appeared to be a French dictionary on the other.

The office was full of people waiting to see the official. Manocher's uncle looked in bemusement at the activity around him. In his mind it resembled nothing more than a common bazaar. He wondered how many were on government business and how many were there in connection with the official's more lucrative side-business of people smuggling. Manocher's uncle had been a director in the Ministry of Mines and Public Works, and under the Soviets he had been a general in the intelligence services. He remained in that position until sacked by the Mujahideen. He had aged considerably in the last few years, becoming a shadow of his former self and developing a distinct stoop which made him look much older than his fifty-five years. His self-esteem was totally destroyed; he was racked with shame having to rely on his daughter in Pakistan to be the main breadwinner in the household when she should have been happily married and giving him grandchildren. And now he was reduced to this, taking a note of introduction from a friend to see an official so minor that, before the Taliban, the official would have had difficulty in getting past the guard at his office.

Life at the Izzatyaar household had changed a great deal since the murder of Manocher's father. With no social welfare system even under the Soviets, the family were left to fend for themselves. In a scenario being played out in countless households suffering a similar fate in Afghanistan, Manocher's eldest brother, Eshan, who was barely a teenager, had had to take over responsibility for his mother and his seven siblings. This enforced necessity for children in Afghanistan to be the breadwinners was the beginning of what were to become the lost generations in the country, whole generations who were forced into scrabbling around doing whatever menial work they could find in order to keep their families alive or who bypassed their childhood to join the Mujahideen forces and fight the occupying Soviet regime.

Eshan Izzatyaar was one of these 'lost children', studying in high school one day and the next working as a coolie, pushing a cart in the market to earn a few Afghanis to feed his family. Rent for accommodation had become an unaffordable luxury, so home for Manocher's family was a succession of floors, or, when they were lucky, spare rooms in the homes of relatives. This state of homelessness, buffetted from house to house, continued for several years until the authorities provided them with a small flat in Macroryan, a development especially constructed for the families of the martyred. By this time other brothers were also working, and the family had reached a level of stability which might vaguely have been regarded as normal. However, the Izzatyaar family's more stable existence was short-lived.

Macroryan became the frontline of some of the fiercest fighting between forces loyal to Massoud and to the Pushtun Warlord, Gulbudeen Hekmatyar. When the first missiles fell on the housing complex, once home to the occupying Soviet administration and where Manocher's family had been moved after the departure of the Russians, the attacks came as no surprise to the residents. If anything, the rocket-propelled grenades that fell upon them came as a blessed relief to the insecurity and terror that had slowly been gripping Kabul over the preceding eight months since the Mujahideen had entered the city. The dream of being ruled by an Afghan government had soured. All semblance of normal life had been well and truly scotched long before the first missile landed in their front yard: schools, offices and workplaces had been closed for months and nearly half the population had fled the city, leaving it eerily deserted with only rabid dogs and Mujahideen fighters wandering the streets. Basic food supplies had virtually run out even for the few who still had money. The frequency of running street battles had increased to the point where a simple trip to get water from the communal well meant diving for cover a number of times to avoid getting caught in the cross-fire.

The first missiles, fired at the crack of dawn to alert civilians not to venture out, signalled the beginning of an onslaught that was to last day and night almost continuously for eight days. A blitz-type mentality gripped the residents of Macroryan as they moved into the basements of the buildings to escape the missiles and bullets that were raining down on them. In spite of the predicament they found themselves in, morale remained high, and food and water were shared amongst neighbours. A genuine spirit of camaraderie spread amongst the families, and they swore that they would survive this together or die together.

Conditions in the basement of Manocher's block, with no light and in the sweltering heat, were harsh to begin with but deteriorated further as close to two hundred anxious souls attempted to survive yet another twist of fate in their wretched lives. If Hekmatyar's missiles or bullets didn't get them, the poor sanitation they were enduring definitely would.

The barrage was relentless. On the third day, with all food in the basement gone and not much remaining upstairs in anybody's apartment, the young men decided to launch a foray in the hope that they could bring back some provisions, stealing if necessary.

Emerging outside for the first time since their incarceration, the sight that greeted the young men of Macroryan was horrifying. Most of their homes lay totally destroyed. They had heard the shelling from their lair in the basement, but no-one could have imagined the sheer scale of devastation that had been wreaked in just three days. Apocalyptic fires burned all around. The few cars that residents of Macroryan had owned lay scattered and broken. Telephone and power pylons littered the ground, twisted into obscure shapes.

Then they saw the bodies: bodies of those unfortunate

enough to have had to venture out for something to quench the thirst of a crying child or to try and find a morsel of food for an old parent dying of hunger; bodies of relatives and friends who had once been neighbours; bodies raked with bullet holes testifying to the effectiveness of the Kalashnikov AK47 as an efficient killing tool; bodies which had been blown apart by missiles and no longer even looked like human bodies. The young men looked at the scene in shock.

Manocher found the body of a young girl near the well. Her green eyes stared into oblivion, a single bullet hole in the middle of her temple the only flaw on an otherwise beautiful face. Most of her hair was still covered by the scarf that she wore, and the clay pot of water that she had been carrying lay shattered next to her body, her hands still firmly gripping the handles. The precious water for which she had sacrificed her life lay in a puddle on the ground mixed with dust and blood and the contents of her skull. Manocher recognised her as a neighbour from an adjoining block. She was a schoolmate of his sister, and she had often come round to his house to play. She was just twelve years old.

That morning in Macroryan, a remote, forgotten corner of the world, the dead buried their dead.

By the fourth day the battle had taken on a discernible pattern, a cycle that the residents of Macroryan were able to decipher and thus pre-empt the lulls in shelling to get supplies and water with relatively less danger to their lives. Even the shopkeepers, fearing large-scale looting, began to risk opening their shops during the lulls and found business brisk; everything and anything was snapped up. Nothing was deemed useless or superfluous. Queues formed and fights broke out just to buy matches and toilet paper.

A battery-operated bell – a strange warbling noise like a bird – rang, silencing the crowd in the room. The official's official PA got up from behind his desk and ushered Manocher and his uncle into the inner office amidst much shouting and protestations from others that they were next in line.

The official's room was in total contrast to the waiting room. The silence was deafening. The walls looked as if they had been freshly painted, and beautiful Afghan carpets in shades of red and burgundy adorned the floors. The matching chairs were new, while the Quranic verses on the wall were expensive original works of art. Garishly coloured artificial silk flowers festooned the large coffee table in the middle of the room. An air conditioner whirred in the background, making the temperature in the room more tolerable than the hot cauldron outside.

The Talib official's presence dominated the room. A naturally large man, with the regulation beard and turban, he dwarfed everybody else. He was leaning back on his swivel chair, barely managing to balance himself without the chair toppling over, and laughing loudly into a satellite phone as the three men entered his room. The official's official PA made his way around the side of the desk and handed him the letter of introduction. Manocher and his uncle remained standing in front of the desk. They were not offered a seat. The Talib glanced at the note and, finishing his call, swivelled his chair to face the visitors. 'So, you want to go to London,' his voice boomed as he looked Manocher up and down.

'Yes sir,' replied Manocher meekly.

'It will be 10,000 US dollars. Can you afford it?'

'I thought that the deal was that we can give you 5,000 dollars now and pay the rest after I…'

'I want 10,000 dollars paid to my brother in London by the end of the week. If you can do it, I have a group leaving next week and will send you with them. If you can't pay – please stop wasting my time.'

'But… But…' spluttered Manocher.

'We will pay your brother the money you ask,' interrupted Manocher's uncle before Manocher could say anything more. 'Please give me the details where to make the payment.' Manocher looked quizzically at his uncle, knowing that they did not have that sort of money.

'Good – my PA will give you my brother's details.'

'If we get the money, what about my passport? What route will I be going?' asked Manocher.

The official stared hard at Manocher, insulted by these questions. 'There is an Afghan expression, "You should enjoy the fruit – not worry about the tree." With a devious smile he added, 'You just pay your money and turn up here next Friday. How I get you to London is my problem.'

With this comment he dismissed them and returned to his phone.

The official's official PA quickly ushered them out and handed them a business card from a drawer in his desk. 'Make the payment to this man and then let me know.' With that, the PA also dismissed them and turned his attention to the others in the room who were crowding his desk.

The bird-warbling bell rang again as Manocher and his uncle left the office.

Those eight days in the basement at Macroryan changed Manocher's life in more ways than one. He fell in love for the first time.

Manocher had noticed Farishta almost the moment that she had moved into the apartment on the second floor with her family, several months earlier. From Kandahar in the South, Farishta, at fifteen the same age as Manocher, had classic Afghan looks: a porcelain clear complexion, beautiful bone structure, blonde hair and the penetrating aquamarine eyes native to that part of the world. Manocher, a shy gawky teenager who had not yet felt the need for girls in his life, was smitten the moment he set eyes on her.

Unable to meet with or speak to her, Manocher conducted his wooing of Farishta in the conventional age-old tradition practiced by lovers in Afghanistan – through meaningful looks exchanged whenever their paths crossed, in this case in the stairwell on the way to and from their respective schools. Their departure and arrival from school began to coincide a lot more than would have been warranted, given that Manocher attended the morning sessions and Farishta the afternoon.

Satisfied that his feelings were reciprocated, Manocher pushed his pursuit of Farishta to the next level – poetry and flowers, which he delivered by balloon to her whenever he saw her alone on the balcony. While she would still not talk to him or write back, she made sure that she was always on the balcony whenever he was around. Like a latter-day Juliet, a whistle or a ring of Manocher's bicycle bell was enough to summon her out, even at five in the morning when he returned from Fajr, the early morning prayers at the mosque. When alone in the starlit night, their souls entwined across the heavens in an embrace that, without touching, still touched every fibre of their being. Like so many others who had trodden this path before them, what was not said remained as explicit a declaration of their feelings as countless empty words spoken by lesser mortals.

The eight days of shelling forced Manocher's object of desire into a proximity that he would not have deemed possible in his wildest imaginings. In the confines of the basement, prevailing circumstances meant that the normal rules of decorum amongst the sexes demanded by Afghan culture and customs were relaxed. Even though men and women remained segregated, they were still forced into sharing the same space. So there she was, just a few feet away from him, continuously in his sight, breathing the same air. In spite of all the horrors and misery around him, Manocher was in heaven; such was his feeling of ecstasy at times, that if he had come face to face with Gulbudeen Hekmatyar, he might have even thanked him.

As the siege continued, a level of fatalistic complacency set in. Many more errands were being undertaken by the young who, getting restless in the basement, were scurrying up and down the blocks for any tiny excuse. Gone was the fear that they might be hit by a bullet or missile; if their life was to end in this way, so be it.

By day six, the men had taken to venturing into the compound and spending most of the daylight hours outside, having found a section of the yard out of the direct line of fire of both Massoud's and Hekmatyar's forces, although they had to dive for cover several times a day to avoid being hit by rockets flying overhead or landing close by.

This relaxation of the regime in the basement was a godsend to Manocher and his burgeoning romance. Whenever he went to the apartment on an errand, or out to the yard where the men were hanging out, Farishta always appeared miraculously in the corridor.

On one occasion while he was standing with the men, Manocher saw Farishta going up the stairs and immediately ran after her. Alone in the stairwell he caught up with her and took her wrist. 'Please stop, talk to me.'

'No, leave me alone.' Farishta released her hand from Manocher's grip and ran upstairs to her apartment. Manocher stood there, savouring the first four words that she had spoken to him. Never had a rebuff been so sweet, and never had a brush-off been as welcome as it was for Manocher that day.

He raced up to his own apartment and out onto the balcony. Sure enough, Farishta was already on her balcony, waiting for him in the private world that they had created.

Manocher picked up a broken plastic rose that was lying on the floor and, attaching a message which simply read, 'If I die, keep this as a reminder of these times', he threw the flower onto the balcony.

All he heard was sigh and a gentle voice saying, 'God forbid.'

Unfortunately, the moment he had thrown the flower was the exact moment one of the more conservative neighbours in the yard below happened to look up and see what was going on. Affronted by Manocher's antics, he stormed up to the apartment, kicked in the front door and accosted Manocher on the balcony with a gun.

'I let you live today because of the respect that I have for your mother. This stops now. Do anything this stupid again and I personally will take care of you.'

Manocher was not able to test how resolute the neighbour's threat was, for that very afternoon, after eight days and nights of non-stop shelling, common sense prevailed and Massoud and Hekmatyar's militias agreed a temporary ceasefire to allow the evacuation of families from Macroryan.

Manocher's family packed a few belongings and set out for the relatively safe haven of Khair Khana, an area that somehow always managed to remain clear of the main skirmishes. With transport non-existent, the journey had to be undertaken on foot, and the fact that the family arrived at their destination several hours later unscathed was nigh on miraculous. Throughout the journey, bullets and missiles had whizzed overhead. On two occasions, the family had to seek refuge in a stranger's house to allow the street fighting to subside to a point where it was safe to continue.

Within an hour of arriving at his uncle's house in Khair Khana, Manocher had convinced his mother that he needed to return immediately to Macroryan to look after the possessions they had left behind. Most men had decided that they would be going back after they had evacuated the women and children to safety, to ensure that nobody looted their homes. Manocher left before his brother-in-law returned and could veto the idea of re-crossing the battleground and living back on the front line as one of sheer stupidity and foolhardiness. In his view, the black and white television set and ancient Chinese cassette player would not have been worth risking anyone's life for.

Travelling alone, Manocher made good time and was back home in the early hours of the morning, just as the sun was *rising. Macroryan was silent. With almost all the families having been evacuated, there was no sign of life. Only the green flags marking the spots where martyred residents of Macroryan had fallen and been laid to rest moved gently in the light early morning breeze, reminding Manocher that this had been a living breathing suburb just a few days before. As he surveyed the scene, a stray dog wandered across the yard, sniffed at a pile of rubbish and moved on.*

Manocher went upstairs to his apartment, and after washing, offered his morning prayers. While prostrated towards Mecca, he heard a commotion in the yard below and finishing off his worship went to the window to see what was happening, Outside the apartment building he saw a taxi and a man whom he recognised as Farishta's father helping the driver to load and secure several metal trunks on the roof. The family was leaving. As soon as the thought registered, he dashed out and bumped into Farishta in the corridor outside her apartment. The rest of the family was already downstairs. As soon as she saw Manocher, Farishta stopped and faced him. In her hand, firmly clasped with the three overstuffed plastic bags of clothes that she carried, was the plastic rose he had given her.

'You are going?'

'Yes.'

'To Khair Khana?'

'No, to Kandahar.'

Manocher noticed her eyes moisten and the tears well up as her mother shouted up the stairs for her to hurry up. Farishta leant forward, placed a delicate kiss on his forehead, turned and quickly descended the stairs. Manocher followed and stood in the doorway watching in disbelief as the family piled into the taxi and drove off. Farishta looked back at him, her face pressed against the back window.

A missile hit the car before it had even crossed the threshold of Macroryan. Six more green flags were planted that morning.

SAN FRANCISCO 04.15 HOURS

Abi went into autopilot mode the moment the alarm roused her from the restless sleep that always preceded an early shift at the station. Switch off alarm. Shed the oversized 49ers shirt left behind by an ex-boyfriend which now served as a nightdress. Brush teeth. Floss. Take shower. Put on work clothes. Take fix of caffeine to sustain drive to work. Leave note for flat mate, Rachel, about dinner arrangements. Apply lip gloss. Remember briefcase. Leave apartment. Make sure the dead lock is bolted. Locate vehicle. Get into vehicle. Switch on radio. Point vehicle in direction of office. Drive.

Abigail Brooke, in her late twenties, was the typical All American Girl. A straight 'A' student, born and raised in the rural Western United States, she did not leave her home state of Idaho until she started college in Seattle. Blessed with looks that many remarked resembled Cameron Diaz, Abi had a journalistic talent to match, which meant that she had found herself rapidly rising up the ranks of KTVU, the local Fox affiliate in San Francisco. The steps from intern, to freelance reporter, to staff reporter and finally news producer that would have taken lesser mortals ten or more years to achieve had been managed by Abi in less than five. In spite of rumours to the contrary, this feat had been achieved solely on the basis of her journalistic talents.

Abi was returning to work after a ten-day break following an embarrassing freak accident. Wet marble floors and fashionable high heels do not go together, as Abi had discovered to her cost. Rushing back from Starbucks, balancing a Grande Skinny Latte, umbrella and handbag, while simultaneously talking to a colleague on her mobile, had been her undoing. Slipping on a step in front of the office, Abi had landed with most of her weight on her right arm. The result: a broken ulna, a dead mobile, a new white DKNY blouse covered in coffee, and a tremendous loss of dignity. An injury sustained while skiing, or in the line of duty, would have counted as glamorous, but slipping in the rain on the office steps did nothing to enhance Abi's reputation.

She felt good being back as she manoeuvred her red Jeep Cherokee into the station car park – no mean feat with one arm still in plaster. Her car, the only indulgence she had allowed herself since she had started working, had recently become a real bone of contention between Abi and her boyfriend, Mo. Mohammed Al Moody, an Iranian whom Abi had known since college but only recently started dating, had become a fundamentalist-green-tree-hugging-eco-warrior. He had spent the past few weeks trying to convince her that her Jeep alone was responsible for the depletion of the entire ozone layer above the North Pole. He insisted that she trade it in for a more eco-friendly model, or better still, cycle everywhere like he did. She gathered her bags from the vehicle and made her way to the entrance. The city of San Francisco was not exactly designed with cycling in mind, and she was certainly not going to try and cycle up and down those hills.

Samuel, the security guard on duty, held the door open for her. 'Good morning, Miss Brooke. Good to see you back again.'

'Good morning, Samuel – it's good to be back and, by the way, thanks for your help the other day.'

'All in the line of duty, Ma'am, all in the line of duty.'

'No really, I am most grateful,' she replied, as she disappeared into the lift.

Getting out at the second floor, Abi entered the open plan newsroom, almost deserted at this time of the morning. It was a great white cavern with countless television monitors and computer screens all spewing out the fodder that Abi and her team packaged into more palatable chunks for their audience. Newsrooms around the planet are all the same: sterile, impersonal nerve centres that are the life blood of a broadcast organisation producing the channel's single most important programme, while at the same time managing to be a Feng Shui practitioner's worst nightmare.

Glen, the blond-haired, blue-eyed breakfast anchor, looked up from his computer terminal as she went past him. 'Hi Abi, did you enjoy the trip?' Glen laughed loudly at his own joke, having spent the better part of a week thinking it up.

'Very funny, Glen, very funny.' Abi said as she made her way to her own desk. She knew that this was not the last time that she would hear this quip today. She just wondered who was going to be at the receiving end of her plastered fist when she had finally had enough.

PESHAWAR – 17.30 HOURS

Farida arrived home and, to the consternation of her mother, went straight to the computer and sat down. She did not want to be enveloped in domesticity, nor did she want to go and sit with her head in her mother's lap as she did every day, unburdening herself of whatever problems might have plagued her at work.

The family lived in a modest, two-bedroom house in one of the better neighbourhoods of Peshawar close to where Farida worked. It was a far cry from the spacious villa they had left in Kabul. Living with Farida were her mother and three brothers, all with their respective families. Her father had gone back to Kabul several months earlier, unable to bear the shame of having to live on his daughter's earnings. The house was overflowing with people, children running here, there and everywhere, all constantly demanding attention from Farida, their favourite aunt.

Angeza, the eldest niece, was holding a tea party in one of the bedrooms for her dolls and the other children in the household. A place had been set for Farida. Angeza was pouring water from a plastic teapot into small plastic teacups, and her guests were sitting drinking the make-believe coffee, tea, Coke or whatever they wanted it to be. There was a lot of yelling and screaming following Farida's uncharacteristic refusal to join the party.

The smell of lamb, onions and rice – traditional Afghan fare – simmering on the stove wafted through the house from the kitchen.

Farida felt an inexplicable sense of impending doom as she raced out into the street from the school where she was working as an English teacher towards the site a few hundred yards further down the road where she had just seen the two missiles strike. The primeval screams and unnatural wailing from the large crowd of men who had already gathered around the spot where the missiles had landed did not bode well, and a tight knot formed in the pit of her stomach as she ran down the road. Struggling to throw off her all-encompassing blue burka, and fighting her way through the throng to the front of the crowd, Farida saw the cause of this spontaneous outpouring of grief from men for whom death and violence had become a daily way of life; lying there were the shattered bodies of fourteen schoolgirls who had taken a direct hit from the missiles that had been fired from the nearby hillside. Those girls who had somehow miraculously survived the blast stood around the crater in the road either crying hysterically or staring dispassionately in a state of total shock at the carnage that lay in front of them. The girls, who less than a week ago had been celebrating the fact that their school had been one of the first to re-open its doors in the city, in that split second had been taught the harshest lesson about the fragility of the time in Afghan history in which their childhoods were unfortunately rooted.

So badly destroyed were the bodies that no form of identification was possible from the mashed pulp of human flesh that remained on the road, but Farida saw something that made her retch and throw up; lying at the side of the hole in the road was a distinctive pink schoolbag that she recognised as one she had only recently bought for her youngest sister. Regaining her composure, Farida took a deep breath and mechanically started to sift through the rest of the debris that littered the road. It didn't take her long to find what she was looking for. A favourite school shoe and the broken remains of a beloved hair band confirmed her worst fears: all three of her sisters had perished in the attack. Farida did not cry; a lifetime of tears would not have been enough to drown the grief that she felt at that moment. She dropped to her knees, and cradling the last few physical reminders that remained of her sisters, she stayed there staring into oblivion, openly cursing a God who would allow this sort of unnecessary bloodshed to take place in His name. She was still in the same position when her father, Abdul Karim, found her several hours later.

Farida was pre-occupied, oblivious to everything going on around her.

The computer was positioned on the dining table in the living room in such a way that Farida could keep an eye on BBC World on television at the same time. Steven Cole, the presenter of a programme called Click Online, was talking to some computer expert about the vulnerability of networks to some virus called Melissa. Farida was not listening. Staring at the monitor screen in front of her, she began to type.

'Mr President,

Two days ago, Ahmad Shah Massoud, the leader of the Northern Alliance, was assassinated in cold blood. With him the Afghan nation's last hope of salvation from the Taliban also died. On behalf of the twenty-six million people of my country, I implore you to intercede and save us.'

Farida sat back and thought. Here she was, writing to the most powerful man on earth asking him to commit the lives of Americans to come and help save her country. Why should he? After all, Afghanistan had no oil. The reality was that Afghanistan had nothing of any redeeming value that could warrant American intervention. This thought preyed on Farida's mind. She continued writing.

'We have nothing to offer you but the prayers of a nation beaten into submission by a repressive regime. Sir, you must act now before this fanatical brand of Islam that the Taliban is breeding gets out of hand and the battlefield extends itself beyond the borders of Afghanistan to your own doorstep.'

With the death of his daughters, Abdul Karim knew that the perfect world he had painstakingly put together through the years had unravelled. He never thought that he would live to see the day, but the time to leave their homeland had come. Even his ability to survive through several regime changes had deserted him; under the Soviets he had joined the Army and risen to General in the intelligence service, then with the subsequent puppet regime of President Najibullah he had managed to get himself restored to his old position in the Ministry of Mines and Public Works. But with the advent of the current Mujahideen administration, Abdul Karim's fall from grace had been dramatic. He had been unceremoniously fired from his position in the Ministry and publicly branded a collaborator which made his chances of re-employment anywhere in Mujahideen-controlled Afghanistan next to zero. One by one, all the trappings associated with high-profile public office began to disappear, and within a remarkably short period of time the beautiful house in the suburbs, the cars, the privileged lifestyle, everything was gone. Home for the family for the last few months had been the floor of a friend's spare room and the family's only income was the small stipend that his wife received from her work in the hospital. Farida, the once pampered eldest daughter who had had her own driver and maid to see to all her needs, had to pull out of her studies and take work as a teacher to help the family survive.

Less than a week after the death of the girls, the family packed their few belongings into two small suitcases, said their farewells, and took the well-trodden refugee route into neighbouring Pakistan: by bus to the eastern town of Jalalabad followed by a three-day, sixty-kilometre trek along the age-old smugglers' donkey tracks through the Khyber Pass and on to Peshawar. These back-door routes into and out of Afghanistan were often more congested than the more legitimate ones, particularly since the Soviet invasion of the country had caused a tidal wave of refugees to flood into Pakistan. Those who had once made a living smuggling contraband through these mountains now made a much more lucrative living smuggling people.

After the family arrived in Peshawar, they immediately made their way to Faisalabad, a small industrial town in the heart of the country and the home of Safi Ullah, an old friend with whom Abdul Karim had conducted a great deal of business in his previous incarnation at the Ministry of Mines and Public Works. Safi Ullah had constructed a flourishing business empire based on the favourable contracts that Abdul Karim had negotiated for him.

It was late at night after six days of continuous, gruelling travel when Abdul Karim and his family turned up on Safi Ullah's doorstep. To Abdul Karim's mortification, his friend whom he had made rich, his friend for whom he had risked his own life to help safely evacuate across the border during the height of the Mujahideen insurrection, his friend who had taken a blood oath to repay the debt if Abdul Karim ever needed him, his friend on whose word Abdul Karim had undertaken this hazardous journey with his family, that very same friend turned around and denied even knowing him. To add insult to injury, Abdul Karim and his family were manhandled roughly off the property and thrown onto the road by gun-wielding guards.

A broken Abdul Karim arrived with his family at Old Shamshatoo refugee camp on the outskirts of Peshawar two days later. Shamshatoo refugee camp, one of the oldest camps in Pakistan, came into existence soon after the Soviet invasion of Afghanistan in the early eighties. By the time in the mid nineties that Abdul Karim arrived at the camp, it was home to nearly 100,000 people, a thriving village with solid mud huts and an established community infrastructure. On registration, Abdul Karim received a tent, six bowls, six tin spoons and a cooking pot; he also received his ration card allowing him limited supplies of flour, oil, millet and the occasional cupful of sugar. Queuing up with the great unwashed for such insufficient rations, Abdul Karim's humiliation was complete.

For the next two years life went on hold for the Karim family while they learnt the art of survival in an environment totally alien to the life they had led. In her previous life, the only hardship for Farida had been to decide which restaurant to take her friends to each evening or which of the family cars would take her to school. Now, barely sixteen years old, she had to be up at four each morning to catch the bus into Peshawar to find whatever work she could, often working as a maid to supplement the family's frugal food supplies.

Following the Taliban's capture of Kabul in the autumn of 1996, there was much celebration in the Shamshatoo camp, and many families, fed up with their wretched existence in a hostile foreign land, viewed the coming of the Taliban as a heaven-sent blessing for their country. Seeing that a semblance of peace had descended on their war-ravaged homeland and that the Taliban were very much an honest Islamic administration who were keen to root out corruption and malfeasance in government, many excited families began the long trek back home. Abdul Karim's was one of the families that willingly left Old Shamshatoo camp to return to Kabul for a better life under the Taliban.

STRATFORD UPON AVON – 13.30 HOURS

My battle with travel expenses continued. However, I took some time out to make myself a sandwich and watch the BBC lunchtime news. It was pretty uneventful. After the news had finished, I sat there looking for an excuse to delay my return to the study. Channel 4 started showing an episode of Friends that I had not seen. Great! Joey, Rachel, Ross and the gang had bought me another half hour of freedom. This episode was pivotal in my understanding of why Ross had not married Emily in London. They were very much in love when I had left for Nepal a few weeks earlier… Oh my God! Ross had invoked Rachel's name instead of Emily's when he was saying the wedding vows. No wonder Emily had ditched him. Served him bloody right – he should never have started a relationship with Emily if he was not over Rachel.

I got up to go back to the study and switched the channel back to BBC. Then I heard: 'We interrupt this programme to take you over to the BBC Newsroom for a newsflash.' While the continuity announcement was still underway, the journalistic part of my brain had already analysed the various possible scenarios that the newsflash could be about and I settled on the death of the Queen Mother as the most likely. A couple of friends who worked in BBC News had been sent to Scotland the previous weekend on what they called Queen Mother death-watch. Should Her Majesty die, it was their responsibility to co-ordinate the coverage. Yes, that was it, the Queen Mother, God rest her soul, was no longer with us.

As the caption disappeared, an aerial shot of lower Manhattan appeared. There was smoke streaming from one of the World Trade Centre twin towers. What the hell was going on? The voice-over tried in vain to explain.

'We are just receiving these pictures live from New York. There seems to have been an accident – a plane has crashed into one of the twin towers of the World Trade Centre. There is no information yet on the cause of the crash or any casualty numbers.'

I stood there watching. As I did so, a second plane appeared behind the towers, banked slightly and flew straight into the second tower, exploding on impact into a massive fireball. Oh my God. This was no accident. Even Peter Sissons, the veteran BBC newscaster, was, for once, lost for words. The pictures flickered silently as the BBC anchor and I, together with countless billions around the world, watched the drama unfold.

I was riveted to the spot, unable to comprehend what I was seeing.

Peshawar – 18.00 hours

Farida had prised herself away from the computer and was eating the evening meal with her family when images of the World Trade Centre appeared on the television screen. Silence descended upon the room. Even the children realised that something serious was happening and sat motionless. Farida turned the volume up. Only a gecko moved, scurrying across the wall in pursuit of a fly.

In addition to the attacks on the World Trade Centre, another plane had gone into the Pentagon and yet another was reported missing. Further unsubstantiated reports were coming in of hijacked planes heading towards famous landmarks in almost all the major cities in the world. The Houses of Parliament, Golden Gate Bridge, Eiffel Tower, The White House and Buckingham Palace had all suddenly become targets. Within minutes paranoia had gripped the entire world.

This was the nightmare scenario Farida had envisaged and had been wanting to warn President Bush about. But now she was too late. Part of her was consumed with guilt – perhaps if she had managed to send her letter to The White House this might have been prevented.

Within an hour of the first plane crashing, the news broadcast mentioned 'Muslim fundamentalists trained in Afghanistan' being responsible for the atrocity.

When President Bush appeared on television later in the day and promised the nation 'to hunt down and to find those folks who committed this act', Farida knew that Afghanistan would now get the American military intervention that it so needed to save it from total destruction. Nearly a million deaths in Afghanistan nobody had cared about, but now, with 3,000 dead in the streets of Manhattan, the world suddenly took notice of her country. Not that Farida was pleased about the attacks or the loss of innocent lives; quite the contrary, she was appalled by the futility of it all. America now had thousands of unnecessary widows and orphans to join those in Afghanistan, all bereaved in the name of *Jihad*, the Islamic holy war.

San Francisco – 06.00 hours

The titles for the Breakfast Show had just begun rolling when the pictures from New York started coming into the newsroom. Abi was in the studio control room overseeing the transmission of the programme. So intensely was everybody involved in his or her own jobs that nobody paid any attention to the small monitor in the bottom right-hand corner on which the network feed was being relayed.

In the moments before transmission, the gallery was a hive of activity.

'Standby studio. Standby, Glen and Jenny. Coming to Camera 3 first for two shot then Glen on 2. Here we go. 10, 9, 8, 7, 6, 5, 4, 3, 2, 1 cue and mix, camera 3, 2 next, standby VT.'

The titles on the screen mixed to studio and Glen and Jenny appeared on screen – the King and Queen of autocue.

'Good morning and welcome to the Breakfast Show on KTVU. I'm Glen Madden.'

'And I'm Jenny Kroll.'

Both smiled to camera and cut to Medium Close Up shot of Glen. Glen shuffling papers. Serious look into camera. 'First the headlines…'

At that point, Cameron, the fresh-faced intern and the only one from the small breakfast team left manning the newsroom, burst through the door of the control room totally out of breath.

'For God's sake, Abi,' hissed Tom, that morning's studio director, 'can't you control your staff? I'm trying to direct a live show here.'

Cameron rushed round to Abi who was seated at the far end of the room in front of a bank of monitors pouring over that morning's script, trying to lose five minutes of overrun. 'Abi, plane, twin towers... accident, happened ten minutes ago.'

'What are you babbling about, Cameron? Can't you see we're on air?'

'A plane has gone into the World Trade Centre, look at the network feed.'

'What? Tom, punch up the network on preview.'

The familiar skyline of lower Manhattan appeared on the screen. The twin towers of the World Trade Centre were in the centre of frame. The North Tower was billowing fire and smoke from somewhere near the top.

Silence descended upon the control room, punctuated only by Glen's dulcet tones as he continued to read the news headlines oblivious to what was happening.

'So, what do we do, boss?' Tom asked. 'Want me to cut to it?'

'Yeah, go with it.'

She switched the talkback to Glen. 'Glen, there's been an accident in New York. We are cutting out of this story to breaking news from network, just cue it in and I'll brief you when we are off air.'

Glen picking up from Abi linked to the feed. 'We'll bring you the rest of that story later. We now take you across to New York for some breaking news.'

Tom punched up the network feed. As the team in the studio watched the feed, a second plane lined itself up and smashed into the South Tower. They all watched in stunned horror.

'Holy Shit…' Glen's impeccable professional façade dropped. Jenny, the female anchor, started sobbing uncontrollably. Cameramen, sound and studio technicians, journalists and the entire production team just stood there staring at the screens mesmerised. Many of the hardened professionals in the studio, veterans of reporting death and destruction from all corners of the world, fought back tears. The line that news people are never supposed to cross – remaining detached and not getting involved in the subject matter they cover – had well and truly been breached by the events of the past few minutes. No amount of guidelines or training could prepare anybody for this sort of thing.

'What do we do now?' Tom asked.

It took less than a minute for Abi to get over the initial shock, regain her composure and click back into professional mode. 'Okay guys, I am scrapping the running order and sticking with network. We'll do localised updates every ten minutes.'

The studio buzzed back into life, everyone thankful for having something to do and occupy their minds.

'Glen, can you get Jenny to the green room and then get back to studio ASAP, we'll do an opt-out in ten.' Abi turned to Cameron. 'Okay Cameron, I want you to phone the entire team and call in the cavalry – we are going to need every person we can get. This could be a long day.'

KABUL — 19.00 HOURS

Manocher had gone to the *Shoha-e-Maiwand*, a bodybuilding club located on the Macroryan housing estate in the east of Kabul where he lived.

Bodybuilding was the only form of recreation deemed acceptable by the Taliban. Playing football, a traditional favourite of Afghan youth, had virtually died out, since playing in the baggy *shalwar-kameez* as ordained by the Taliban — for whom wearing shorts was seen as 'un-Islamic' — had proved an impractical proposition for most players. Cheering or clapping at matches, a sign of Western corruption, would also land spectators in jail, often suffering severe beatings. Matches, when they were played, would be regularly interrupted by the *Munkrat* — the religious police — who would herd the crowds and players into mosques for prayers. Playing an uninterrupted ninety-minute match often proved impossible. But the local clubs really lost the will to play football when the Taliban commandeered the stadium they used to carry out the weekly public executions and amputations. They found it difficult to play football using goalposts that doubled as gallows every Friday.

The *Shoha-e-Maiwand* bodybuilding club had become a refuge for the young men of Macroryan. They could vent their frustrations and channel excess testosterone. Calling it a 'bodybuilding club' or 'gym' was a very liberal use of the words. In reality, the *Shoha-e-Maiwand* bodybuilding club was just a large dusty room, which in the absence of electricity had to be illuminated by candles and gas lanterns. It was equipped with just a flea-bitten punch-bag precariously suspended from the ceiling, a single set of ancient dumbbells and two rusty bench presses. Even so, at any given time there were between forty and fifty men making use of the facilities, often spending more time waiting for their turn to use the equipment than actually using it. All exercising had to be carried out while wearing the *shalwar-kameez*, and even in the gym the omnipresent *Matawan* were always on hand to ensure compliance. The heat combined with the sweat of forty or so fully-clothed men exercising in close proximity created a stench so potent that it could nauseate those not used to it.

It was here that Manocher spent all his evenings. Today, however, his mind was not really on training. He was concerned where his uncle was going to get the 10,000 dollars that they had promised to the Taliban official. They certainly did not have that much money – even the initial 5,000 dollars had been raised by selling almost all of what little they owned and the remainder had been borrowed from friends and relatives. His uncle had returned from the office with Manocher in total silence and had refused to be drawn on how he intended to get the rest of the money. All he had told Manocher was to prepare to leave the following week. This thought preyed heavily on Manocher's mind as he held the punch bag for a Talib boxer, trying to make sure that the ferocity of the punches did not bring the bag down.

Lost in his own world in the gloomy, smelly atmosphere, Manocher did not notice Jamshed who had come in a few minutes earlier and was now standing behind him. 'Manocher Jaan, have you heard? New York has been bombed.'

In Manocher's frame of mind, Jamshed's words barely registered. Somewhere else in the club somebody had switched on a small transistor radio tuned to Radio Shariat so that they would be able to hear *Azan*, the call to prayer, leaving them enough time to get to the mosque in time.

Jamshed tugged at Manocher's shirt and said, 'Manocher, listen.'

'Praise be to Allah. Today, brave Mujahideen have struck a mighty blow at the heart of the great infidel.'

All activity in the club ceased as the men stopped what they were doing to listen to the radio.

'Today, the Satan Bush and his cronies have learned that Americans are no longer safe in their own homes. The fires of hell are raining down on the *Kafirs*. The streets of New York are littered with their dead and the streets of Washington are running with their blood.'

A shout of 'Allah o Akbar', 'God is great', reverberated around the room. Some of those now gathered around the radio broke into spontaneous cheering. The Talibs in the room hugged each other offering congratulations. Others were silent, listening intently to the ranting of the newscaster, trying to discern what had actually happened in New York from the scant information offered by Radio Shariat.

Manocher grabbed Jamshed. 'Come, let's go.'

Jamshed followed as Manocher made his way out and across the Macroryan.

A couple of Talibs from the club followed them out and started firing AK47 rounds into the air, the traditional Afghan show of celebration and jubilation. Other sporadic bursts of automatic gunfire were echoing across the city. Red tracers, from the rapid-fire bullets arching up into the sky, lit up an otherwise dark skyline like some bizarre pyrotechnic display orchestrated with cheap fireworks.

Manocher entered the apartment block opposite his own building and made his way up the dark stairwell to his friend Ghafar's home. Jamshed followed. Manocher knocked quietly on the door. 'Ghafar, are you in there? It's me.'

The front door opened quickly, and Manocher and Jamshed were ushered into the small flat by Ghafar's mother. The two boys exchanged pleasantries with her while they took off their shoes. As she went into the kitchen to make tea for the visitors, she nodded towards the sitting room where they would find her son. To define a room in an Afghan household with a Western label is something of a misnomer. In estate agents' jargon, this flat was a 'two bedroom, lounge, kitchen and bathroom'. In Afghanistan, with such large families to accommodate, rooms were just spaces serving multiple purposes. The 'lounge' which they had just entered also served as a bedroom for Ghafar and his two younger brothers. Another room served as a dining room during the day and bedroom for the parents at night. In Ghafar's household, only his two sisters managed to get a room that was a bedroom. Most homes were sparsely furnished to facilitate this multiple use – most often just with traditional Afghan mats and bolster cushions which served both as seating for guests and bedding for the family.

The room was in virtual darkness as Manocher and Jamshed entered. The only source of light was a bare sixty-watt bulb which glowed and waned with the fluctuations of the Kabul power supply. The room, like most in Afghanistan, was in dire need of decoration; the paint had long since lost any colour. Afghans had put every aspect of their normal lives on hold since the arrival of the Taliban, and aesthetics such as decoration came very low on people's list of priorities. The Taliban ban on photographs of any kind meant that the walls of Ghafar's room were bare, with the exception of a framed certificate from a computer course that one of Ghafar's younger brothers had completed a year earlier. In spite of its position of prominence in the room, how much of a real qualification the diploma represented was debateable since the entire course had been taught without the students going anywhere near a real computer at all. The computer department at the university where he had studied computer science actually had no computers at all – the nearest the students got to seeing a computer was courtesy of an ageing wall chart salvaged from an old Compaq catalogue. All practical instruction had been based on this improvised teaching aid.

Even in the dim light, however, it was still possible to make out the faded areas on the walls where the once-proud family had exhibited a veritable gallery of images representing key moments in their lives. Dominating the room now, on the wall just above where Ghafar was seated reading, was the damage created by an RPG missile which had happened during the factional fighting a few years ago. Ghafar had been sleeping in the room when the stray Mujahideen missile had hit their apartment. Such was life at that time that, instead of becoming hysterical, all Ghafar had done was to dust the debris off his sheet, turn over and go back to sleep. A framed certificate of indeterminable value and an un-repaired missile hit just about summed up life under the Taliban.

Ghafar put down his book and rose to welcome Manocher and Jamshed. They kissed one another on the cheek and exchanged the Afghan greetings that could take several minutes. Satisfied about the health and welfare of virtually all of each other's living relatives, age-old customs having been upheld, they were able to proceed to other matters.

'Something big has happened in New York,' started Manocher.

'Can we hook up to CNN and see what is really happening?'

Ghafar had pre-empted the request and was already moving towards his sisters' bedroom where he retrieved a portable six-inch black and white television which had been secreted there.

'Give me a hand setting it up. The signal is not very strong here so I will need someone to move the dish while I tune it in.' He also brought out a rudimentary satellite dish that he had fashioned himself out of old tin cans. The logos on the tins created a weird mosaic of Western consumerism, totally at odds with the surroundings. Ghafar proceeded to set up the television and the receiver while Manocher and Jamshed secured the dish to the balcony making sure that it remained out of sight. *'Thou shalt not have a television set or satellite receiving equipment'* still remained high on the list of Taliban commandments. Ghafar was taking great personal risk maintaining this last link with the outside world.

A fuzzy picture appeared on the screen and the three friends looked hard at it, trying to make out what was happening. The commentary left them in no doubt. Islamic fundamentalists had hit the World Trade Centre and the Pentagon. The finger was pointed very much at Osama Bin Laden's al-Qaeda based in Afghanistan. Inevitable retribution would follow. George Bush had promised his nation that these acts would not go unpunished.

Ghafar's mother entered with tea and stale toffees for the three boys. She poured each of them a cup from the oversized thermos.

'So Beta, your mother tells me that you are going to London very soon?'

'No, Auntie, I am not going anywhere. After tonight I will be staying put here in Kabul.'

Jamshed looked at his friend with a heavy conscience, hoping that it was not his prayers earlier that day for a miracle to keep Manocher in Kabul that had brought on this devastation.

STRATFORD UPON AVON – 15.00 HOURS

I called John on his mobile just after the South Tower had collapsed. The mobile was switched off and I was put through to the answer-phone. The familiar voice came on the line. 'You have come through to the answer machine for John Murray. This means that I do not wish to speak to you right now. Leave a message after the beep, and if you are a young blond female I will get back to you. If not, I probably won't, but try your luck anyway. That includes you, Mum.' Beep.

The message, which John had recorded on his personal mobile to wind up his priggish-semi-feminist Danish assistant, always brought a smile to my face whenever I heard it. But at that particular moment I found it extremely irritating. Quite out character, I just wanted to slam the phone into the wall. I took a couple of deep breaths and calmed myself down.

'JM, if I don't get through to you before you pick up this message, call me immediately. This is urgent.'

Travelling as much as we did, both John and I had favourite hotels in each of the cities that we worked in; the familiarity of the same surroundings and staff made the experience as much like 'a home away from home' as was possible when staying in so many different places. In Tallinn we both opted for The Hotel Olympia, a huge concrete monstrosity built by the Finns. Situated just outside the old city, it was central and ideally positioned for our needs. In addition, the hotel gave our organisation a special rate and, much to John's delight, was mostly staffed by stunning blondes who all looked as if they had walked straight off the catwalk.

I dragged through my digital diary and found the number for the hotel. I got through first time.

'Good Afternoon. Hotel Olympia. How may I help you?'

I immediately recognised the voice. Only two of the girls on reception were as fluent in English as this.

'Hello Svetlana, it is Mr Mahmood – can you put me through to Mr Murray's room?'

'Hello Mr Mahmood, how are you? When will you be in Tallinn again?'

I was in no mood for idle chitchat even if it was with the gorgeous Svetlana. 'I am sorry Svetlana, this is an emergency. Can you put me through to John straightaway?'

She sounded hurt. 'Mr Murray has requested a DND on his phone.'

'Sveta darling – ignore the DND, please just put me through to his room.'

I heard the phone ring several times before John's distinctly befuddled voice came on the line. 'Whoever it is – piss off.' Whenever John got worked up, his choice of language and accent always betrayed his Brummie roots.

'John, it's me.'

'Look mate, I mailed you to tell you I was alright. Just go away and leave me alone. I haven't had any kip in two days.'

'John, shut up and listen to me, switch on to BBC World or CNN or whatever. Listen, just switch on the bloody television.'

'What? Pakistan finally won at cricket or something?' John still sounded asleep.

'Trust me, John, for Christ's sake, just do as I say NOW!'

The urgency in my voice must have got through to some part of John's subconscious and made him realise that something serious was happening.

'Alright, calm down – don't get your knickers in a twist. Let me just grab the remote.' I heard the television come on in the background. 'Trust me, this had better be good or you die!'

It took several seconds for the images to register in John's mind. He woke up pretty swiftly after that. 'Oh my God! What's happening? That's New York? The twin towers? Oh shit! What's going on?' He must have been reading the captions that were crawling along the bottom of the screen. 'A tower has collapsed? Terrorists? Tell me that this is a dream.'

'No John. I just wish it was.'

While I brought John up to date on events as they had unfolded up to now, the North Tower also started to collapse.

We watched – no more than helpless voyeurs. Even the barrier of television could not sanitise the horror of death and destruction unfolding in front of us.

As we watched, as if to reiterate some unsaid point, pictures of Palestinians celebrating in the Gaza strip appeared on the screen. As the news had filtered through that Muslim fundamentalists were responsible, I had felt disgusted to be a Muslim; now seeing these images of jubilation, I felt positively sick. I knew what I was seeing but my brain didn't want to process or compute the images.

We both felt the monumental significance of what we were watching unfold in front of us.

'I think everything's changed now.'

John agreed. 'It seemed the last time we spoke, just a few hours ago, we lived in such an innocent world.'

'Yes, and now, in a matter of a few minutes, it has become a world of distrust, of hard-heartedness, of revenge. Nothing will ever be the same…' I mused almost to myself.

'The strange thing is – these terrorists in their minds are doing a good deed – even a holy one. Twisted, but it's true.'

'That's what I'm afraid of. The lines seem to be drawn. Who knows who will win? This time it really is a different kind of war. A war of ideas.'

The pictures on the screen switched back to the Pentagon. Something suddenly clicked in my mind. 'Hang on, John, I want to check something.'

Taking the cordless phone with me I walked into the study. I quickly found what I was looking for – the envelope addressed to Gifto Travel was still lying in my out tray on the table. Even though I had cancelled my flights to the US a couple of weeks earlier, I had not yet got around to posting the tickets back to the travel agent for refund. I ripped open the envelope and looked at the ticket. '*Waseem Mahmood AA77 Washington Dulles to LAX, Los Angeles, September 11th, Confirmed OK.*' A wave of nausea swept over me. My head began to spin. My legs gave way and I slumped to the floor.

John must have heard me fall. 'Waseem! Waseem, mate, what is going on? You okay?' I heard John yelling into the phone.

I found it difficult to speak. My chest constricted and I was having difficulty breathing. 'John, I was … I was…'

I closed my eyes to try and gather my thoughts. In that split second, I felt myself where I should have been that morning, sitting in seat 34G on a plane helplessly flying over Washington. I saw the Lincoln Memorial, the Congress building, the Washington Monument, all whizz past the window. I saw the Potomac River looming up. Arlington. The Pentagon. Then I felt the impact, a huge bang and explosion after which nothing – just an oblivion of infinite darkness.

'For Christ's sake, Waseem, what is going on?'

'Flight 77… Pentagon… I was booked on it…'

SAN FRANCISCO – 20.00 HOURS

Abi had been on the go for nearly fifteen hours without a break, sustained only by caffeine and adrenalin. For her, telling the world what was happening was a good way of not having to deal with it herself. Professionalism bred detachment. Many others in the newsroom were also grateful to be working that day. Team spirit and a shared sense of duty to the audience pulled them all through. The newsroom and studio gallery had taken on the semblance of a wartime bunker where those within were in some way disconnected from the reality of the events taking place on the television screens.

The mood of the broadcasts had also changed during the course of the day, reflecting the feelings of those broadcasting and with them the mood of the nation. At the beginning of the day, broadcasters overwhelmed by the immediacy of the sequence of events that were unfolding just transmitted the raw pictures live as they came in with little or no commentary; as the day progressed, the questioning had begun, but more importantly the attribution of blame had started. Finally, as the day ended, virtually all the broadcasters had embraced a patriotic stance with almost religious zeal. The Stars and Stripes dominated every frame, and objective news anchors had started talking about the attack in the first person. The attacks were 'on our great nation' and 'against our way of life'.

With only one more news programme to do that evening before the relief shift took over, even the hardiest of staff had begun to show signs of fatigue. Abi made her way from the cocoon of the studio back to her desk for a short respite from the relentless barrage of news and information.

The newsroom buzzed with activity, just like any other day, the sombre mood of those working being the only tangible difference. Heads were bowed and nobody could make eye contact with anyone else. Almost all expressions were blank and the news team was mechanically going through the required motions. The usual laughter and gossip that formed part of newsroom life was conspicuous by its absence.

Abi poured herself a coffee and took it back to her desk. Cameron had thoughtfully left her a sandwich. When she saw the food, Abi realised that she had not eaten since the morning and that she was very hungry. A healthy eater who never missed a meal, she wondered how she had got through the day without any sustenance. She felt grateful to Cameron for having had the foresight.

Abi's cubicle was untidy as usual, not that any of the neighbouring cubicles were any better. Tidiness and journalism have never gone well together in the best of cases, but in Abi's case they came nowhere close. This was surprising because in her private life Abi was a fastidiously organised person whose need for order and tidiness often drove her flatmate Rachel crazy.

Abi logged on to her computer to check her emails, and saw that during her absence from work more than 600 had accumulated in her in-box. She didn't feel up to looking at emails at that moment and decided to give them a miss till the next day. Instead she switched on her mobile phone. The voicemail flashed, indicating that she had messages. While she ate the sandwich she connected to the voicemail service. There were six messages; one was from her parents who were concerned about how she was coping on her first day back, two were from Rachel who frantically wanted to talk with her about the tragic events of the day, and the remainder were from Mo.

'Message left at 09.15hrs. Abs I cannot get a hold of Mumu, am beginning to get concerned. Call me if you can.'

Mumu was Mo's younger brother who had just started grad school at Columbia University specialising, ironically, in security issues in the Middle East. They had been smuggled to America as young children when the Islamic revolution in Iran had claimed the lives of their parents, both of whom had been close allies of the Shah. Growing up in exile, living with a succession of uncles, the two brothers had developed a very close bond.

'Message left at 09.45 hours. Cannot get through to New York at all. Call me as soon as you pick this up.'

'Message left at 12.05 hours. Just managed to speak to an uncle in New Jersey on his cell. Mumu was doing the early shift this morning... Abi, please, please call me, urgently...'

Even though the desperation was evident in Mo's voice, for a moment Abi did not immediately register the significance of the messages. Slowly it dawned on her.

Mumu had been in San Francisco a couple of weeks ago, and a conversation that she had had with him at the Cheesecake Factory atop Bloomingdales department store replayed in her mind. Mumu proudly boasted to her that he was going to pay his own way through school and not rely on his family. To prove his point he had got himself a job as a waiter at The Restaurant At The top Of The World in the Twin Towers. In between bites of strawberry cheesecake and cream, he had joked a great deal about how he was starting his career at the top.

The colour drained from Abi's face. Till now, she had been isolated from the reality of the horrors taking place on the East Coast by the barrier created by her professionalism. She had not really thought of the casualty figures she had been broadcasting all day as representing real people. They were just statistics. Suddenly, the thought of Mumu being one of those who might have perished put it all into perspective. She prayed fervently that Mumu, her young brother-in-law-to-be, was not amongst those who had lost their lives.

Abi picked up the phone and started dialling Mo's number. She stopped before she completed it. She replaced the receiver and retreated to the sanctuary offered by the studio.

Abi ended her day just as she had begun it – on autopilot.

Part 3

The Road to Kabul

We are more than the sum of our knowledge.
We are the products of our imagination.
Ferdi Serim

What difference does it make to the dead, the orphans
and the homeless, whether the mad destruction is wrought
under the name of totalitarianism or the holy name of
liberty or democracy?
Mahatma Gandhi

COPENHAGEN — 10 OCTOBER 2001

The plane began its descent to Copenhagen's Kastrup Airport. I put down the file of papers that I had been trying to work on during the flight and looked out of the window at the familiar geometric patterns of the Danish landscape unfolding below. I hate to admit that subconsciously my attention for most of the flight had been fixed on a Mediterranean-looking passenger sitting across the aisle from me and that I had suffered discernible palpitations each time the poor guy got up to use the toilet or get anything out of the overhead locker. Another hundred pairs of anxious eyes had also followed his every move. Such was the mood of the post 9-11 environment that suspicion and mistrust amongst fellow travellers were on a knife-edge. In the US a captain had offloaded a respectable Indian doctor with whom the other passengers had refused to travel.

Even in the cool, air-conditioned climate on board the aircraft, nervous sweat was making the shirt cling to my back. My stomach reeled from the sickness I had felt for most of the flight.

Events had moved swiftly after 11 September. Two days after the attacks, President Bush emerged from a meeting with his key military advisers at Camp David and told the American people: 'Everyone who wears the uniform should get ready. We're at war.' Bush had gone on to warn the grieving nation to brace themselves for a long and bloody conflict. 'I will not settle for a token act. Our response must be sweeping, sustained and effective. This act will not stand.' He swore that there would be full and proper vengeance for the atrocities that had violated the very heart of America. 'We will find those who did it. We will smoke them out of their holes, we'll get them running, and we'll bring them to justice.'

The exodus from Afghanistan had begun the day after the attacks had taken place in America. In a land without television where no one had actually seen the footage of the two hijacked planes crashing into the World Trade Centre, nobody had any doubts that the US was about to launch attacks on their country – and that these reprisals, when they came, would be devastating. Even Afghans, for whom war and conflict was a way of life, now feared worse.

Residents in the more affluent districts of Kabul started packing their bags and began to leave the city. Battle-hardened men no longer possessing the will for yet another fight padlocked the gates to their homes and drove off in battered Toyota pick-up trucks towards the Khyber Pass, to the safety that they believed lay beyond the mountainous border with Pakistan. Women hidden underneath billowing blue burkas were packed into the backs of the trucks beside the few possessions that the men took with them. The crying of children, too young to understand the spectre of death that hung over them, combined with the spluttering of ancient engines to create the cacophony of a frightened nation in flight. Those who remained behind began barricading their already battered homes for yet another onslaught. Fuel and food supplies, already in short supply because of sanctions, began to run out very quickly. Many lives were lost in the fighting that broke out in the streets over a few litres of diesel oil.

The Afghan people's fears were justified. A few days later, President Bush addressed Congress with a firm warning for their rulers, 'The Taliban must act and act immediately. They will hand over the terrorists or they will share in their fate.' With British Prime Minister, Tony Blair, standing by his side, the President continued, 'Our grief has turned to anger and anger to resolution. The hour is coming when America will act.' Congress stood and gave the President a standing ovation that went on for what seemed like an eternity.

The mood within the Taliban regime remained equally resolute. Mullah Omar, the one-eyed fanatic who led the Taliban, addressed the Afghan people over Radio Shariat with passionate vitriol. 'Don't be cowards. Every Muslim should be ready for holy war and take strength from their faith in Islam. Paradise awaits those who find martyrdom in the fight against the Great Infidel.'

On the evening of 7 October President Bush appeared on national television. 'On my orders, the United States military has begun strikes against Al-Qaeda terrorist training camps and military installations of the Taliban regime in Afghanistan. More than two weeks ago, I gave Taliban leaders a series of clear and specific demands... None of these demands was met. And now, the Taliban will pay a price... At the same time, the oppressed people of Afghanistan will know the generosity of America and our allies. As we strike military targets, we will also drop food, medicine and supplies to the starving and suffering men and women and children of Afghanistan. The United States of America is a friend to the Afghan people.'

I sent a mobile text message to John the moment I disembarked from the plane at Copenhagen: 'Touch and go @ times, but made it 2 CPH in 1 piece. Will call U after meeting. WM'.

The single spotlight blinded me as the curtain parted and I stood on the stage facing the audience. I could sense my classmates sitting in dark anonymity just a few feet away, but from where I was and with the light shining directly in my eyes, I could not see anybody beyond the footlights. The perspiration trickled down my forehead into my eyes streaking the little grease paint make-up that I had reluctantly used. My hands felt clammy and my knees had trouble supporting my weight. My stomach began to churn and I felt rather sick. Surely there was something wrong; this could not be what acting and performing was all about. Why had I chosen this profession?

I repositioned the cheap plastic chair in a way so that the back of it faced the front of stage; I then sat, straddling it as one would a horse, with my elbows on the back rest and my chin resting on my hands. I looked intently into the dark void, waited for a few beats and began.

> *'Now is the winter of our discontent*
> *Made glorious summer by this sun of York.'*

The first lines out of the way, I began to relax a little and decided to let Shakespeare's writing do the hard work. All I had to do was to make sure I remembered the words, a great feat in itself.

Just then someone sitting in the audience on the studio balcony coughed, reminding me that proud parents were also present at this performance. My parents, however, had not come to see me perform – but then, they had never come to see me perform, not in the primary school nativity, not in school plays, not in school concerts, not tonight – never. Alas, I was destined to tread the boards of my glittering stage career without the support of my family in the wings.

In that instant, I understood Richard; I understood the bitterness towards his family that was manifesting itself through the scene. At that moment, I wanted to be Richard – his solutions seemed so much more pragmatic than my lame acceptance of the situation.

The applause took me somewhat by surprise and broke the spell; no longer Richard in a London street, I was back in Sutton Coldfield College of Further Education Drama Studio performing to an audience that did not include my parents.

As I came off stage John Murray's bulk blocked my exit. I tried to dodge him but felt his hand on my shoulder, stopping me. He looked totally absurd dressed as a 1930s American gangster holding a mocked-up wooden Tommy gun under one arm and with an oversized fedora on his head. He was chewing on what looked like a cigar poking out from the side of his mouth.

'Yes?'

'Sublime. Intense Stanislavski performance. Minimalist Brechtian staging – loved it… '

With that he turned and swaggered onto the stage to begin his contribution to the evening: a performance of 'Macbeth' set in 1930s American gangland delivered in a pseudo Italian-American accent.

This critique of my performance from John was the longest conversation we had had since the start of college several months ago. But where the hell had he learnt of Stanislavski, living in Castle Vale? I can't imagine that the works of nineteenth-century Russian writers were the major topic of discussion at the Artful Dodger public house on his council estate.

As the first year of college reached the final semester, John and I had managed, for most of the time, to maintain a diplomatic détente that Henry Kissinger would have been proud of. We simply kept out of each other's way. However, all this was to change during the Easter holidays when fate set our stars, till then in respectively divergent orbits, on an irrevocable collision course.

Holidays in second-generation Asian homes were strange affairs. We never went anywhere or did anything interesting as our neighbours' children always seemed to be doing. Holidays for me were a diet of daytime television and playing cricket 'up the park' with other Asian kids in the neighbourhood who were in the same position. During this particular Easter break, my parents, as always, were at their respective work places, making the most of the overtime that was available during the holidays when their colleagues took time off to be with their families.

I was just watching Bagpuss putting the toys back to sleep when the phone rang. It was Anne-Marie Greene, a girl from the drama course and the only person there that I was remotely close to. Much to the chagrin of others in the group, in particular John Murray, we always sat together in classes and always chose to work with one another for group exercises. Anne-Marie Greene was without doubt the most beautiful girl in our class if not the whole college. She was trained as a dancer and had already carved herself a budding career as a model. Looking at her, it was not difficult to see why. She was quite tall with naturally blond hair almost down to the small of her back, dazzling green eyes and a very-seventies-in-vogue Twiggy figure. She knew that her legs were her best feature and did everything she could to accentuate them – her jeans looked as if they had been sprayed on. But more than anything else it was her smile that captivated everybody.

Anne-Marie's voice sounded frantic on the phone – she and John had just managed to have a major fracas with the three others in the group that they had been working together with for their drama practical exam. John had felt that the others were not taking the assignment as seriously as they should have been, and when one of them had wanted to leave rehearsals early for a tennis class, John had hit the roof. Apparently, Anne-Marie had had to physically restrain him from rearranging little Geoffrey-with-a-G's smug face. The nice Sutton kids, who saw drama as a nice hobby and not as a vocation, had unilaterally decided that they could not work with an uncouth slob like John and had walked out in a huff. This left John and Anne-Marie with five days to come up with an alternative exam piece. I calmed Anne-Marie down as much as I could over the phone and told her that I would be with her as soon as I could get there, reassuring her that between us we would sort it out.

As soon as I walked into the drama studio, Anne-Marie rushed over, gave me a tight hug and started babbling nineteen to the dozen. I hardly heard a word she said because my eyes were fixed on John Murray who was standing behind her. I had spent most of the time on the journey to college trying to pre-empt his reaction when he saw me, since I was sure that he had been press-ganged by Anne-Marie into calling me for help.

Much to my surprise, he offered me his hand and said, 'Thanks, mate, for coming in and helping us out.'

'That's okay. Until Annie called, watching Bagpuss had been the highlight of my day.'

He laughed. 'So that's where you pick up your acting techniques!'

John had flown in to spend the weekend with me in Stratford, ostensibly to provide his qualified input to the strategy paper on a humanitarian radio service for Afghanistan that I had been working on, the one I was going to be presenting to the Danish Foreign Ministry for funding. But in reality, as a good friend, he had taken the first opportunity that his work schedule had allowed to come and provide the moral support that he knew I needed. He was aware that I had not told anyone in my family of the greater significance of my cancelled trip to America. This was a conscious decision; I felt that my ability to continue to work in international development, already a sore point, would have been heavily curtailed if Farah or the boys had known the truth.

Trying to keep the semblance of normality, I had taken the whole family, together with John, to the Royal Shakespeare Company to see *Julius Caesar* on the Saturday evening, after which we had had dinner at the Thespian Restaurant, a strange name for an Indian restaurant and surprisingly the only place that appeared to be open in Stratford for post-theatre meals.

On the Sunday, John and I managed to escape from the family under the pretence of a working lunch and had spent most of the day sitting together on the banks on the River Avon watching the last of the summer tourists enjoying the delights of Shakespeare's home town; old couples trying to recapture the magic of their courting days; young teenagers enjoying stolen moments away from the grind of urban living; youthful fillies in diaphanous summer dresses – potential conquests a few years ago, now totally out of our league; toddlers feeding the geese and swans on the river oblivious to the hallowed significance of the ground they were standing on. All this, combined with endless cups of frothing cappuccinos and delightful paninis at Cox's Yard, had made for a quintessential English afternoon, something that was now totally foreign to the realities of our recent lives. Many of our salad days as drama students had been spent at this very spot discussing the finer points of Mr. Shakespeare's work, but now John and I found our lives helplessly adrift; a once familiar world was becoming increasingly alien and in its place an unnatural world was becoming uncomfortably real. Discussions of Taliban, collateral damage, surgical strikes and flak jackets that John and I engaged in that afternoon seemed so much at odds with our surroundings. The *theatres* we now referred to were *theatres of war* where different sorts of dramas were enacted – dramas where not all the players survived long enough to take the final curtain call.

I had been going through a major crisis of conscience since the attacks on September 11th. John knew it. I needed to talk and he needed to listen. He had always been my sounding board and at that moment more than any time in my life I needed him to say the right words. I didn't know what the right words were, but I knew for a fact that no matter what, John would say them.

'John, do you think what we do really matters? What we saw on TV – all that suffering, the horror – how can we ever begin to imagine that what we do makes a difference? In the end, it's all selfishness, isn't it?'

'I don't know, Waseem. There are no answers, are there? We just have to be who we are – and that is goodness. The terrorists don't like us for being who we are. But will that stop us from being who we want to be – I don't think so. Maybe being ordinary is the very essence of goodness. Maybe when we pursue our little projects, our desires, we are perpetuating goodness – and it is this goodness that these murderers want to destroy.' John looked over at me intently. 'Where is all this doubt suddenly coming from, Waseem?'

I turned my gaze from the river to look John long in the eye. 'Maybe guilt, John, guilt...'

For once, I think that I had actually floored John Murray. 'Guilt?'

A wave of torment washed over me and I knew that John could sense it. I heaved a deep sigh and steadied myself. 'Guilt – because when I didn't show up on flight 77, they gave the seat to someone else. I was even assigned a seat number – 34G. Some poor soul sat on my seat and went down with the plane when it should have been me. Me, John – me!' My eyes began to well up, 'Is what I do so damned important, or that worthwhile, that I was saved – and someone else died in my place?'

John listened intently, looking as if he was beginning to understand the demons that had been screwing up my head.

'I can't just forget, John. You and I have been in many horrible places. We've seen too much that decent men shouldn't have to see. But this time it's different. This time it is personal. I have to make a difference. In my own small way, I have to prove to myself that saving me was important. Do you understand, John?'

Tears welled up in John's eyes, too, and he nodded. 'I understand, Waseem. I do.'

As I walked through customs into the arrivals hall at Copenhagen Airport I saw that Soren, my boss, was waiting for me. This had very rarely happened in the four years I had been working for the organization, Soren personally picking me up from the airport. John had obviously briefed other colleagues about my near brush with death. I presume that with the amount of time that we all spent travelling, the possibility that any one of us could have been a victim of 9-11 had spooked everybody.

Soren was a typical Dane, with blonde hair, bushy beard and the most piercing deep blue eyes – the only reason that Lena, his wife, claimed that she had married him. Towering a good six inches above me, Soren was dressed in his trademark 'uniform': a crumpled brightly-coloured cotton shirt, frayed jeans belted below the waist but still managing to be a good two inches above his ankles, an oversized suit jacket whose matching trousers had been condemned to a charity shop long since by his wife, and

Jesus sandals – *with socks*! He looked more like a hippy professor, a 60s time warp, than one of the world's leading authorities on the reconstruction of post-war media. In spite of his outward appearance, Soren's presence exuded an authority that demanded respect.

The Danes are one of the most-laid back nations I have come across and Soren was even more laid back than the average Dane. Nothing ever fazed him, but this morning at Copenhagen airport he looked almost sullen and lost for words. He attempted a smile as he saw me approach. 'Hi. Glad you made it.'

I tried to be cheerful. 'Hi Soren. Good to see you again. Hey, thanks for coming out all this way to pick me up.'

'No problems, my pleasure. I thought that you could brief me on what you and John have dreamt up this time on the drive into town.' A few beats of uncomfortable silence ensued. 'How are you?'

'As you can see I'm fine… I appreciate all the concern, but honestly, I am okay.'

He moved towards me and instead of shaking my proffered hand embraced me in a tight bear hug. We parted abruptly. Another uncomfortable silence followed.

'How was the flight?'

'As good as BA can be, I guess. The sandwiches and tepid coffee will never improve on these short-haul routes. Of course, most of the passengers spent the duration of the flight worrying that I was a terrorist who was going to hijack the plane and crash it into… I don't know… the Little Mermaid.'

Soren didn't know whether to laugh or not. After a few seconds he said, 'Did you hear that someone has stolen the head of the Little Mermaid?'

'Islamic fundamentals?'

'No… No… some TV reporter did it for a silly publicity stunt.' Soren smiled, sensing that my old dark sense of humour was back.

'So let me get this right, the Little Mermaid is in the middle of the harbour without a head?'

'Yeah, the authorities have only just recovered it and apparently it will take a few days to replace it onto her body.'

I just burst into fits of giggles. The thought of the headless Little Mermaid was just too much to bear.

We made our way to the car park. The airport was eerily deserted, even though it was nearly a month after 9-11. More nervous souls than me had obviously not yet regained the confidence to get back in the air.

'So who else is going to be at this meeting?'

Soren briefed me as he eased the car onto the motorway for the short drive into the centre of town.

The Danish Ministry of Foreign Affairs is a modern steel and glass building on one of the backwaters of Copenhagen harbour. It is directly opposite the parliament building on the other side of the Knippelsbro Bridge, one of the more famous landmarks in the city. The new buildings that form the Asiatisk Plad development along the harbour are strangely in harmony with the green-roofed baroque buildings that make up the rest of the government offices in the area – a rare feat in urban redevelopment which the Danes seem to have managed rather well.

Soren and I were ushered into the Ministry with the minimum of fuss and within minutes found ourselves seated in a large anonymous meeting room awaiting our hosts who had gone off to arrange coffee. It is routine in Denmark that officials, no matter their rank, are responsible for providing the refreshments for their visitors.

The room had the most beautiful view over the harbour, but unfortunately I was seated with my back to the windows looking instead at a large white board on which someone had drawn a colourful flow chart. Other than this splash of colour on the board and the ubiquitous blue chairs which seem to be in every Danish office anywhere in the world, the rest of the room looked rather sterile. It could have easily been a hospital waiting room rather than the nerve centre where the Danish Government made some of its most important foreign policy decisions.

As Soren and I arranged our papers in preparation for the meeting, our hosts returned carrying the various accoutrements necessary to provide a steady stream of caffeine-fuelled beverages. Bottles of mineral water – still and sparkling – were already on the table.

We went through the perfunctory exchange of business cards. The usual comments followed about the design of our organisation's cards which uniquely carried our photographs – they are, as we always pointed out, a useful aide-memoir to jog people's memory and not some act of misplaced vanity. Whatever the reason, they always served as a great ice breaker.

The meeting was chaired by a woman from the humanitarian aid department. In her mid-twenties, she was one of the people responsible for managing aid to the South Asia region. Her colleague was of indeterminate age and someone I recognised as a deputy director of some quango or other in the United Nations. My organisation had had close dealings with him about work we had done in the Balkans for the Ministry, and I vaguely remembered that I had shared a bus ride with him from Zagreb to Opatia on the way to a media conference. Now, if his business card had had his picture on it like ours did, I could have been sure whether it was him or not.

Introductions over and with coffee cups charged, the woman whose name was Pia called the meeting to order. She thanked us both for coming at such short notice and me in particular for having flown from Stratford.

She then went on to describe her departmental policy position, and made it clear that her department was still in the process of deciding on a political level what the Danish Government's response to the unfolding Afghanistan crisis would be. She also made it very clear that her department's definition of 'Humanitarian Aid' meant only food, water and shelter; media was not part of their remit. I was dumb-founded. I had specially flown in for this meeting. What was the purpose of it if she was not going to be able to fund my humanitarian radio station. Controlling my temper, I asked her, 'So, unless I am missing something here, what exactly is the reason for this meeting?'

'I was intrigued by your plans and wanted to know more. I believe in cross-cutting synergies.'

My eyes de-focussed. I felt the room spinning. The ticking of the electric clock on the wall began to pound like a hammer on the auditory sensors in my brain. Even in this huge room I felt claustrophobic, as if the walls were closing in. I fought back waves of nausea.

'So let me get this right. The hundreds of thousands of refugees fleeing their homes, the hundreds of thousands of Afghans now stranded in the middle of nowhere because the borders with Pakistan and Iran have been closed...' She listened dispassionately. '... these people caught up in the middle of a battlefield. You are telling me that the Danish Government does not regard this as a humanitarian crisis.'

'No. What I am saying is that the department has not yet decided on a suitable intervention strategy.'

The pounding in my head intensified. I hate it so much when officials hide behind bureaucratic mumbo jumbo. 'So when will the department decide? Perhaps when a few more thousands die? Can't you see that now is the time that these people need our help? Don't you think that they have suffered enough?'

'That is very unfair; the Danish Government is constantly monitoring the situation and will take the most appropriate action when it deems the time is right.

We have already authorised several million dollars of multilateral aid through the relevant UN agencies.'

I glared at her. She glared back. The tension in the room was palpable.

Her UN colleague coughed. 'I have a suggestion. My organisation has money to undertake a fact-finding mission to Pakistan next week. Why don't you guys join us and do a proper feasibility out there and then I am sure that Pia's department will take another look at the project proposal when you get back.'

Soren, who seemed stunned by the way that the proceedings of the past few minutes had developed, suddenly snapped out of his dazed stupor. 'I think that is a very good idea, Claus. I am sure that Waseem would agree that there are a lot of practicalities that still need to be resolved. We will be happy to take you up on your offer.'

I collected my papers and addressed Pia as I rose to leave. 'Thousands of innocent people have already died in New York and Washington. We'll be looking at thousands, hundreds of thousands, even millions of deaths if you don't take action now. I just pray that you are the one your department decides to send to Afghanistan after the winter snows have thawed and you will see for yourself the death and devastation that your damned remits will have caused.' She looked completely taken aback, and I should have stopped right then but found myself carrying on, almost involuntarily. 'You know something? In my mind this attitude of yours makes you no better than those who carried out the attacks in America or even the Taliban. You are all equally responsible for the deaths of innocent people.' With that I walked out and started making my way shakily down the corridor. As I got to the main lobby I stopped and waited for Soren who was following a short distance behind. I was bent double, hyperventilating, trying to catch my breath as he caught up with me.

'That was a bit dramatic. Whatever happened to professionalism in there?'

I listened in silence, unable to look Soren in the eye. I stared down uncomfortably at my shoes and wriggled like some naughty schoolboy being admonished, except that this was a lot more serious than being caught smoking behind the bike sheds. 'We do a lot of work with the Ministry of Foreign Affairs; you really cannot treat one of their senior officials with that sort of contempt. Emotion has no place in our line of work.'

'I hate desk jockeys who sit in their plush offices making these sorts of decisions on the fate of people's lives with a single stroke of a pen. It is you and me, Soren, who have to pick up the pieces out in theatre.'

'Look, we both know that she was only trying to do her job. Why can't you see that she only agreed to see us because she was interested in the project? Just get it into that thick brain of yours that our survival as an organisation depends on donors such as her department.'

'As will the deaths of a few thousand more innocent people while we do our feasibility.'

'Let's be realistic. We both know that there are more than a few holes in your proposal. Damn it! You don't even have the Pakistanis' permission to site your transmitters there yet.'

It was amazing how Soren managed to express his utmost anger without raising his voice a single decibel. Part of me knew he was right, and so was Pia.

'So I suggest that you co-operate with Claus, take the opportunity of the feasibility and plug those gaps. I promise you, if you tie up all the loose ends I will get you the money you need for your bloody radio stations.' As always, Soren had presented the voice of reason.

'But Soren, you know what I feel about wasting aid money on fact-finding missions, feasibilities, needs analyses and all that administrative crap. This is about saving lives, not writing reports on how to save lives.'

'Don't think of this trip as a fact-finding mission if you don't want to, think of it as a way of getting into theatre. Both of us know that that's where you want to be... so just shut up and go.'

I was sitting at the departure gate about to board the return flight back to Birmingham before I managed to finally get hold of John.

'How did it go, then, Big Man?'

'We got two places on a three-week frigging fact-finding mission led by the United frigging Nations.'

'Is the shattering of an illusion the aesthetic equivalent of one?'

John Murray sat next to me, grinned at the obvious discomfort that my question had caused Millicent Turner-Browne, our prissy tweed-loving drama lecturer. Fed up with the mediocrity of her theory classes, John and I had declared intellectual anarchy and spent all our spare time in Birmingham Central Library digging up obscure references to provide the ammunition for our insurrection. The more obscure the reference the better. Millicent's classes lacked the informed discussion we craved. Her pedagogical style relied solely on dictating to us the regurgitated notes of a former student, Andy Bow-Your-Head Lynch, who had got straight 'A's' and gone on to Oxford University to major in classical Greek drama. While this seemed to be acceptable to the rest of the class who lapped it up without a second thought, John and I found that Andy Lynch's work didn't even begin to scratch the surface of the subject. The sport of Millie baiting became an obsession for us both.

When John followed the 'aesthetic equivalent' comment with a reference to Artaud's theatre of cruelty, it proved to be one step too far for Millicent who burst into tears, got up and stormed out of the class leaving us at the mercy of our indignant classmates. We were only saved from a lynching by the summons a few minutes later to the deputy principal's office, where we were severely reprimanded for being disruptive influences. As a consequence, we achieved notoriety amongst our contemporaries, we became academic revolutionaries, comrades-in-arms despised by the teaching establishment and regarded with contempt by out petite bourgeoisie classmates.

It was around this time that I had my first epiphany: I discovered to my utmost dismay that I was not cut out to be an actor. Standing there in a drama improvisation class with my arms stuck out at a ridiculous angle, I realised that I was not being a tree. As hard as I tried to experience the emotions of a tree swaying in the forest I could not. Not only did I feel very stupid, I also felt a total failure. In the greater scheme of things, I guess that divine revelations have a tendency to work like that; you find out that you've arrived at a painful truth without realizing that you were even looking for it in the first place.

After the intense five days that I spent directing their exam piece, John, Anne-Marie and I had become inseparable. John and Anne-Marie's performances as Brick and Maggie in the first act of Tennessee William's 'Cat on a Hot Tin Roof' in their exam practical had earned them both 'A's' and a rare comment from Ernest that our interpretation of the play had been far more insightful than the Liz Taylor and Paul Newman film. My move into direction was as painless as it was inspired.

Our salvation from what we saw as the mundanity of the drama course and the fact that we felt increasingly cut off from the rest of the group came from the most unusual quarter. Wulstan Wilson, the Spanish teacher, a time-warp hippy whose colourful kaftans were a psychedelic aide-memoire to the fact that he was still living in the fag end of the sixties, started a television course at the college. In spite of his own life being firmly grounded in the era of flower power, free love, long hair and tie-dyed tee-shirts, he was an educational visionary who had the foresight to realise that media was going to be one of the buzz careers of the eighties.

He had spent two years convincing the powers-that-be to donate some space and money to set up a television studio. Fortunately for us, he succeeded in his quest during our first year at the college, and an old stock room and what seemed like a broom cupboard were furnished with two black and white cameras, rudimentary lighting and an ancient, second-hand video recorder.

In spite of its technical shortcomings, the studio became a refuge, and even though the course was still classed as an extra-curricular activity, John and I found ourselves spending more time there than we did in the formal classes, much to the annoyance of Millicent Turner-Browne and the other regular tutors. Wulstan turned out to be a real cool dude who on more than one occasion put his own neck on the line to cover for John and me, as we were increasingly bunking more and more lessons to carry on the production of our television programmes. Here in a sea of indifference was someone who genuinely believed in our daydreams. Was it really tobacco that he always had in his pipe?

Just before we broke up for the summer holidays John cornered me in the television studio. It was one of the rare occasions that we were alone without the third musketeer, Anne-Marie.

'So Waseem, what's going on between you and Annie?' The question was not entirely unexpected; in fact I was only surprised that it had taken John so long to build up the courage to confront me on the issue.

'Nothing John – I am just not interested in Anne-Marie in that way.'

'Why? Are you gay or something?'

'No. I am not gay,'

'Don't you fancy her?'

'It's not that. She is a very beautiful girl and I confess that I love Annie dearly but I am not in love with her, John.'

The difference between loving someone and being in love with someone was beyond John's comprehension and something that was to elude him for years to come. 'What do you mean?'

'Look mate, there's someone else.' I didn't bother to elaborate and John didn't bother to ask, but the last item of contention impeding our friendship seemed to have been well and truly demolished.

John's first shot at Anne-Marie was to come a lot sooner than I could have imagined, just a few days after our conversation.

One morning before class, I found Anne-Marie sitting on the large convector heater in the drama studio in virtual darkness. She looked very fragile, almost like a little girl, small and vulnerable, sitting alone in the dimly lit studio.

'What's up Annie?'

I went over to her, jumped up beside her, and put my arm around her. Sensing the comfort of my body, she burrowed her head deep into my body and started sobbing. In between her sobs, I managed to extract from her that Steven Doyle, her childhood sweetheart, had dumped her for some floozy who worked in the local chip shop. I pulled Anne-Marie tighter into me and tried to reassure her the best I that could. John walked in a few minutes later.

'What's wrong? What's happened?'

'Steven's dumped Annie.'

A grin slowly spread across John's face. I tried in vain to pass telepathic messages to him to stop right there and not go any further, but failed miserably. Don't do this John. John opened his mouth and uttered the two small words that were to change the course of his life. His reaction to Anne-Marie's devastating news was, 'Oh great.'

Peshawar, Pakistan – 5 November 2001

Peshawar, the old garrison town near the border of Afghanistan, has been a centre for travellers, traders, smugglers and soldiers for centuries. The city of

Alexander the Great and of Rudyard Kipling's *Kim*, it is inextricably linked with the Khyber Pass, the silk route, the spice route and more recently the opium route. The old city is a remnant of those bygone days, a mosaic of bustling bazaars of every kind imaginable. Balconied buildings with intricately carved wooden doors line the narrow, winding streets, and kebab stalls and spice and perfume shops fill the dry air with fascinating aromas. Media reports describe the city as a place of terrorism, drug smuggling, arms-trading and random violence; it is said that in Peshawar it is easier to buy a RPG rocket launcher or a Stinger missile than a pair of decent socks.

The ornate marble lobby of the Pearl Continental hotel in Peshawar was teeming with people as I entered with my small mission. This was made up of a couple of nondescript idealists from Claus Nielsen's UN group, my trusted driver/guide/fixer Aga Jaan, a Pathan whom I had called on from Islamabad, and my main point man, Alexander Graziani, a mad Brummie biker skinhead with a dragon tattooed on his shaved head, who was not only responsible for the technical feasibility of the project but had also taken it upon himself to be in charge of the team's security. Fortunately, after much debate I had managed to convince him to remove most of the iron work that had adorned his face prior to our arrival in Pakistan.

The last time I had seen Alex was when we had had the altercation over the transmission of the Mitrovica tape. He had stayed on after I had left (I did the politics, John did the training and Alex stayed behind to make it all happen – that's how we worked). It is fair to say that we had all noticed that Alex's behaviour had become increasingly erratic after the incident. His drinking had increased and the rate that he was going through girlfriends was alarming even by his usual Lothario standards. More disturbing, though, was his growing tendency to go AWOL for several days at a time; he would suddenly vanish only to reappear days later with no recollection of where he had been. The problem was that this was now happening not only when he was in the relative safety of his home but also when he was on mission in war zones. It was obvious that he needed professional help but he was too much of a man to admit as much, and, as always, the adrenaline rush of the next big gig proved too great a temptation to miss out on.

With the Afghan war being fought less than fifty miles away across the other side of the Khyber Pass, Peshawar had found itself under siege once more – this time by the world's media. The Pearl Continental, situated on the Khyber Road between the old and new city, had attracted television crews and journalists from as far away as Korea and Portugal. As a consequence, its 150 rooms were so overbooked that the American news network, CNN, had been forced to commandeer the ballroom, turning it into makeshift studios, edit suites and bedrooms. A camp bed in a dining room was costing up to $300 a night, and rumour had it that a well-known photographer from a British tabloid was paying $150 to sleep in a corridor on the third floor.

In spite of our confirmed reservations, a gold Pearl Continental loyalty card and a three-year on-first-name-terms friendship with the manager, it still took a call from the personal spin doctor of the president, General Musharraf, to secure two rooms for us. Our UN colleagues were about to say something about having to share a room when a glance from Alexander told them that it would be in their best interests to remain quiet on this issue.

Anywhere one looked around the hotel, one saw familiar faces from the world's media – Rageh Omaar, the BBC journalist, walked across the lobby sipping a diet coke and talking to someone on the phone, Christina Amanpour, the doyenne of CNN, was seated in the Marco Polo coffee shop holding court while eating a

Pearl burger, and a new girl, Laura something or other, whom I vaguely recognised from some British breakfast programme, was coming out of the beauty parlour holding her hands in front of her in a way that indicated that she had just had a manicure.

In addition to the world's press, practically every local Pakistani journalist and television producer I had ever come across had also descended upon the hotel. The rumours that the streets of Peshawar were paved with the gold of media dollars had spread quickly and everybody was scrambling for jobs. They were having a field day earning ridiculous amounts of money working as fixers and translators for the international news organisations. Most were earning more in a day than they had earned during the entire preceding year. I had already had to change my mobile phone number twice since I had arrived in Pakistan because I had been plagued by friends and relatives (I had not realised I had so many cousins...) calling me at all hours wanting me to use my old BBC connections to set up jobs for them.

The once serene surroundings of the hotel had turned into a media circus. Wires ran everywhere, huge satellite dishes littered the car park, and on the roof terrace scores of reporters were doing live updates to news programmes around the world. The Marco Polo coffee shop had become the epicentre for the entire world's media coverage of the Afghan war. Most tables had been commandeered by competing news crews with their fixers and assorted hangers-on spilling over several further tables making it very difficult to find any space to eat. Camera equipment lay strewn on the floor, an obstacle course for guests trying to take their croissants and freshly squeezed orange juice from the breakfast buffet to their tables. Loud intrusive mobile phone conversations were setting up live satellite feeds or reassuring family back home that Peshawar was not being bombed by the Americans. The nature of rolling news channels around the world meant that this circus carried on around the clock without a minute's let up.

Pakistan remains technically a 'dry' county where possession of alcohol can be punished by lashes under the Sharia Law, but the media's collective thirst and inability to last even a few hours without lubrication persuaded the hotel management to set up a bar on the roof-top terrace. The sign on the door of the bar – which had been named the Gulmaar – advertised *Happy hour – 4 and 6pm – all drinks half-price for non-Muslims only*. I wondered, as I entered with Alex, did this mean that I, as a Muslim, would have to pay full price for my drinks even though it was still 'happy hour'?

Amongst the drinks on the tables of the Gulmaar Bar lay numerous yellow plastic packs I immediately recognised as the food packages that were being dropped into Afghanistan at the same time as bombing sorties were being carried out by the American forces. The packages contained peanut butter and jelly, items though nutritiously sound, did not readily appeal to the discerning Afghan palate, so a flourishing trade had been established – the food packages were harvested in Afghanistan, smuggled across the border into Pakistan and sold off to the hoards of homesick American press corps who devoured them with relish.

The people of Peshawar had not impressed Marco Polo when he visited the city in the thirteenth century. He described them in his journal as 'having a peculiar language, worshipping idols and possessing an evil disposition'. Several hundred years later those sentiments echoed my own feelings, not about the indigenous Pathans who lived in Peshawar, but about the international media who were swarming over the hotel and the city; to me they all spoke a peculiar language, worshipped idols and definitely possessed an evil disposition!

As the lift doors opened on the first floor, a familiar face got on board. I recognised the lanky frame of Saad Uddin, a protégé John and I had trained in Pakistan a couple of years before. He was so engrossed in his thoughts that he didn't recognise me.

'Going down?'

'No Saad, we're going up.' My use of his name pricked his subconscious into recognition.

'Waseem Saab?'

'Yeah, 'fraid so. So, what you up to?'

Saad had landed the big one. He was the official fixer to the official fixer of John Simpson, the veteran BBC reporter. Saad had apparently just been sent to the bazaar to buy two blue burkas for John Simpson and his cameraman to wear as they slipped inconspicuously over the border into Afghanistan. Weaving through the tables of the Marco Polo, it was not difficult to discern that the main topic of discussion, with the Taliban having closed all borders, was – how to get into Afghanistan for that scoop from the front line? John Simpson had obviously decided to call the Taliban's bluff and use their strict dress rule for women as a Trojan horse to get himself into the country. The mere thought of John Simpson, all six-foot-something of him in a burka, cracked me up.

That night Alexander and I watched a triumphant John Simpson reporting on BBC World Service from Afghanistan how he had managed to smuggle himself into the country disguised as a woman on the back of truck. He even did part of the report with the distinctive blue burka still draped over his shoulders. The very next day the Taliban border guards began to hassle every burka-wearing woman at the border. Another British journalist, a woman working for *The Express* trying to cross into Afghanistan in a similar fashion, was arrested at the border. Needless to say, Simpson was not very popular in the Marco Polo café.

Our motives in Peshawar were less clandestine. After ditching our two UN companions who were busy enlisting a non-partisan board of governors and developing editorial guidelines for the proposed radio station to ensure that the humanitarian programming we transmitted conformed to internationally-accepted freedom-of-information models, Alexander and I decided to recce possible sites for locating our radio transmitters. Having poured over detailed maps showing the topography of the area, Alexander had decided on two sites that would give the transmitters the best coverage – the only problem was that they were both on the Afghan side of the border.

Alexander was very gung-ho about getting into Afghanistan. The thought had crossed my mind that I should suggest to him that we also buy a couple of burkas and do 'a Simpson', but I thought better of it.

The British Foreign Office had issued the highest level travel advisory for Pakistan, stating that it was 'Unsafe for travel' and that 'all non-essential personnel should evacuate the country immediately'. The travel alert specifically warned British nationals against going to the 'tribal areas' in the North West Frontier Province where the Khyber Pass was located. Even in less turbulent times, the Pakistani government had never really had any jurisdiction in the region, preferring instead to relinquish control to the bands of roving Pathan tribesmen. To my knowledge, these Pathan tribesmen whose loyalties openly lay with the Taliban regime and who were well known for imposing their own brand of tribal law, were not signatories to either the Geneva Convention or the Universal Declaration of Human Rights. Pakistan's tribal areas remain a no-man's-land where the only law is that of the gun and the tribe. So it was with some trepidation that I found myself in a car with Alexander, an armed guard, and our driver/guide/fixer who had developed an unhealthy passion for old Boney-M songs which seemed to be continuously looped on his car stereo, heading out of Peshawar on the Khyber Road towards the Afghan refugee camps. Alexander had come up with the wonderful idea that, in lieu of on-site inspections in Afghanistan, talking with some of the newer arrivals from the region would provide him with the necessary up-to-date security information he needed about his proposed transmitter sites.

The smell of the Jallozai Camp hits you well before you arrive there. My expensive cologne and the lemon car-freshener could not disguise the putrid smell of a collective mass of humanity living in the most squalid of conditions.

Even before the current conflict, there had been over two million Afghan refugees residing in refugee camps in Pakistan. Most lived in well-established camps like Old Shamshatoo with thriving bazaars, businesses, and even a payment system for utilities like water and electricity. Those in Old Shamshatoo who didn't live in solid mud-bricked structures had been provided with canvas tents with small windbreaks made of plastic as protection from the constantly blowing dust. The children in Old Shamshatoo attended overcrowded schools and played games, making dry-earth sandcastles or flying kites made from sticks and plastic sheeting salvaged from ripped tents, unaware that anything was amiss in their lives.

Jallozai Camp, however, was a different matter. Created just after 9-11, it already housed 70,000 lost souls, and in spite of the fact that all borders were closed, hundreds more were still managing to arrive each day. It was located where one wouldn't ordinarily expect a settlement to bloom, on a burning, parched and cracked plain without a single shade tree in sight and several miles from the nearest source of water. To make matters worse, the camp had not yet been officially recognized by the authorities, and as a result the inhabitants were living under conditions that would be deemed wretched even by the normal standards of refugee life. Many were without adequate shelter, surviving under whatever roughly-sewn-together plastic sheeting and rags they could find. With winter approaching, it was evident that few of the residents of Jallozai Camp would see Nao Roz, the Afghan New Year, traditionally held on the first day of spring.

As Alexander and I made our way through the peripheries of Plastic City, the name given to the sprawling camp by locals, the refugees looked broken, spent, unkempt and ill. Faces etched with years of suffering sported blank looks; some hardly noticed us as we walked past, others followed our every move with deep-set suspicious eyes.

Aga Jaan, our driver/guide/fixer, went off in search of the camp's head elders, leaving Alexander and me alone with the guard. The atmosphere was becoming palpably tense as we stood there waiting. Dishevelled bearded men and naked children began emerging from the makeshift tents and slowly began to surround us. Some, it seemed, were just plain curious and had come to see the skinhead *Kharjee* with a tattoo on his head, others definitely seemed hostile towards our intrusion into their miserable existence.

A small boy about six years old came up behind me and started tugging at my jeans. He was wearing a tattered shirt but no pyjamas, thus signifying his position in the camp hierarchy as above that of the numerous younger children who remained naked, but still not important enough to warrant him the luxury of total modesty. Irrespective, the rags he wore provided little protection against the harsh extremes of weather that the North West Province experienced at that time of year. He stood there, looking at me with his big puppy dog eyes and smiling. I squatted down on my haunches and offered him my hand. Suddenly shyness hit him and he started tugging at the front of his shirt and took a couple of steps back. I dug into my pocket and drew out a packet of Tic-Tac mints and held the pack out to him. He hesitated, looking at the mints, then at me, unsure of what to do. In that faltering split second, the decision was taken out of his hands when a much older boy pushed him to the ground, and, grabbing the mints from my out-stretched palm, tried to make a run for it. Several other boys in the crowd who had obviously been harbouring similar avaricious thoughts about the mints pounced on him, bringing him to the ground. The plastic sweet container was hurled away, breaking in the process and thus spilling the half-dozen or so mints across the ground. The scrum that ensued, with twenty or so children scrambling in the dust to retrieve the sweets, resulted in several split lips and bloody noses.

Appalled at the scene that I had caused over six or seven pathetic sweets, I turned to the little boy to whom I had first offered the Tic-Tacs. He was still lying on the ground face down, crying his eyes out. I helped him to his feet and dusted his shirt. Tears and a watery stream of mucus from his stubby nose had left his face weirdly streaked which made him look feral in spite of his beautifully feline green eyes. I frantically searched through my pockets for something to placate him, and failing to find any other sweets or pens, I made the fatal mistake of taking out my wallet and offering him a hundred rupees. If the Tic-Tacs had created a scrum, what happened next could only be described as a stampede.

Alex, who had been watching all this unfold with growing disdain, sprang into action, and in one swift movement grabbed me by my shoulders, hauled me to my feet and with a mighty shove pushed me through the growing crowd towards the driver/guide/fixer who was returning from his meeting with the village elders. 'Get the crap out of here. Now!'

Irrespective of the mini riot that my hundred rupees had instigated, it seemed that the camp elders had already decided that we were not welcome in Jallozai and that we should leave the camp immediately.

I managed to make my way to the car with the driver without too much of a problem but Alexander and the guard had disappeared and for several long minutes were nowhere to be seen. Alexander reappeared in typical Alexander style, running towards the car accompanied by a hail of stones and with a baying crowd on his tail. The armed guard who had been charged with our security was also running for his life. Obscenities were being exchanged in a multitude of languages and Alexander was still hanging out of the window giving his Afghan pursuers the single finger salute as we sped away.

I never found out what Alexander had done to provoke such an outpouring of emotion from the Afghans, but as many on the terraces at Birmingham City Football Club could testify, sometimes Alexander's appearance alone was enough to start a fight.

That morning in Jallozai camp I had allowed myself to cross the line that anyone working in media knows full well should never be crossed – I had allowed myself to become involved. I had made the fatal mistake of becoming the story. I had allowed my raw emotions to usurp years of professionalism – perhaps I was turning back into a human. Alex's admonishment was swift. 'You twit!' was all he needed to say.

On a mission of this nature it is an unfortunate fact that not all the meetings you undertake are directly relevant to work that you are ostensibly there to carry out – some meetings you have to attend at the behest of the donor just to appease them. Thus, on a bright October morning, we all found ourselves seated at the conference table of a Danish NGO in Peshawar working with the rehabilitation of Afghan widows – a worthy and necessary endeavour, but not entirely relevant to the job in hand of setting up my radio stations. It was obvious to everybody that Alex and I were not fully engaged. Less than fifty miles away from where we were sitting a war was being waged, and here we were talking about how handicraft bags made by Afghan widows were being marketed at bazaars around Peshawar. Luckily for us, our UN colleagues were more than fascinated by the presentation to compensate for our total lack of interest.

I started to round up the meeting so that at least Alex and I, if not our UN colleagues, could return to the real task of trying to prevent any more women joining the ranks of those already supported by this organisation. Just as I began expressions of gratitude, into the meeting room walked a young girl carrying information packs about the organisation for us to take away. She must have been in her early twenties, and I immediately knew from the way she was dressed – wearing jeans, a long tunic and a headscarf as opposed the more traditional *shalwar-kameez* favoured by the local women – that she was not Pakistani. What struck me about this girl was the natural confidence that she exuded, confidence that had a depth of experience behind it rather than confidence that came about as a result of daddy's bank balance or daddy's position like many of the Pakistani girls working in these international organisations. She was very fair and her skin was flawless, her complexion as clear as fine porcelain. Her features were exquisitely chiselled. And then there were her eyes: large, almond shaped, a light greyish colour, alluring, beautifully captivating, but sad, lost and vulnerable at the same time. In the split second that our eyes met as she handed me my information pack, I knew everything about her that I needed to know: she was a lost soul buffeted from pillar to post by years of suffering, she was Ariana, she was Afghanistan.

Having totally lost track of what I was saying by this stage, I began to stutter and waffle. Our Danish host, sensing my discomfort, stepped in and proceeded to effect an introduction. 'Ah Mr Mahmood, allow me to introduce Farida Karim, our principal information officer. She arrived from Kabul less than a year ago and is studying at Peshawar University to be a journalist.'

Suddenly, this meeting, which was originally scheduled purely as 'protocol', was becoming relevant.

'Would Ms Karim mind joining us for a few minutes to discuss our radio project?' Alex ventured, almost reading my mind.

Farida looked hesitantly at her boss who nodded his agreement, and she pulled up a chair and joined us at the table. We outlined our plans for the radio stations to her and asked her what she thought.

She was brilliant. Speaking in faultless English, she briefed us about the state of the Afghan media, refugees, potential transmitter sites... in fact, she was able to brief us about almost everything that we needed to know. More impressively, she did it with an air of authority that could only have come from real first-hand experience. Less than thirty minutes later, by talking with Farida we had achieved something that we had not been able to achieve in countless meetings with various local officials and several international experts: we had developed a full game plan for the implementation of the radio project.

As we were gathering our papers to leave, Farida caught my eye. 'Mr Waseem, I would not waste too much more time on the humanitarian radio station if I were you. Instead, I would be giving more thought to what you will be doing in Kabul when it is liberated.'

I didn't understand what she meant until twenty-four hours later when it was reported that the town of

Jalalabad in the east of Afghanistan had fallen, that the Taliban had capitulated without a fight and that Northern Alliance forces were on their way to Kabul.

On our last night in Peshawar I lay awake ordering my thoughts and trying to formulate a way forward for the project. Farida's prediction about the war finishing sooner than we had all expected had cast a real shadow over the validity or indeed the need for what I had been proposing. Expert analysis was suggesting that the war was going to go on for several months, but would the prediction of this young student journalist in Peshawar prove to be more accurate and would we have the opportunity to set up a radio station in Afghanistan itself?'

Suddenly, Alexander, who had gone to sleep several hours earlier, sat bolt upright in bed. His eyes were as blank and vacant as those that I had seen earlier at the Jallozai Camp. He padded across to the fridge and poured himself a large vodka from the secret stash he had managed to smuggle into the country secreted in bottles of mineral water. He opened a bottle of pills and knocked back a handful, unaware that I was watching him. He kept repeating over and over again, as if repeating some mantra, 'You should've run the story, Waseem, you should've run the story!'

KENYA – 13 NOVEMBER 2001

I could hear Natasha's soulful voice singing in the shower as I sat on the bed in my sumptuous room in the Stanley Hotel in central Nairobi after an all-day trip into the Kenyan bush to look at a rural television station. I kicked off my shoes, plumped up the pillows, lay back and flicked on the television as I waited for the young girl to finish.

As the television sprang to life, out of the corner of my eye I noticed that I could see the bathroom reflected in the mirrored door of the closet in the hallway. The door was open and I admit that I could not avert my gaze. I saw Natasha's body through the shower curtains, her brown skin glistening under the water... then I saw John Murray crouched in a corner of the bathroom near to the door... I saw Rodney, the cameraman, suspended on top of the vanity table... I saw Surjinder, the director, sitting on the toilet seat... I saw the soundman and his boom perched somewhere between the bathtub and the bidet trying hard to stay out of the shot. Outside the bathroom, seated on the floor, were another four members of the film crew which had commandeered my hotel room for the shoot.

Whilst undertaking consultancy and training work that we were contracted to do at the Kenyan National Television Station, John had been bullied by these youngsters into giving up his evenings to teach them how to make professional pop videos on zero budgets. John, always one to encourage young talent, had given up his time freely and volunteered my bedroom as a location into the bargain. Apparently my balcony, being on an upper floor, afforded a good view of the Nairobi skyline which was needed for some of the later shots. After having part-exchanged John's socks and beloved Aston Villa tee-shirt for a four-foot wooden giraffe on Mombassa beach the previous weekend, I was hardly in a position to turn down his request.

'I hope that you're going to bloody well apply for this.'

John Murray stood on my doorstep. He had turned up out of the blue. This was the first time I had seen him in the two years since we had both left college and gone our separate ways, in my case to go to university to study further the theory of drama while John went to drama school to hone his acting skills. His hair, though longer, was better styled and he was sporting a trendy goatee beard. The acne had all but disappeared. However, his dress sense had obviously not benefited from his time at drama school; the lumberjack shirt and the torn jeans he wore for most of the time he was at Sutton must have been surgically grafted onto his body because he was still wearing them. Other than the few outward cosmetic changes, this was essentially the same John Murray I had last seen disappearing prematurely out of the examination hall where we had both been sitting our drama theory 'A' level.

John was holding a copy of the local newspaper, The Evening Mail, open at the situations-vacant page which he thrust under my nose. Dominating the top right-hand quarter of the page was an advert announcing the BBC's desire to recruit television production staff.

Still taken aback by John's sudden reappearance, I tried to dismiss his frivolous doorstep career advice. 'Don't be stupid, Murray, the Beeb don't hire from outside the organisation. And they definitely do not take this level of staff at the age of twenty-one.'

'But you're good at it. Some of that stuff you did at college was brilliant.'

'Get real, John. That was college, this is the real world.'

John's return suddenly piqued me. He had totally vanished off the face of the earth after college, without so much as a phone call or a letter, and now boldly decided to turn up, expecting to pick up from exactly where he had left off. 'Anyway, what the hell brings you crawling out of the woodwork after such a long time?'

'I had one of my dreams a few months ago. I saw you working at the Beeb which didn't make sense at the time, but when this ad appeared a few days ago, everything became crystal clear. So I decided I had to track you down.'

I looked at him standing there grinning and snatched the paper from him with a sigh.

'Fancy a cup of tea?'

'You know me, mate, never say 'no' to a good cuppa.'

With that, he stepped into the house and back into my life, this time never to leave. There had always been a spirituality *about John that I had respected all the way through college and my faith in his visions remained resolute, even though on more than one occasion belief in Murray's capabilities as a soothsayer had proved my undoing. This time, however, his revelation proved to be a little more accurate.*

Six weeks later, after a rigorous selection procedure, which I admit that I approached half-heartedly never once expecting to succeed, John's faith in my abilities was rewarded and I was appointed a producer in the General Programmes Unit at BBC Pebble Mill in Birmingham. From that point life became one long blur. With the proverbial foot through the glass-fronted doors of the BBC, the rest was relatively easy. Within a very short time I had everything that I could ever have wished for: my own house, a sports car, showbiz friends, and a glamorous lifestyle befitting my new status.

'Cut.' John's voice boomed out. The music playback stopped and John strode out of the bathroom, a big smirk on his face. 'Admit it, Waseem, this is the only way either of us will ever get a half-naked girl into our hotel rooms these days.'

I scowled at him. A comment like that didn't warrant a response.

I turned my attention to the television screen. The BBC World Service headlines came on. Kabul had fallen! How the hell could this be possible? Only a few days before, military analysts at the Pentagon were preparing everybody for the long haul, Taliban forces were reported to be digging in for a protracted battle for Kabul, and even the fount of all knowledge, John Simpson, had said that he did not expect a significant Allied military breakthrough till after the harsh Afghan winter.

As I juggled with the remote control to turn up the volume, John Simpson's imposing presence filled the screen. He was walking down a hillside surrounded by a throng of excited Afghans.

'It's an exhilarating feeling to be liberating a city.' Simpson's dulcet tones filled the room. 'It was BBC people who liberated the city – we got in ahead of the Northern Alliance.' Farida's predictions had proved to be spot on.

The day trip out of Nairobi had left us incommunicado from the rest of the world, so we had been totally unaware of the momentous events which had been taking place since early morning.

John Murray cancelled the rest of the evening's shoot, we ordered room service and settled ourselves in front of the television to watch the events unfolding in Kabul: people shaved their beards off, danced in the streets and lynched Taliban.

'Well, I guess it's next stop Kabul for both of us,' said John.

His prophesy was closer to the truth than he could have imagined.

We found emails waiting for us the next morning as soon as we logged on. Soren had taken a call from the European Commission and agreed with them that we would launch a humanitarian programme on Radio Kabul within six weeks. He signed off his mail, 'You guys wanted to be in theatre. I just got you your tickets.'

LAHORE – 10 JANUARY 2002

It never fails to amaze me the amount of luggage that Pakistani travellers feel obliged to take with them when they fly. The baggage carousel at Lahore airport was positively heaving with a mountain of consumer goods piled high on its worn rubber belt. I watched as enough colour televisions, fridges, sewing machines and ghetto blasters to fill a moderately-sized British High Street shop made their slow procession around the carousel. Battered suitcases were spewing out their contents, and garishly coloured clothes, various unmentionables and a variety of exotic foodstuffs littered the belt. A cavalcade of huge red and blue tartan plastic sacks that seem to breed in Sub-Continental airports sailed past me together with bicycles, cooking pots and even what looked like half a side of a goat.

In spite of being marked 'Priority' by Lindsey, the friendly check-in girl at the Emirates desk in Birmingham Airport, an hour after disembarkation there was still no sign of the single suitcase and flak jacket that was the sum total of my luggage.

Then, to make matters worse, the ancient air conditioners serving the baggage area spluttered, coughed, and died. Without the flow of cooler air to keep it at bay, the humidity seeped in and even at three in the morning in the middle of winter it became desperately clammy, making the wait for my luggage more intolerable.

Eventually, when my baggage finally appeared nearly thirty minutes later, it made two circuits of the carousel before I managed to penetrate the hordes of passengers and airport workers jammed into a crazed jigsaw by a heap of trolleys, most of my fellow passengers obviously being of the opinion that the closer they stood to the belt and the greater their numbers at the belt, the quicker their baggage would appear.

After doing my 'O' levels I had taken a gap year and decided that I wanted to travel to Pakistan to find 'my roots'. Like most second generation immigrant children, I had found myself suffering a major identity crisis through my adolescence, not really being Pakistani but not really being English either. I knew that I supported Pakistan when they played cricket, even when they played against England, but that was the extent of it. To confuse the issue further, I supported England in every sport other than cricket and squash. I had long since guessed that there had to be more to being Pakistani than just cheering for Imran Khan and the lads at Lords and I felt that I needed to find out what it was for myself. I needed to experience Moenjadaro and Harrapa in the Indus valley where modern civilisation had first taken root, I needed to wallow in the grandeur of the Mogul culture and to learn first-hand about the turbulent blood letting of the partition in order to find out who I was. However, all visions of hitchhiking along the Indus basin or trekking up into the Karakorum Mountains quickly vanished when it was decided that my voyage of self-discovery would be orchestrated by my parents and that I was going to be accompanied on the trip by my mother.

With a chaperone watching my every move, the journey was virtually doomed from the moment that the Pakistan International flight took off from London Heathrow. Once in Pakistan, with my grandiose plans of travelling through the country already vetoed, my mother and I ended up staying for the entire time at the home of a close family friend of my father's. In place of the spiritual search for the meaning of life that I had embarked on, all I ended up searching for was every English novel that I could lay my hands on in the bazaar to while away the monotony of my incarceration. I am sure that the works of Sidney Sheldon and even Jackie Collins were never so eagerly lapped up by anyone as they were by me during those days. However, I did learn one very important lesson in those six months which was that boredom was a universal phenomenon and felt the same whether you were in Pakistan or at home in Birmingham.

Then Rosie happened. She was the sixteen-year-old second-born of the friend at whose house we were staying. Spending six months in close proximity to a good-looking teenage girl after five years at a boy's school, I guess it was inevitable that she would have had an effect on my hormones. Her fresh-faced looks and coquettish behaviour had me captivated from the moment we had arrived in Lahore, but I was at a total loss what to do about it. My *knowledge of girls and particularly Asian girls was limited to what I had gleaned from the Bollywood Hindi films that my mother was addicted to. However, after I had ruled out running around trees singing songs professing my feelings as a viable wooing option, I could not really see anything else I might have picked up from Hindi movies being of much use. Knowing how to simultaneously beat up six villains terrorising a poor downtrodden village without upsetting one's hairstyle is indeed a very handy skill, but unfortunately not much use to me in this particular instance. So for five months and three weeks, I suffered the pains of unrequited first love. I had all the symptoms: sleepless nights, loss of appetite, and loss of all powers of meaningful conversation, or even for that matter speech, whenever she was in earshot.*

This all changed a few days before my departure. Somehow Rosie and I found ourselves alone on the veranda. 'Alone with girl I fancy' was not a situation that my brain was programmed to compute, and thus, as a purely protective reflex, it started to go into shut-down mode. However, just before brain function entirely ceased, I heard her speak.

'We will all miss you when you go back home.'

I looked up, and like some hackneyed Hindi movie scene, our eyes met. In that instance, we both knew that nothing further needed to be said. Invisible orchestras played, flowers bloomed, and somewhere in the distance fireworks danced beautiful waltzes across the night sky. My hand found hers and we sat there for what seemed an eternity just holding hands looking into each other's eyes. Hers were deep hazel, bright beacons glowing with the discovery of first love. In the brief few minutes that we managed together before the rest of the family returned from wherever they had been, many pacts were made and many endearments exchanged, all without a single word being uttered between us.

'Shall I compare thee to a summer's day? Thou art more lovely and more temperate.'

I didn't even know her real name, only the ridiculous Anglicised nickname that all Pakistani and Indian parents bestow on their offspring, but it still seemed as if I had known her all my life. This was meant to be and we both knew it. Unfortunately, others did not seem to see it the same way.

That very night, Romeo, Rosie's elder brother, rather unusually took me with him to the bazaar when he went to get the naan bread for the evening meal from the tandoor, the communal oven. He had made no secret of the fact that he had resented my presence in the house from the very first day. Most of the time I was there, he had kept well out of my way and had tolerated me only in deference to the long-standing friendship our fathers enjoyed.

As we walked back home down a dark alleyway, he suddenly grabbed me by my collar and pinned me up against a wall. With his eyes spitting pure venom and the grip on my collar rather frighteningly moving closer and closer towards my neck, he enlightened me as to the reason for the 'friendly mugging'. The provocation for this act of violence was apparently the fact that he held a firm suspicion that there was something going on between his sister and me. This guy was good. I had only found out less than an hour ago that there might be the possibility of something going on between his sister and me.

As his hand reached my throat and his vice-like grip began to tighten, he continued to inform me that because of his undying respect for my father, much as he wanted to, he was not going to harm me; neither was he going to make a major family issue of his suspicions. In return, if I wanted to stand any chance of staying alive, I would have to disappear back to London and give up any hope of ever seeing his sister again, and if he so much as caught me in the country again, his would be the last face that I would see before I died. To prove his point, his grip tightened even more. I tried to nod my acceptance of his terms of ceasefire, no mean feat when the life is slowly being squeezed out of you. Honour apparently restored, he let go of me. I fell to the ground, doubled up and gasping for air. Shakespeare was right, 'The course of true love never did run smooth.'

By the time we got home with the naans, Rosie was gone. I never found out where she had gone and nobody deemed it necessary to enlighten me. In the circumstances, I did not think it wise to ask.

In the Jackie Collins that I was reading I found a simple note with a poem by the Pakistani poet, Iqbal, written in Rosie's unmistakeable flowery handwriting.

Khudii ko kar buland itnaa	Elevate yourself to such a position
ke har taqdiir se pehle	that before every fate
khudaa bande se khud puuche,	God, himself asks man
bataa, teri razaa kyaa hai?	Tell me what is your wish?

This was so bizarre; not even in love for an hour and I already found my life had taken on the momentum of a very bad Bollywood film. Barring Romeo being involved with a group of international smugglers, which, with the dodgy company he kept, I knew I could not totally preclude, all the other masala ingredients necessary for a Hindi blockbuster were present in oodles, right down to the ridiculously named villain.

Given the EC's notorious reputation for mind-numbing bureaucracy, events had moved comparatively fast after I received Soren's e-mail in Kenya. A not-at-all unexpected delay with procedure in Brussels had bought me a brief respite over Christmas, but in reality, even with the additional time, I was none the wiser how to achieve the objectives that we were now contractually obliged to deliver in less than six weeks.

On the flight into Pakistan I had continually reassured myself that in my favour was the fact that I was a Moslem, and as such, shared a common heritage and culture with the Afghan people. Perhaps on that basis I would be able to persuade them to trust me. However, on the converse side, being of Pakistani parentage and given the Afghans' antagonism towards Pakistanis whom they blamed for having bred the Taliban, I wondered whether I would be treated with the same suspicion reserved for my parents' countrymen and find myself with a one way ticket to Guantanamo Bay.

In the course of all normal interventions that we undertook we were able to do some preparation in advance, or at least find a starting point. In this case, with virtually no communications possible with anyone in Afghanistan and the country still a live conflict zone, the odds of success were definitely stacked against us and I knew it.

That is possibly why I had opted to transit through Lahore and turn to the only starting point that I felt might be appropriate in the circumstances. Though not overtly religious, I really felt that I needed a fix of spirituality, and thus, as soon as I had rested and showered, I made my way to the old city and the shrine of Data Gunj Bakhsh, the sixteenth-century saint and 'the bestower of favours'. According to legend, any person who visited the mausoleum every Thursday for forty consecutive weeks would have his wishes fulfilled. Unfortunately, I did not have that luxury and would have to be content with whatever blessings that I could muster in the brief overnight stopover that my schedule permitted.

At any time, day or night, devotees are always to be found at the shrine in large numbers. Thursdays, being the eve of the Moslem Sabbath, were considered more auspicious than other days, and each Thursday the Saint's shrine took on a magical fairground-like atmosphere with tens of thousands of visitors. Rickety rides and hawkers selling cheap religious baubles and food from makeshift stalls crammed into the narrow lane leading to the shrine.

I sat in a corner for nearly an hour watching both the poor and the well-to-do bringing their hopes and desires to the saint. Childless couples, the terminally sick looking for miracles, students about to sit exams, businessmen embarking on new ventures, pop stars launching new albums, the homeless just looking for a place to rest their head for the night, all came to pay homage and seek patronage from Data Gunj Bakhsh. I listened to the Qawwali, the traditional Sufi devotional song extolling the virtues of the great saint. The repetitively chanted mantra, 'Nobody goes back from Data Sahib empty-handed', echoing through the shrine was positively reassuring. The rhythmic drumming proved infectiously hypnotic. In front of me, a single dervish dressed in green rags spun around in a mystical trance, performing 'Dhamal', an ancient ritual known to few and a way of achieving a higher spiritual plain for believers. Smells, colours and sounds assaulted my senses.

As I sat there that cold January evening taking in everything around me, I experienced a strange inner peace, a state of nirvana – a spiritual dry-cleaning if you will – which, for all my Westernisation, I needed to come to the shrine of a sixteenth-century saint in the old city of Lahore to find. The irony that Data Gunj Bakhsh was himself an Afghan hailing from the Ghazni province was not lost on me. Perhaps I should have taken that as an omen.

As I left, an old fakir caught hold of my sleeve and looked me straight in the eye. 'Beta, Data sahib said, 'You must know enough to know that you do not know'.'

Another omen? Perhaps. I put a hundred rupee note into the beggar's bowl and made my way out through the crowds queuing up to be fed at the shrine by those whose requests had been fulfilled by Data Gunj Bakhsh. 'Nobody goes back from Data sahib empty-handed.'

Our Bollywood hero, now a big shot television producer in the BBC, decided that he was sufficiently well settled and respectable enough to be able to go back to Pakistan, take on the villain and claim the girl who he knew would be waiting for him, tearfully counting down the days to his return. He decided that even if he could not have the girl in his life, at least he would die trying. 'Cowards die many times before their deaths; the valiant never taste of death but once.'

Unfortunately, true life has a tendency to be as detached from Hindi movies as Hindi movies are detached from real life. There was no running down the street into each other's open arms, no fight to the death in the rain with the wicked brother for the girl's honour, and definitely no riding into the sunset atop a white horse to the strains of joyful wedding songs. No, in the real world I found that Rosie, my muse, my inspiration, the reason that I didn't get off with Anne-Marie and the whole reason for my existence for the past few years, was gone. She had been married off to someone else and was now already a mother of two children with a third on the way.

I took out the dog-eared scrap of paper from my wallet, looked at the familiar flowery writing one last time then ripped it up and threw it onto the tarmac of Lahore airport just before I boarded the flight. Lord Tennyson said, 'Tis better to have loved and lost, than never to have loved at all.' The guy obviously didn't have a clue what he was talking about.

I had been appointed mission leader on the project by Soren and it was my responsibility to sort out all the diplomatic and political permissions necessary to secure the transmission of the programme and get the show on air. It was also my responsibility to pull together and lead the consultancy team which would help me accomplish the mission. I felt a bit like Jeff Tracey, the patriarch from International Rescue, choosing which of the Thunderbirds to send out to save the world. Without knowing what tasks necessarily needed to be fulfilled, it was difficult to start to assemble an appropriate team to undertake them. Nonetheless, it went without saying that the first person I called upon to join the team was John Murray whose task would be to train the locally recruited production crew, if and when we found anyone suitable, and then assist them to get the programme on air.

Alexander, my original point man on the project, had once again vanished off the face of the earth and nobody knew where he was. To be frank, in a funny sort of way I was secretly pleased because Alex was becoming a liability that I could not afford to carry in a live conflict zone. Once I was back in civilisation, I decided that I would physically take him to counselling if I had to – but at this moment I had a job to do and Alex being AWOL did not figure as a priority.

Joining me in Lahore was Saad Uddin whom I had come across in Peshawar where he had been buying burkas for John Simpson. As a television producer, his credentials were impeccable; several years earlier we had worked together with John on launching Pakistan's first pop show which had gone on to become one of the most popular programmes ever. His abilities as a fixer were also growing by the day. What the BBC had only recently discovered about Saad I had known for several years; coming from one of Pakistan's chosen families, he was someone who could get anything that I ever needed in Pakistan done with the minimum of fuss, be it printing a thousand tee-shirts overnight or getting a seat on a closed flight manifest; he always seemed to know somebody who knew somebody who could help. However, what he could achieve in Afghanistan, particularly with the antagonism that Afghans felt towards Pakistanis, remained to be seen, but he had relentlessly bullied me to include him on the advance team from the moment we had met in Peshawar. For sheer peace of mind alone, I had decided to allow him to come along to Kabul. Persistence, arrogance and being a general pain in the butt were qualities which sometimes outweighed his undoubted talents and the reasons that John had never really taken to him. To Saad's credit, however, even before my arrival he had already managed to secure four seats for my team on the UN flight from Islamabad into Kabul by having some British tabloid journalists taken off.

In an ideal world, the fourth person on my team would have been Farida, but alas we had to accept that that was not going to be possible, so instead I had asked her to nominate an appropriate proxy. She had recommended her cousin, Manocher Izzatyaar, who had arrived in Peshawar from Kabul days after 9-11 to escape the war; he had worked with an international relief agency in Kabul and had been studying what he could of journalism at Kabul University. He also spoke good English. It didn't take long for us to realise that in recommending Manocher, Farida had once again come up trumps.

As soon as we met, Manocher struck me as being the perfect choice to act as guide and interpreter for the team. I found him an unassuming character with a complex personality, and his youthful looks did a great job of hiding a sharp articulate mind and all the years of suffering that I was to learn later that he had endured. John summed it up well when he described him 'as wise beyond his years, but at the end of the day still twenty-three years old'. For all his intellect and streetwise bravado, Manocher was very naïve and innocent in many respects. I found his choice of 1980s attire, flared jeans and colourful flowery shirt, engaging.

On the eve of our departure to Kabul I had managed a very brief call from Islamabad to a number in Kabul given to me by a BBC friend, and secured two rooms in a guesthouse used as a BBC safe house. Before I could get any further details the phone connection was lost and reconnection had proved impossible.

When John arrived in Islamabad later that same evening, he came complete with two suitcases full of toilet paper, tins of tuna, dried milk, tea bags, baked beans and enough over-the-counter medications to start his own private drug cartel. He told me that he had been forced to leave two crates of mineral water behind at Gatwick airport when excess baggage charges to transport them to Islamabad had proved prohibitive.

As we made our way back to our rooms from the security briefing that I had just held with the team, John caught up with me. 'So Asia Major, what's the plan this time?'

'John, you remember the Christopher Hampton play, *Treats*, we did at college?'

'Vaguely.'

'The character you played had a wonderful line in that play: 'I don't make plans anymore, just cover the exits.''

'In other words, you haven't got a bloody clue, have you?'

John had hit the nail right on the head. I really didn't have a bloody clue.

BAGRAM AIRBASE – 16 JANUARY 2002

John Murray, Manocher Izzatyaar, Saad Uddin and I arrived at Bagram Airbase in the north of Afghanistan on a very cold January afternoon.

During the most recent conflict, the airbase had been one of the prime targets for coalition bombing, and the rotting remains of the Taliban's dilapidated air force strewn on each side of the runway bore testament to that. The base was now in the hands of the coalition forces and had become the nerve centre for the on-going military action in northern Afghanistan. Sophisticated military hardware, the paraphernalia of modern warfare, littered the base. Camouflaged tents took the place of buildings destroyed during the bombings. Helicopters that were used to ferry soldiers in and out of the base during the hours of night lay silent, but I could clearly see them as we taxied along the airstrip: the fat-bellied Chinooks, the menacing Black Hawks and the lethal Apaches. In the distance American flags flew over the countless rows of khaki-coloured tents that obviously served the troops as living quarters. Someone sitting next to me on the UN flight had pointed out that one of these tents actually housed a Burger King outlet. Sand-coloured Humvees buzzed around keeping a close eye on us. I sensed that the military was not too pleased at this invasion of civilians on their territory. Since it was the only runway in Afghanistan left intact they had no choice but to live with our intrusion.

As we disembarked, Manocher so pleased to be back in a free Afghanistan, he fell to his knees, Pope-style, and started kissing the tarmac. Saad, who had misplaced his beloved mobile phone, had gone back onto the plane and was proceeding to tear it apart in an attempt to find it. How he could have lost something that seemed to have been surgically grafted onto his right ear escaped me. John surveyed the scene and then turned to me, saying, 'What now, big guy?'

I looked around; the location of Bagram, surrounded on three sides by big snow-capped mountains, was absolutely stunning, but at the same time it was also totally remote from the rest of civilisation, hence its choice, I guess, as a strategic airbase. I had been led to believe that the UN would be running a shuttle service into Kabul which was about fifty miles away from the airbase. However, after the immigration and customs checks were completed while still on the tarmac, our fellow travellers, all journalists or aid workers, made their way to a fleet of minibuses waiting for them at the edge of the apron and sped off into the distance.

The plane on which we had arrived took on the departing passengers and, with Saad's phone still on board, taxied out to the runway and took off back to Islamabad. The UN personnel servicing the flight had also vanished into thin air almost as quickly as they had appeared.

Soon there were only five of us left – the four members of my team and an Italian journalist, all standing on the tarmac looking like lost sheep. Around us, the young American marines based at Bagram were visibly growing more and more restless about our continuing presence.

Satellite phones are a notoriously bad method of communication. In order to make and receive a call, both parties have to be in direct line of sight of the satellite, and since there is no signal available inside buildings, the chances of that happening are pretty remote. By pure fluke or maybe the divine intervention of Data Gunj Bakhsh, I managed to get through to Rafiqi, the owner of the guesthouse, on my third attempt. However, during this conversation and before I was able to make any definite arrangements with Rafiqi, my sat-phone ran out of power and totally died on me.

John was becoming increasingly agitated. Admittedly, being stranded on an American military airbase in the middle of a hostile conflict zone with members of the coalition forces eyeing you up suspiciously was nobody's idea of an auspicious start to a mission. But irritating John even more was Saad who stood there whimpering in the cold, trying to look cool in his Armani shades, going on about his damn phone and cursing the stewardess whom he accused of having stolen it. If he kept this up much longer, he would be close to being throttled by John. His continuous barrage of corny jokes about John's weight during the past few hours had not made him popular with John to start with.

Leaving the two of them to slug it out, I went in search of Manocher who had worryingly gone missing since our arrival in Bagram. I finally tracked him down amongst a small group of Afghans working as support staff with the coalition forces, huddled around a fire drinking cups of tea. Such was the emotion of the moment that Manocher was greeting and hugging everyone as if they were all long lost friends. I pulled him away from his cosy tea party and asked him to see whether any of his new-found acquaintances could source us any form of transport to Kabul. At that moment even a train of mules would have sufficed.

As if by magic, a minibus appeared. Physically dragging Manocher away, we piled our luggage into the back and took our seats. Following our lead, the Italian journalist also proceeded to pile his bags into the van and then made himself comfortable in the seat next to mine. Off we set in the rust bucket of a van that in some other incarnation had been a Toyota Hi-ace, chugging slowly towards some unknown fate. I closed my eyes, allowing myself a few moments of quiet contemplation before the proverbial shit hit the fan, as I knew it would sooner rather than later. I didn't have long to wait.

At the exit to the base we stopped at the military checkpoint, waiting for the guards to raise the barriers. Two American marines came around to the passenger side and asked to see our papers. We handed over our passports. Dissatisfied with something, they asked us to step outside the van. Before we could do anything, our driver and his conductor, both affronted that guests to their country were being treated in this way by foreigners, jumped out of the van and started yelling at the marines. In one swift movement the marines had slipped off the safety catches of their automatic rifles and were pointing the weapons at us.

'Get out of the van, now!' shouted the slightly taller of the pair, the two stripes on his arm signifying that he was in charge of this checkpoint. 'Get out of the van with your hands above your heads.'

The van driver had by now stepped into the gap between the marines and the van door, preventing any of us from getting down. Pointing guns at him was having no effect; if anything it seemed to be provoking him further and his yelling was growing louder. The soldiers were also beginning to shout. Volume, it seemed, was the only common language that the two cultures seemed to understand.

The commotion had alerted several other marines who had been on duty nearby, and within seconds we were surrounded by a group of about eight or so teenage, spotty-faced, American marines, with rifles primed and pointing at us. They looked nervous. Suddenly, as if out of nowhere, several red laser targeting beams began dancing all over the scene, criss-crossing my small group and ending up most alarmingly with a red dot coming to rest on each of us.

The situation was deteriorating fast – one false move now and we could all be dead in an instant. Rule number one of survival in a conflict zone that I had rigorously briefed my team about the previous evening was – never argue with anyone holding a gun: the gun means that they are right!

As inconspicuously as possible in order not to attract any attention from the marines, I nudged Manocher gently in his ribs with my elbow. He immediately understood that it fell upon the two of us to do something to diffuse the situation before we were all arrested, or worse still, shot. He had to deal with his two Afghan compatriots while I handled the Yanks. Manocher slowly put his hand on the shoulder of the driver who was standing in front of him and tried to calm him down, while I started yelling in English at the marines, telling them that we would comply with anything they wanted us to do. Gently manoeuvring around the driver who was still blocking the passenger door but was now beginning to calm down and listen to Manocher, John and I got down from the van with our hands in the air. The red dots followed us, hovering a few centimetres above our right breasts.

'We are aid workers,' I yelled above the commotion to the person I presumed was in charge. 'Our accreditations are in the van.'

John joined in the yelling, 'What actually is the problem here?'

'Sir, we just need to know, the gentleman with the Pakistani passport, is he also with you?' So it was Saad's presence that had sparked this off. I had had a bad feeling about his being on this mission from the onset. My fears were beginning to come true and we hadn't even got outside the airfield.

'Yes, he is part of my team.'

'You have his papers?'

'Yes, do you need to see them?'

'No, that is fine, sir. I believe you.' With that the marines stood down and dispersed almost as quickly as they had appeared. The one in charge clicked his heels to attention, saluted, and said, 'Have a good day, sir!'

We boarded the van again. The barriers were raised and we left the base.

The road from Bagram to Kabul had been the scene of major fighting between the Taliban and Northern Alliance forces. It was full of craters from numerous missiles and bombs from decades of fighting. The roadside was littered with the debris of war: rusting tanks, discarded shell casings, abandoned heavy artillery positions and the rotting skeletons of numerous vehicles that had been caught in the bombing. Boots and helmets lying by the side of the road provided a constant reminder of the human cost of the war.

A number of decaying freight containers, riddled with bullets and blown up into obscene shapes, dotted the roadside at regular intervals. Many of these had served as makeshift prisons. Piling hundreds of prisoners into these huge metal boxes, and then tossing grenades into the centre of the pathetic human cargo, had proved a quick and efficient method of dealing with the problem of overcrowded prisons. I closed my eyes, trying hard not to picture the scenes that had been played out along this stretch of road just a few weeks earlier.

We were the only sign of any sort of life as far as we could see. Ruined villages lay on either side of the road, pounded into oblivion by years of fighting. Save the occasional lizard scurrying in and out of the rocks, animals had long since migrated from this God-forsaken terrain. Parched dust plains devoid of vegetation stretched out to meet the majestic mountains of the Hindu Kush towering in the distance. Only the odd burnt tree broke the monotony of the arid landscape. Brightly painted red rocks, signifying un-cleared mine fields, lined both sides of the road, the only colour in the bleak monotone surroundings. The vapour trail of a B52 bomber flying high above us reminded us that Afghanistan was still a live battle zone.

Suddenly, two trucks appeared on the distant horizon. Side by side, they were hurtling towards us at great speed on the single lane freeway. They weren't overtaking, and it quickly became apparent that they were actually racing one another. Our presence on the same bit of road made no difference. The gap between us diminished at an alarming rate. They must have seen us but they continued to race, neither prepared to concede defeat. Afghan warrior code was very simple, 'Thakt ya Thakta' – the throne or the coffin – no discussion, no compromise.

Our driver was screaming profanities in Dari, John started swearing in the most colourful English he could muster, Saad sat slobbering behind me, and the Italian journalist who seemed to be praying began digging his nails into my arm. I prepared myself for rapidly approaching death, a victim to a misplaced display of machismo that allowed no room for second best.

It is true that you do see your life flash before you just before you die; I had definitely begun to see the first reel of mine when, with inches to spare, our driver bit the bullet and swung our mini bus hard to the right, over the red-painted rocks into the dusty field. Over my shoulder as I looked back I saw the slogan 'Trust in God' painted on the tailgate of one of the trucks as they rapidly receded, still racing, into the distance. Then I braced myself for the explosions. As the van careered to a halt, a good twenty feet into the minefield, there was silence, deafening silence.

As the dust began to settle around us, I burst into nervous laughter. 'Welcome to Afghanistan, John!'

'You bastard! Only you, only you, Waseem Mahmood, could have contrived to try and get me killed twice within the first hour of the mission. You'll pay for this, I promise!'

About an hour later, thankfully without further incident, the city of Kabul suddenly appeared, stretched out in front of us as we went over the brow of a hill. No signs, no defining city boundary line, no suburbs, nothing to signify that we had actually arrived. We entered down the same road that I vaguely remembered John Simpson reporting from when the BBC had 'liberated' the city.

What caught my eye immediately were the numerous dwellings that seemed to be carved out of the dark granite mountains. As we drove down into the valley, everywhere I looked precariously-balanced mud huts filled all but the crest of the mountains which surrounded the city. Natural-eco-friendly-skyscrapers, I guess you could call them, but in reality they looked like a random splattering of old Lego bricks stuck in oversized mud pies that some child had made in kindergarten.

While not enthralled by the place, I was struck by the medieval quality of life in Kabul as we drove through the streets. It was as if time had stopped some five hundred years ago, and we, as twenty-first-century travellers, had stepped back into a time-warp. People milled around on the streets looking totally lost, as if they had all come out of a collective twenty-year coma into an unfamiliar world. Having been told what to do and what not to do for so long, now that the puppet masters had all gone and nobody was left to pull the strings, the marionettes were definitely finding it difficult to adjust to a life without manipulation.

We heard music playing at street corners and bazaars. Markets, though austere, seemed to be relatively well stocked for such a recent post-conflict zone. Pictures of Ahmad Shah Massoud were everywhere, from covering a dangerously high proportion of the windscreens of Mujhahid jeeps to being machine-woven into Afghan rugs. His face beamed down benevolently wherever you looked. A few traders had also dared to put up pictures of Hindi film stars in their shop windows. On the face of it people were going about their normal everyday jobs but everything seemed to be running in slow motion, and during our drive through the city we hardly saw any women on the streets.

Small ragged children surrounded the van at every street corner shouting 'Thank you'. I assumed that that was because those were the only English words they knew, but Manocher informed us that the children were really thanking us – for having got rid of the Taliban from their country. It was a humbling experience.

Manocher could hardly contain himself. 'You know, this is a totally different city to the one I left a few weeks ago. Instead of just existing, people are now beginning to live again. I've seen folks actually smiling.' Whoa, reality check – if this was an improvement, I cannot even begin to imagine what he must have left behind. As I saw it, what we were seeing was not so much 'ground zero' as 'civilisation zero'.

After we deposited the Italian journalist at the Intercontinental Hotel, it dawned on me now that we were in Kabul that I did not actually have the address for Rafiqi's guesthouse.

The driver was beginning to get agitated, so being ex-BBC and maybe because a part of the organisation will always remain ingrained in my genetic make-up, I decided that the only thing we could rationally do was to make our way to the local BBC office; they would surely know Rafiqi since he ran their safe house or at the very least they would offer us a friendly welcome and a cup of tea. Old school BBC camaraderie was the stuff on which the great broadcaster built its reputation.

We went to the BBC offices situated in the affluent Wazir Akbar Khan district of Kabul. A converted villa, this was the place from which the veteran journalist, William Reeve, had been famously broadcasting live when a missile had hit the Al-Jazeera offices less than a block away. Wazir Akbar Khan looked untouched by the twenty-three years of fighting; driving through these streets you would be pushed to remember that you were in post-war Kabul. Patrols of the international peace keeping force, ISAF, that regularly drove around the city in conveys were the only tangible clue to the city's most recent history.

On arrival at the BBC offices, we were refused entry. After what seemed an eternity, I managed to use my old BBC identity card – which I had kept on my departure from the broadcaster as a keepsake – and an awful amount of judicious bullying to get myself past the all-too-efficient Afghan guards. The inside of the building totally belied the surroundings outside. State-of-the-art communication equipment filled most of the rooms and the welcome smell of freshly brewed English tea permeated my dust-filled nostrils. I made my way to the only Englishman I could see. He was seated behind a bank of computer screens in what seemed like a makeshift edit studio. He didn't even bother to look up as I entered.

I introduced myself and enquired about the directions to Rafiqi's place. The rather pompous journalist didn't know what I was on about, but reluctantly agreed to allow me ten minutes 'and no more, mind you' to charge my sat-phone. No tea was offered and, leaving me alone in the improvised edit suite, he went off rather rudely to another room. I had a good mind to remind him that it was my television licence fee that was paying his salary, but thought better of it.

When I finally made my way out *exactly* ten minutes later, a crowd had gathered around the van where what seemed like a mini riot was taking place. At the centre of the commotion were John, Saad, and Manocher. They were arguing with our driver, yelling obscenities in a variety of languages. After the escapade in the refugee camp with Alexander, a lot of these words were becoming familiar. The driver's assistant was physically restraining the driver from hitting Saad, who for no apparent reason was yelling the loudest. The second rule of my security briefing the previous evening had been, 'Do not draw unnecessary attention to yourself in public places.' Obviously nobody in my team had paid an iota of attention to the rules I had drawn up.

Apparently the driver, under the misapprehension that we were journalists, was demanding one hundred dollars from each of us for the drive from Bagram to Kabul. As much as John, through Manocher, had been insisting that we were not journalists, the driver reasoned quite logically that since our destination was the BBC, we had to be journalists and obviously on unlimited expense accounts.

After a lot of gesticuling and pleading, we managed to convince the driver that we were, in fact, poor aid workers here to help the country and that the only reason we had come to the BBC was because we were lost and looking for a friend. Finally a compromise was reached and we settled on fifty dollars each.

It was late evening when we finally arrived at Rafiqi's. The guesthouse was a villa similar to the one occupied by the BBC. The well-manicured front lawn was littered with a number of small satellite dishes signifying ownership by other residents in the guesthouse of the more expensive satellite telephone models that, unlike our sat-phone, could take calls inside buildings. The paved driveway housed three or four of the ubiquitous, white, four-wheel-drive land-cruisers that seem to plague every post-conflict area. The house was well guarded, set a good safe distance away from the roadside with large walls on all sides topped with broken glass and razor wire. Two rather large Mujhahid types sat to attention at the front door armed with AK 47s. We were subjected to as hard a time getting into the guesthouse by these two as we had been at the BBC offices, and though irritating after the long day we had had, it was a very reassuring sign of the high level of security maintained.

The inside of the guesthouse was functional; one would be pushed to equate it with a one-star establishment in any Western country. However, the atmosphere was homely and welcoming, not at all what any of us had expected in Kabul. The place was dimly lit and the light bulb was noticeably fluctuating with the ebbing electricity current. Beautiful Afghan carpets and rugs in varying shades of red adorned the marble-chip floors. The walls were covered with massive oil paintings of landscapes and enough antique guns and swords to equip a militia group. A television was blaring in the main room as we walked through. It was switched to DW-TV, the German news channel. A mix of Germans and Afghans sat on the colourful sofas dotted around the perimeter of the room, drinking tea, watching the news or having conversations. An open bottle of brandy was strategically placed between two of the Germans. A wood stove burned in the corner, heating the room and creating the unique ambience one associates with real log fires. The smell of fresh food cooking wafted through the living room, an obvious shock to John who had been expecting to live throughout the entire mission on his tins of tuna and Pot Noodles. The gathering could easily have been mistaken for an après ski party in a Swiss chalet.

We were met in the lobby by the only member of staff who could speak passable English, Azim, a diminutive man from the Hazara tribe with distinct Mongol, almost Chinese, features. Azim was hyperactive, rushing around the house like a gnome on speed. After welcoming us with much needed cups of tea, he tried to explain to us, in a mixture of broken English and hand gestures, that the group of Germans who were to have left that morning were still there, and as a consequence all he could offer us was one single room to share and a mattress in one of the Germans' rooms.

John refused outright to accept the idea of sharing a floor with any of the Germans. War-zone or no war-zone, there are certain compromises that John Murray will never make and one of them is sharing a room with anyone, never mind a German. With nowhere else to go, a shoot-on-sight curfew minutes away, John unwilling to budge or consider a compromise on the issue and Azim unable to produce another room out of thin air, I was left at a loss as to what to do next and slumped down exhausted on the stairs. Fortunately, common sense prevailed, and John agreed that he would grudgingly put up with my snoring for one night and share a room with me. Saad, therefore, would have to share with the Germans. Manocher excused himself to get to his home before curfew.

As we began to move our stuff upstairs, John and I saw a bedroom at the far end of the house which looked suspiciously unoccupied to us. We looked at Azim accusingly.

'No Mr Waseem, Mr John. Very important man live in this room. Big man, he come morning and make phone call.'

John pounced on this. 'So this big man, he does not sleep here?'

'No, no, he not sleep here. He sleep at Minister house. He come early, have breakfast and make call.'

John put his arm around Azim who only came up to John's shoulders, and began to try and sweet talk him into allowing him to use this room for the night.

'No, no, Mr Rafiqi get very angry if you sleep here. Very big man. Very important.'

Ten dollars, two packets of Benson and Hedges and a bar of Cadbury's Fruit and Nut later, a compromise acceptable to both parties was reached. John could use the room on the condition that he was out by 6.30 a.m., well before the time that this big important man arrived. John got his single room and Saad was spared the Germans' floor and moved into my room.

The atmosphere in the guesthouse the following morning was reminiscent of a cheap British seaside bed and breakfast like the fictitious *Fawlty Towers* complete with a manic Azim scuttling around like some latter-day Manuel. Even the German guests lived up to their national 'towels on deckchair' stereotype, hogging all of the bathrooms in the morning and totally exhausting the limited supply of hot water. They also hogged the breakfast table long after finishing their breakfasts, and worst of all, they hogged the television remote control making us suffer more of the intolerable DW-TV.

Azim cornered John and me just as we were coming down for breakfast and whispered to us, 'Mr John, Mr Waseem. Big man come back. He want sleep here. He not happy, Mr John, you in his bed. Mr Rafiqi, he very angry...' With this he scuttled off into the kitchen.

Now that Azim had mentioned it, I did vaguely recall a lot of shouting and door slamming taking place on the peripheries of my consciousness during the night, but in my pharmaceutically induced state of sleep I had dismissed it as a bad dream. John looked at me, shrugged his shoulders and went in for breakfast. I followed him.

Seated at the dining table having breakfast was the largest specimen of homo-sapiens that I had ever seen. Both John and I consider ourselves to be large, but this guy was massive. This was apparently the 'big man' whom John had managed to upset by taking his bed.

He glared at us menacingly as we took our seats opposite him. From somewhere in his vast beard, a fierce grunt emanated. Other than that, breakfast continued with an uneasy silence hanging over the meal and the atmosphere growing discernibly more tense with each passing minute. When an arrival at the front door summoned the big man away, both John and I breathed a sigh of relief and physically relaxed as we watched him sway across the room and go out onto the front lawn.

Unfortunately, in Afghanistan this was not just as simple as having taken somebody's bed for a night; this had become a convoluted honour thing that Afghan culture seems to thrive on.

The incident proved highly amusing to Saad and provided him with a whole lot more material with which to bait John, whom he now insisted on calling 'Goldilocks'. And if he said, 'Who has been sleeping in my bed?' one more time, even as a confirmed pacifist I might have had to resort to violence.

Thankfully for Saad, at that instant Manocher arrived at the guesthouse. The Manocher who appeared in the doorway that morning was a changed person. He was positively beaming, his smile infectious. He was no longer the rather timid creature who had met us in the Islamabad hotel just a couple of days before, unable to look anyone in the eye. Spending less than twenty-four hours in a free Afghanistan had transformed him beyond recognition. He seemed to have grown physically in stature. Standing before us was a confident young man who would no longer take any rubbish from anyone. It was an amazing metamorphosis; our caterpillar had emerged overnight from the cocoon of repression into a free butterfly.

The welcome he had received the previous evening was so rapturous – there were so many people there to greet him – that it had taken him more than four hours to get from the taxi to his uncle's apartment in Macroryan, a journey of less than a few hundred feet.

'I never believed that I would ever live to see this dawn... waking up in a free Afghanistan.' Manocher repeated those words slowly, savouring every syllable, 'A free Afghanistan. It seemed so much like a dream only a few weeks ago... last night we were laughing and joking, something that was forbidden under the Taliban. For the first time we are in charge of our own destinies.'

As idealistic as it sounded, I guess that is why we were there, to give the Afghans a voice and to try to make sure that they did not have to suffer a future like the history that they had endured. Manocher's happiness, his words, his hopes, his dreams had all just validated what we did and why we did it. Racak felt like a million miles away, a lifetime ago.

Without a telephone system in Kabul, all meetings had to be set up in person, and whether or not you got your meetings depended heavily on the ability and, more importantly, the contacts of the fixer you engaged. Luckily, in Timur, our fixer, a young Australian Afghan returnee provided by Rafiqi, we seemed to have hit gold. Within one hour of understanding the project brief he had managed to set up three meetings with the relevant Ministers and one with the head guys at Radio Television Afghanistan.

We made our way to the first meeting with the Minister of Information and Culture, the man in whose hands the fate of the entire project lay. As we entered the powder blue Ministry building, with no glass in any of its windows, nor electricity to power heat or light, Timur casually briefed me that he felt that the meeting would be easy because the Minister's right-hand man, the person upon whose opinion the Minister's decision totally rested, was our 'roomie'. 'Small world, isn't it? This is how we get business done in Afghanistan. It's not what you know but who you know that matters, mate. And, trust me, we are seeing the main man.' Timur was really pleased with himself.

Timur's comment about the 'roomie' whizzed around in my head without me making any connection until we were ushered from the ante room into the office of Mansoor Shiraz, and sitting there larger than life was the 'very big man' whom John had made bed-less the previous night.

As I pondered the possible political ramifications of John's need for undisturbed beauty sleep, Mansoor slowly got up from behind his desk and, stroking his beard with his right hand in a most threatening way, made his way towards us. This was it. John's stubbornness had put paid to the project before we had even begun. Timur stepped forward to introduce us and Mansoor stopped him and began to speak in a pronounced mid-western American drawl. 'Yeah, I know these guys.' He nodded knowingly.

I could hear my heart beating; beads of perspiration began to form on my forehead. I was so convinced that we'd blown it that I was already beginning to think of various excuses to explain away this unmitigated disaster to Soren.

'It's Goldilocks and the three bears.' Then, amused at his own joke, he started laughing.

Within twenty-four hours of landing in Kabul we had secured a daily one-hour breakfast slot on Radio Kabul.

Click. A full length shot of Saad and Manocher standing in front of the decaying Eid Ghar, the famous yellow and green mosque in the centre of Kabul sited at the spot where Immanullah Khan first announced Afghanistan's freedom from the British in 1919.

Click. A panoramic view of Kabul taken from the Majaran Hill, in the foreground looming awkwardly the crumbling mausoleum where the body of Nadir Shah, founder of the Afghan Royal Family, lies interred. The cityscape looks serene, almost beautiful.

Click. John and I posing with a couple of British ISAF troops we met patrolling the area of the mausoleum. All of us giving silly thumbs-ups to the camera.

Click. A close shot of a rather morose Saad standing outside the cage of a brown bear at Kabul zoo. The bear which is peering over Saad's shoulder has no nose. A young Talib soldier had decided to cut it off after feeling offended by the bear's stare.

Click. A shot of the traffic police control booth where the Taliban brutally hanged President Najibullah and his brother after dragging them from the UN compound across the road.

Click. A wide angle shot of the Olympic Stadium.

Click. A bearded man begging for mercy sacrificed like a goat, his throat slit by the brothers of the Talib that he allegedly murdered.

Click. Fuzzy shot of the goalposts.

Click. Three Mujhahids hanging from the goal posts.

Click. Shot of the empty stands.

Click. A young boy running around the stadium with several severed hands tied together, showing his macabre trophy to the cheering crowds.

Click. Shot of the goal mouth, the penalty spot barely visible in the mud.

Click. A woman clad in a blue burka kneeling cowering on the floor, her hands held up to the muzzle of the AK47 to try to stop the bullets.

Click. A postcard picture of Darul Aman, the old defence ministry building, once a magnificent palace, now lying in ruins, beautifully framed against the bright blue sky with just a splattering of light cloud over the distant snow-capped mountains.

Click. A shaky out-of-focus shot of what looks like a Hollywood production designer's vision of a post-apocalyptic landscape. Miles and miles of what were once streets in the west of Kabul now reduced to contours of rubble, stretching far into the distant horizon. Devastation, death and destruction wrought on a biblical scale.

Click. A candid shot of a group of children playing in the ruins.

Click. A close shot of a single child standing apart from the rest of the group. He stares into space with blank eyes, oblivious to his surroundings, no emotion registering on his face, not even tears.

Fate is a concept that seems to have little meaning in the West these days. It is dismissed by many as an outdated notion for our modern way of life in which destiny has no role to play; but in the original Arabic, *kismet* is still the most common way of explaining the toss of a coin that seems to govern every aspect of life, especially in fatalistic societies such as Afghanistan.

The images of the young boy I had encountered in the ruins continued to haunt me for the rest of the night, a barrier standing between my conscious and my unconscious state. He looked about thirteen – the same age as my younger son. Dressed in rags, his bare feet were swollen and caked with mud. I remembered his eyes, a beautiful deep green colour, penetrating but devoid of life.

At that moment, all the great arguments raging in the world – the clash of civilisations, Islam versus the West, the war on terror – were suddenly unimportant, and all that remained in my mind was a child – standing alone in the ruins, his eyes full of hurt and grief. I tried to work out the unspeakable suffering that I seen in those eyes. I was also aware of the role that *kismet* had played in both our lives. He had done nothing to deserve his fate, and I'd done nothing to deserve mine. Yet soon I would go back to Stratford and take pleasure in a good brunch with my young son at Cox's Yard. The Afghan boy would probably be dead before the winter was out.

Manocher was in the bedroom I shared with Saad helping me light the fire in the stove which provided our sole source of heat, my lack of eyebrows a testament to my inadequate attempts at trying to light the stove myself. The initial euphoria of freedom, it seemed, was wearing off and the harsh reality of the huge reconstruction task facing his battered nation was beginning to hit. There was no magic wand that someone could wave and somehow everything would miraculously be OK. This was going to be a hard slog and it would be several years before Afghanistan would achieve any semblance of normality.

Manocher slumped on Saad's bed, his disillusionment apparent. 'Mr Mahmood, you know, our hearts are scorched with tyranny, our souls have become vast deserts, and instead of the brotherhood I expected, I find only scorpions and vipers.' Manocher was becoming glassy eyed and was speaking in little more than a whisper. 'But, you know what? We have returned. We, the guardians of our land. We may find the garden barren and grown with weeds, but we have come prepared, with pruning hooks and saws.'

I listened intently to Manocher's flowery, almost poetic, rhetoric, captivated by the imagery his words evoked. I am sure he was quoting from one of his father's famous poems, but my knowledge of neo-classic Farsi poetry being somewhat limited, I couldn't be sure.

He carried on in the same vein. 'We shall cut away the dead wood, and the grip of poisonous vines. We shall pull up all the weeds – and throw them onto a vast fire. And then we will plant new seeds, and when the rain comes, the seed shall bear fruit – and the name of that fruit shall be – Peace!'

He was a born orator, and I was sure that if the fragile peace lasted for a few years, Manocher would some day surely take his rightful position in the running of his country. He was exactly the sort of person the new Afghanistan needed.

I don't know what he had expected to find in Kabul, but what he had found had sorely disappointed him. I could see that he was a lost soul totally adrift and unsure of how he could achieve his lofty dreams. He knew that he wanted to do something to rebuild his country but had absolutely no idea what he could do.

'Why don't you come and work for the radio station?'

He looked at me blankly. It took a minute or so for the penny to drop and for Manocher to realise what I had said.

'But… I have no experience and know nothing about radio.'

I had obviously caught him totally unawares. He was on this mission as a guide and interpreter and had not at all expected to be actively involved in the radio station. However, both John and I had been observing him over the time we had been in Kabul; his comprehension of the concept, his resolute belief in what we were trying to achieve and his confident handling of officials and even ministers had led us both to the unanimous conclusion that Manocher was the right man to run the show. We both knew that there would be hell to pay in Copenhagen when they found out that we had entrusted the fate of the European Commission's multi-million dollar flagship project to the somewhat shaky hands of a twenty-three-year-old part-time student journalist, but hey, what the hell.

What we needed was a clean slate, somebody totally untainted by experiences of working in radio either under the strict Taliban regime or as an Afghan exile for some Western broadcaster. Both those types carried baggage that we did not need. What we wanted was somebody we could mould to the needs of the project, not someone who would mould the project to his own needs, and Manocher fitted the bill. The speech he had just made in my bedroom had confirmed that decision.

I let Manocher carry on spluttering excuses to as why he was not the right candidate for a couple more minutes before I attempted to address his concerns.

'If Afghanistan is to maintain the peace that so many have given up their lives for, then Afghans will need a voice.' I could see that my words were hitting a nerve. I went in for the kill. 'Do you remember the faces of the little Afghan children we saw at Darul Aman the other day? Remember that boy? He needs you out there, he needs you to give him the voice that he doesn't have, and to know that his voice will be heard. That's why we – just ordinary people – need to make a difference. Even if we make a difference in one child's life, trust me, Manocher, we will have changed the world. Mr John often quotes a verse from the Bible where it says in the Book of Revelation, 'They shall hunger no more, neither shall they thirst any more. For God shall wipe away every tear from their eyes.' That's what we have to do, help God wipe away the tears.'

Even before the fire in the stove had caught properly, I had my programme editor.

The 'towel ceremony' took place at the guesthouse nearly two weeks after we had arrived in Kabul. For some unfathomable reason, towels had been a scarce commodity in Afghanistan during the Taliban regime and the situation did not seem to have eased, even six weeks after the liberation of Kabul. Soap and other toiletries were equally scarce unless you knew someone with access to smuggled contraband; the black market in toothpaste flourished as vigorously as the underground liquor stores. UN sanctions, it seemed, had obviously had the desired effect, hitting the Taliban where it really hurt: in their bathroom cupboards.

Showering and shaving had been driven off my team's agenda from the moment we had arrived in Kabul due to the sub-Arctic temperatures we encountered in the bathroom where most mornings there was a thin layer of ice on the floor which could easily have served as an ice rink for small children. Icicles spouted from the taps where there should have been water. This, combined with all the hot water being hijacked by the Germans, meant that indulging in luxuries such as personal hygiene was not a priority. For what little washing we were managing, we had had to resort to drying ourselves with scratchy pink sheets of Chinese toilet paper and John's blotched skin bore more than adequate testament to its dubious origins. Consequently, we ended up getting through bottles of cologne and growing the trademark 'mission fuzz' that all expatriate men in Kabul seemed to be sporting.

In these circumstances a great fuss was made on the arrival of the first batch of towels in the guesthouse, something that had only been achieved, we were told, by the use of Rafiqi's growing political influence in Kabul. There was almost a party atmosphere as Azim, whose joy on the occasion suggested that he had won the lottery on a rollover week rather than just obtaining small squares of cotton terrycloth for his guests, ceremoniously handed over the bright blue towels to the residents.

The turquoise hue that John's face had taken on after his morning ablutions the next day suggested that the celebrations the previous night might have been premature; subsequently, whenever I managed to wash, I decided to stay wet, or drip dry, or even risk the coarse Chinese toilet paper rather than end up looking like a Smurf.

The Intercontinental Hotel in Kabul, situated in the north of the city and set high on an isolated hill in a commanding position, had assumed the role of the new front line for the world's media. The stunning view of the city from the roof of the IC provided the backdrop to virtually all the reports coming out of Kabul. News crews on the streets seemed to outnumber the ISAF forces by almost two to one.

Nearly two months after the fall of Kabul, Afghanistan remained in the news, though it was slowly working its way down many programme-running orders. Editors were now looking for features, not hard news stories, a sure sign that Afghanistan's time on the world's news agenda was limited. Live broadcasts from the roof of the IC were decreasing in number and one by one the smaller news organisations were withdrawing their staff and relying on agency pictures for their coverage. The major league network stars had already left or were in the process of leaving. However, with CNN and a number of the other major news networks still maintaining a presence in Kabul, the IC hotel remained a hive of activity.

Most of the journalists we had encountered in Pakistan were now entrenched at the IC in unenviable conditions. The dilapidated hotel, which had obviously seen better days, seemed to be so rickety that it felt as if it was being held together by the acres of gaffer tape used by the television news crews.

It was a living testament to the changing fortunes of the city; the crumbling grandiose ballroom and basement discotheque betrayed the intention of the original owners to attract the city's then growing nouveau riche; the austere make-over during Soviet times represented the hotel's transformation into no-frills communist functionality; and finally, the evident neglect afforded by the subsequent Mujahideen and Taliban regimes typified the contempt that they had felt for outsiders visiting their country. The hotel lay crumbling, without even the basic amenities to be able to cater for the hoards that had unexpectedly descended upon its fragile infrastructure. Rooms with glass in the windows were attracting a twenty-dollar premium and the total lack of hot water had spawned a lucrative side business for the hotel porters who were run off their feet selling hot water by the bucket load to the hapless residents.

Almost involuntarily, John and I found ourselves retreating to the IC on a daily basis to escape from Kabul. Like moths drawn to a winking light, we headed to the IC the moment we had finished work. Even though the country was still a live conflict zone, the members of the British press who were staying in the hotel had created an atmosphere in the coffee shop more akin to the Groucho Club in Soho than a run-down café in Kabul. For a couple of hours every night before curfew, we would sit in the crumbling café drinking cups of tasteless coffee, talking with other guests, discussing everything from the fortunes of John's favourite football team, Aston Villa, to the latest BBC gossip.

For John, in addition to being able to follow the fortunes of his beloved football team through the communications systems set up by the news networks, the availability in abundance of smuggled Snickers chocolate bars in the IC gift shop went a long way to compensate for the bland coffee and more than justified the long daily trek to the hotel. War-zone or not, John's daily fix of chocolate remained sacrosanct.

It was also in the IC coffee shop that we had managed to pressgang a number of prominent members of the world's press corps to volunteer for a couple of evenings to help renovate our new studio facility. Whether it was out of a sense of compassion for the less fortunate members of their brethren, or the lure of John's illegal hoard of duty free Burgundy, an impressive number of hardened hacks signed up and agreed that we could rely on their help when the time came.

The Ministry of Information and Culture had magnanimously granted us the use of the old Radio Kabul building in the centre of the city as the base for the project. Situated in the heart of the bustling commercial area, the studio was the spot where broadcasting had begun in Afghanistan fifty years earlier. However, we had been warned by our 'roomie' friend in the Ministry – who turned out to be a high-ranking American marine who had come back to Afghanistan and turned Mujhahid when the Soviets had invaded – that the building had not been used since the departure of the Soviets and consequently might be in a 'mild state of disrepair'. 'Mild state of disrepair' were not the first words that would have sprung to mind when we visited the studios for the first time. But then again, in the context of a bloody twenty-three-year conflict and the decimation we had witnessed in the city, maybe 'mild state of disrepair' was the appropriate term.

Near the Radio Kabul building was the Titanic Market, so named because of its location right in the centre of the dried-out riverbed of the River Kabul where it had a tendency to sink like its illustrious namesake whenever the rains came. The market's name was also a tribute to the Afghan people's favourite movie. For a land-locked country, the Afghans harboured a bizarre love for James Cameron's story of the doomed ship. Maybe they saw parallels between what they suffered and the fate that befell the passengers, or maybe it was the sight of Kate Winslett's breasts that had proved irresistible. Many punishments were endured during Taliban times by people whose passion for the movie fell foul of the regime's ban on any sort of television or videos. Even in the absence of music on Afghan radio stations, the theme song from the movie had become Afghanistan's unofficial national anthem, with most Afghans familiar with the tune if not all the words. Leonardo DiCaprio was revered in Kabul virtually as a holy deity, his face and the movie's logo adorning everything from the side of trucks to household appliances.

The market, which consisted of a couple of hundred small carts, seemed to be selling everything that one would normally expect to find in a British department store. Even in the middle of the harsh freezing winter, the place was alive and buzzing with thousands of people. The odd gaggle of burka-clad women mingled uneasily in the crowd, the blue of their burkas standing out against the deep reds of the traditional Afghan carpets on sale. People crowded around carts piled high with second-hand clothes long since discarded as 'out of fashion'by consumers in more affluent countries. They sifted through the jumble trying to find the right size – colour and style being of secondary concern.

Even in Kabul, the blue burkas seemed to be drawn, like bees to a honey-pot, to the stalls with women's shoes, giving credence to John's theory that all women, no matter where in the world, were basically genetically programmed to shop for shoes. Buying shoes was hard wired into a woman's DNA.

Gathered around big open woks where potato chips were being fried were crowds of small, wide-eyed children, hungrily consuming their country's equivalent of fast food with naan breads so large that they dwarfed many of the children eating them. A smell vaguely reminiscent of a

British chippie, without the vinegar, wafted through the open window of the car. Loud Hindi music blared from several battery-powered cassette players. The cacophony bombarded our senses. Even in the short time we had been in Kabul, the transformation of the city from 'the village of the damned' into something resembling third-world normality had been substantial. This vibrant heaving mass of humanity was very different from the nation which had spent five years cowering under the yoke of Taliban repression.

We were moving at little more than snail's pace, progress through the hoards of shoppers proving difficult. In addition to the teeming crowds, our driver faced the additional hazard of trying to avoid running over the wretched, often limbless, beggars littering the roadside.

We finally arrived at the currency market near where our studios were situated. Here, money dealers armed with sat-phones sat on their haunches behind piles of dollars, euros, rupees and afghanis, carrying out the sort of complex financial transactions that in the West would be impossible without rooms full of sophisticated computer equipment worth millions and teams of brokers earning the equivalent of Afghanistan's entire GNP. There were no worries here about the fluctuations of the Footsie or Dow Indices affecting business; exchange rates in Kabul currency market were fixed by the dealers yelling to each other down the street. For a place where there was easily several million dollars lying on open view in the confined space of a few hundred feet, security seemed pretty lax, but I couldn't really see anybody messing with these guys and walking away alive.

Unfortunately, the repetitive stopping and starting of the minibus finally proved too much for the engine which had obviously not seen the inside of a service depot since it had been stolen from Dubai, and we ground to a halt, literally a few feet short of our destination. All attempts by the driver to restart the vehicle were in vain.

Suddenly the van was engulfed by what seemed like hundreds of blue burkas. They were making a strange wailing noise and tapping the windows of the van like demented woodpeckers. The density of the crowd began to block out the sunlight and the interior of the vehicle became threateningly dark. The intensity of the tapping increased and all we could see were blue shrouds, each with a claw-like hand stretched out in front, their gauze-covered faces pushing right up against the windows. We could feel the concentration of the stares from under the burkas, and John, the only obvious foreigner, who was sitting next to me, was growing distinctly uneasy. Without the engine running, the windows quickly steamed up, heightening the feeling of claustrophobia. The minibus started to rock under the sheer weight of the beggar women now surrounding us, and one managed to get a scrawny hand through the small gap in window and touch John on the shoulder. He jumped and moved to the centre of the bus. What was more worrying to me was the fact that the two Afghans in the van, Manocher and the driver, both looked nervous.

Then we heard the unmistakable rattling of AK47 rounds being fired into the air. The crowd of women dispersed almost as quickly as they had appeared. In their place stood six sinister-looking Mujahideen all armed with AK47s and one with a rocket propelled grenade launcher slung over his shoulder. All had inane grins fixed on their faces and were eying us intently through the windows of the vehicle.

I really do not know which was more frightening, the march of the zombie burkas or the these trigger-happy zealots who, as a result of the on-going peace process, were obviously suffering withdrawal symptoms from not having fired a bullet for nigh on six weeks. One of them roughly yanked open the door and amidst a lot of shouting hustled John and me out. Knocking a very shocked John Murray at the base of his back with the butt of his automatic weapon, another of the Mujhahids manoeuvred us in the direction of the Radio Kabul compound. With two Mujhahids in front of us parting the crowds and clearing a path, two on each flank and the guy with the RPG bringing up the rear, the sorry procession made stately progress. When we reached the Radio Kabul building, the Mujhahids just shook our hands, smiled and left. It transpired that these ex-Mujahideen militiamen were responsible for security at the currency market, and when they saw us in trouble they had come to help us and escort us to our destination. As Manocher explained, we were 'respected guests'.

The studios were hidden down a long alleyway next to a bombed-out police station. Walking down the narrow passageway, it quickly became all too obvious that the ground around the building had served as a public lavatory in its recent past. Human faeces covered the ground in such quantity that trying to weave our way through without stepping in something proved impossible. And the smell... it would definitely need a lot more than a few bottles of bleach to get rid of that!

Fortunately, the building itself was reasonably inspiring. Two stories high, the ground floor housed a beautiful music studio and the upper floor where we were to be based had a single large studio. Both studios had been built and fitted out by the Soviets during their sojourn in the city and were in a reasonable state considering the neglect suffered during Mujahideen and Taliban times. There was also a good-sized control room and a number of other rooms we could convert into offices including a large rehearsal room which would ideally serve as the main newsroom.

Virtually all the windows were without glass and many of the doors were hanging off their hinges. Patches on the walls revealed that they had at some stage been cream but were now a nice shade of dark grey. What little furniture remained was beyond redemption. The building had no electricity, no water and no heating, and everything including the ancient Russian equipment lay under several centimetres of dust. It was obvious to even the most technically inexperienced that none of the equipment we found in the building was salvageable, so everything we required to get the programme on air we would have to bring in ourselves. The building had been ransacked a number of times and thus anything that remained we had to assume either did not work or had no value even as scrap.

The place was dirty, cold and damp, but it still had a certain inexplicable homely feel which immediately drew all of us to it. As John said to the rather perplexed Sky News crew who came later to interview us for a news feature, 'What we see here is not the dust, but the potential.' He was right; what we both saw that day was not what we physically found on site but the phoenix we hoped would rise out of the ashes, or in this case, the dust.

In one corner of the rehearsal room stood a battered piano which I somewhat romantically would always point out to visitors. It was perhaps the only one that had managed to survive the Taliban regime and their edict against music. The piano became yet another symbol for us all, a poignant reminder of why we were there, and an equally poignant reminder of what we could not allow to happen to these people again. Metaphors were the one thing that were unfortunately plentiful in Afghanistan. I even made a point of getting my hair cut every time I visited Kabul, just because the Taliban regime had forbidden haircuts.

With less than three weeks to going on-air, the clock was ticking. We felt that we had reached a hiatus and achieved all we could in the meantime. We now needed to get home, not only for a fix of civilisation but also to sort out a significant proportion of the operation that we could not do sitting in Kabul. We decided to leave on the first available flight.

As is the case with most burgeoning bureaucracies, rules and regulations in Afghanistan changed virtually every day. In the first stage of any regime change, the incoming administration purges itself of all the laws that it has inherited from the previous government, often just to make a point. Then, unsure of what to replace them with and with no judiciary process in place to refer to, individual officials begin to invent new rules, frequently just to create work for themselves. This appeared to be the case with the Interim Administration in Afghanistan, who, a few days before our departure, having got rid of the Taliban ruling that all foreigners needed an exit visa from the Foreign Ministry in order to leave the country, decided to reinstate it. We sent Saad with Timur, our fixer, to the Ministry to sort out the relevant paperwork.

Timur returned a few hours later with our passports. John and I experienced no problems – being British nationals, our passports had been returned with the requisite endorsement without any fuss. However, Saad, who held a Pakistani passport, had been refused an exit visa and the Ministry had impounded his passport. Not only that, but he was 'in custody and under investigation' for being a possible Pakistani spy. Nobody in the Foreign Ministry seemed to have believed his story that he was an aid worker.

By the time Timur got back, Saad had already been transferred to the Interior Ministry for questioning. The interrogators at the Ministry, having dealt with a number of Taliban and al-Qaeda terrorist suspects, were not known for the subtlety of their interviewing methods. With most Afghans still holding all Pakistanis collectively responsible for unleashing the Taliban curse upon them, hatred for their geographic neighbour ran high in Kabul.

It took Rafiqi's intervention and subsequently a personal note from the Foreign Minister and further verification from our donors, the European Commission, attesting to his status as an aid worker before we managed to get Saad released late the following day. He was looking very subdued when he was brought up from the bowels of the Interior Ministry building where he had been held overnight. He seemed to have aged ten years and he looked sullen. Black rings around his eyes testified to the fact that he had not managed to get much sleep during the night and he was also decidedly unkempt. He was uncharacteristically quiet for the remaining few days that we were in Kabul and reluctant to talk to any of us about what had happened during his detention.

Saad did not return to Kabul.

STRATFORD UPON AVON – 4 FEBRUARY 2002

As the Emirates Airbus swooped over the city of Birmingham on its final approach to the airport, the over-riding urge that I had after my brief time in Kabul was to hit a shopping mall as soon as possible. For some reason, above everything else, I needed to immerse myself in the decadence of Western consumerism almost like some security blanket that I had misplaced. I needed the reassurance that food and consumer durables were available in abundance and more importantly that I had the choice and means to indulge in whatever took my fancy. The weekly shop around Tesco or a stroll past the racks of books and magazines at WH Smiths became events, the very thought of which would send me into spasms of joy. An errand to my local Toyota car dealer to replace the wipers on my one-year-old car resulted in my walking out of the showroom having bought a brand new top-of-the-range model, not because I needed it but simply to prove to myself that I could buy a new car. Deprivation in Kabul of the most ordinary things that I had always taken for granted had bred in me an insatiable greed and gross excess that made me despise myself. My cholesterol levels must have gone into orbit with the number of cream cakes and donner kebabs that I consumed on my short trip back to civilisation.

To my utmost annoyance, I also found myself getting hooked on television soaps, a genre of programming that I had tried very hard to ignore in my pre-Kabul life. The lives of a group of make-believe families living in a fictitious borough in East London or the exploits of the neighbours in a middle-class Melbourne street began to matter to me more than what was happening around me in the real world. So involved did I become that even when I was back in Kabul, I had to make regular phone-calls to my wife solely to learn of the fate of Kat Slater or the welfare of Laura Beale, characters in the BBC soap 'Eastenders', both of whose destinies were precariously balanced at the time of my departure. Even a group of multi-coloured blobs called 'Boobahs' masquerading as a programme for pre-school age children held my attention as they were attempting some form of Indian dancing. The harsh actuality of Afghanistan necessitated such escapism that even the outer realms of reality presented by children's television was a blessing.

The purpose of the trip back to UK, however, was not to learn the finer points of Katak dance from overstuffed puppets or to go on shopping trips, but to get together and ship out all the equipment we needed for the radio show. The Danish state broadcaster and the Scottish radio station where John had begun his illustrious broadcasting career many moons before had both generously donated significant amounts of equipment which had been gathering dust in their storerooms. Outdated junk in their eyes, in our estimation this was a veritable treasure trove which the Afghan engineers would be familiar with and not require further training to operate.

Within a few days we managed to amass over six and a half tons of essential equipment: three tons had been rotting in a basement in some remote radio station in the Scottish Highlands, three tons in Denmark Radio's studios in Copenhagen, and close to half a ton of stationery supplies were piled high in various rooms around our town house in Stratford, much to the consternation of my wife, but to the obvious delight of Simba, our cat. However, with no regular flights into Kabul, and courier companies like DHL or FedEx not yet having the balls to open an Afghanistan office, the question arose, how on earth were we going to get all this to Kabul in time?

Various attempts to sweet-talk contacts and friends in the Ministry of Defence to get the British army or the RAF to airlift our equipment had been totally ignored. Apparently, shipping tanks and vital supplies such as Mars Bars for the lads in Afghanistan took precedence over radio stuff. John had even spent an evening in a pub in Hereford getting drunk with SAS friends from his Kosovo days in an attempt to convince them to covertly smuggle the kit in on one of their transporters, but the equipment remained firmly grounded at locations in the Scottish Highlands, Scandinavia and my front room.

Three days before John and I were due to return to Kabul, our hopes of getting the stuff shipped slowly diminishing and alternative plans to get the programme on air being given serious consideration, Soren, by pure fluke, over a lunchtime beer in the local *bodgier*, discovered that the shipment of most humanitarian aid to Afghanistan was being co-ordinated by a Danish company. Not only that, but the whole show was being run from a small airfield just down the road from our organisation's offices. After a great deal of negotiation and judicious arm-bending, the shipping company agreed to carry our equipment, as and when space was available, on the UN cargo planes. The next scheduled flight was in seventy-two hours' time, after which no further airlifts to Kabul were planned for the foreseeable future.

Action stations! Within an hour of the confirmation that the Danes would transport our kit, a well-rehearsed plan was put into operation. Alexander Graziani had resurfaced, and while not agreeing to go to Kabul, had volunteered to transport the equipment to the carrier. He and his brother would collect the boxes of stationery from my house, make their way to Scotland to pick up the equipment, then drive to Denmark and personally deliver the consignment to the Danish shipping company. Meticulous planning meant that Alexander had enough time to arrive comfortably before the scheduled departure of the UN flight. When John and I flew back to Afghanistan again in a couple of days' time, we would be able to enjoy the champagne hospitality of the airline secure in the knowledge that somewhere over the horizon the equipment was also winging its way to rendezvous with us in Kabul.

However, as with most ventures involving Alexander, it proved not to be that simple. The trials and tribulations endured by him in his frantic attempts to deliver the equipment to Denmark on time began to mirror a bad Hollywood 'B' movie almost from the moment he left my front door having collected the stationery. Parallels to scenes from the movie 'Planes, Trains and Automobiles' began to materialise in my subconscious as I tracked their painful progress. In fact, Steve Martin and John Candy's calamitous attempts to get home in time for their family Thanksgiving dinner seemed trivial compared to the adventures they had in delivering our equipment.

To start with, Alexander and his brother managed to get lost in the Highlands. A simple map reading error combined with a blizzard put our intrepid duo nearly fifty miles off course. They turned up at the wrong radio station much to the bemusement of the startled station staff, who had absolutely no idea who these two English 'yobs' were who had just landed on their doorstep and were rather determined to take a significant chunk of their station's broadcasting equipment away with them. A few phone calls, thankfully not to the local constabulary, cleared up the misunderstanding and Alexander was pointed in the direction of the radio station where he was expected.

When they arrived at the correct place, the van which had been hired for the purpose of transporting the equipment proved totally inadequate to carry the load, and a frantic search for a larger vehicle was hastily launched – not an easy task on a Sunday in the remote Scottish Highlands. The rental company had to be bullied into delivering a replacement to them from the nearest English town, several hours away. By the time the substitute vehicle was loaded, Alexander, his brother and, more importantly, the equipment were several hundred miles from the ferry on which they had been booked and which was at that very moment setting sail without them.

The next morning, en-route to Hull to catch the evening ferry which was positively the last ferry crossing for the equipment to have any chance of making the UN flight, Alexander rang to inform me that the front brakes had failed while they were on the motorway and as a precaution they had called out a roadside recovery service to check the vehicle before they went any further. He assured me that they were only a few miles from Hull, and once the mechanic had given the brakes the once-over, they could be on the quayside in less than twenty minutes.

Just an hour before the scheduled departure of the ferry, Alexander called again to inform me that the roadside recovery service had arrived and found that one of the front wheels was about to fall off. The van had been condemned as a death trap and a pick-up truck had been called to tow them back to Birmingham.

With the deadline for the UN flight now long since past, when Alexander got the equipment to the shipping company had become purely academic. However, another brave attempt to deliver the jinxed Scottish equipment was mounted the following morning. When I called them from the executive lounge in Dubai on our way back to Afghanistan several hours later for a progress report, I had expected them to be somewhere in Germany. But they were still very much in Birmingham, this time because Alex's brother had forgotten his passport and they had had to return there to get it. There was also a vague mention of a punch-up with some Newcastle United supporters in some pub, but I wasn't really paying attention by that time. Somehow I didn't care any more. I fixed John a neat double Scotch, poured myself a strong dose of caffeine and we went back to reading our respective books.

My fall from grace at the BBC was as spectacular as my meteoric rise had been. I was directing a live breakfast time show when the floor manager on the show thrust a copy of an infamous tabloid under my nose. The headline said it all: 'Beeb drugs scandal.' It was not that I ever used drugs or for that matter even condoned the use of anything stronger than caffeine. No, what had brought about my downfall was the bye-line – the story had been written by my brother.

What had been private family chatter around the kitchen table had been regurgitated into sensational front page news exposing the party antics of the great majority of my friends at the BBC including, unfortunately, my boss. With only 'an unnamed BBC insider' identified as the source for the revelations, I tendered my resignation on the same day as the article appeared, and when my mother refused to admonish my brother, claiming that it was a good story and that 'he was only doing his job', I packed up my wife and children and left the family home, never to return.

Professionally, I found myself banished to that barren wilderness which was 'disgraced ex-BBC' from which very few ever returned. Suddenly, all the awards and all the successes meant nothing and overnight I had become an unemployable pariah who had allegedly sold out his friends to the vultures of tabloid journalism. While my brother's career shot into some tabloid stratosphere fuelled by his amazing exposé of wrong-doing at the BBC, mine spiralled equally spectacularly downwards towards the gutter. Friends who had been dangling lucrative contracts in front of me while I was still at the Beeb now stopped taking my calls. Even their secretaries, who had been on first-name terms with me, suddenly began denying that they even knew me. Media, for all of its rivalries, remained very much a closed shop where everyone looked out for each other, and before long I realised that my chances of gaining employment in the British media again were rather bleak. In the eyes of my peers and contemporaries I had committed the most heinous sin, and my humiliation was complete when I couldn't even get a lowly job at my local radio station.

It didn't take long for the cars, the designer lifestyle, the savings, the credit cards and all the glamorous friends to vanish. The high life that I had become accustomed to was replaced by an existence where comparing the cost of the supermarket's own brand beans to Heinz made a difference to whether we ate or not. It was only John's generosity and my wife Farah's continued faith in me that kept my head above water.

When we were at our lowest, literally homeless and penniless, Farah, my pampered better half who had never had to do anything more than look good, ended up taking a job in the local shop to make ends meet, while I carried on looking for increasingly elusive rehabilitation in the *media fold. For the time being, helping the local video shop make the occasional Asian wedding video had become my last tenuous link with my chosen profession. If I had to edit one more kaleidoscopic montage of bored relatives gorging themselves on carnivorous delights set to cheesy Hindi film music, I felt that I would slit my wrists.*

My salvation came from the most unusual quarter. A small Danish organisation was looking for someone with some production experience to help them with media development work that they were doing around the world. On a whim I applied. Thankfully, my infamy not yet having spread to Scandinavia, I got the job, and the rest, as they say, is history.

Some ghosts, however, become impossible to exorcise and my brother's betrayal was one of them. It taunted me every single moment and I knew that it would continue to do so till my dying day. There were, and still are, times when the anger is overwhelming, and while I try very hard to forgive him, I find it nigh on impossible to forget what he did. The one question that haunts me to this day is 'why?'.

Helping those less fortunate than myself definitely eased the pain, and what had started off as 'the only job I could get' soon became an obsession which slowly began to dominate my life. Instead of just existing, I once again had a purpose.

Maybe it was my search for some sort of redemption that led me to work in virtually every war-zone in recent history – picking up the pieces of other people's messes became a humbling yet gratifying experience. That, and a firm belief that media should be used as a positive influence to rebuild lives and not as a destructive power which had devastated so many lives, including my own.

One of the most annoying aspects of the Afghanistan project was having to deal with all the media attention we were attracting. Ironically, very few of us who work in the industry actually like being interviewed ourselves. Knowing some of the stunts we have pulled in our own journalistic careers, little wonder we don't trust others in the same profession. In this instance, what had started out as a favour by a few well-meaning journalist friends and colleagues to highlight the work that we were doing in Afghanistan had turned into a full-scale media frenzy which was proving to be as intrusive as it was time consuming. Telling people what we were doing was getting in the way of doing the job itself. Also, more annoying for me was the fact that most of the journalists who were interviewing us seemed fixated by Afghan women and, in particular, their veils. The questions we were being asked quickly became clichéd and monotonous: 'Will you be having women singers on the programme?', 'Are the women working in the station going to wear burkas?', and one French radio journalist actually asked me live on-air whether I preferred my women 'with or without burka'.

As a direct result of this media interest John and I became really sad and started a 'Google sweepstake'. Each morning we would 'Google' each other's name and see how many page hits we had amassed in the preceding twenty-four hours. Rumour had it that Niels, our technical support person at base in Denmark, was running a book in the office and reputedly making healthy beer money by taking side bets on our burgeoning stardom.

Abigail Brooke was just one of the many journalists who contacted me after reading about our work on the internet. She had first got in touch while I was at home in Stratford, and had asked me to do a live guest interview on her breakfast show for a feature she was doing about Afghanistan reconstruction.

Ms Brooke, or Abi as she insisted that I call her, had developed an unquenchable thirst for stories about Afghanistan, and to satiate her need, she took to calling me very frequently. Her boyfriend, apparently, was Iranian and she was fascinated by anything to do with that part of the world, an interest which had been spurred by my interview on her show. She seemed totally in awe of the fact that she was actually speaking to someone who had been in Afghanistan. As pleased as I was about having converted at least one American citizen to believing that there was more to Afghanistan than Taliban, guns and dust, her daily calls were becoming somewhat tedious, particularly in light of the ongoing fun and games I was experiencing with the adventures of Alexander and Co. It was also becoming somewhat tricky to adequately explain to my wife why an American girl was ringing me so many times, often at odd hours of the night – 'it's work' no longer sufficed as justification.

So, in a moment of madness, or maybe as a feeble attempt to get rid of her, I asked Abi to come to Kabul with me on one of my future trips and help us train the Afghan journalists whom we would soon have working for us. I don't know why I did so. Maybe I presumed that she would be too chicken to come to Kabul and that that would have been the last I heard of her. However, I realised how big a mistake I had made almost before I had even finished making the suggestion. But it was too late by then, the damage had been done. Her uncontained excitement at the idea was definitely not part of my script, and sure enough, three days later, she called to let me know that she would be taking a sabbatical from work and was planning to accompany us on our next trip.

John's refusal to sit next to me on the flight to Dubai said it all. 'Since when has 'Come with me into a war-zone' been one of your chat-up lines? What the hell possessed you to invite a girl, and an American at that, into Afghanistan? You dozy git, don't you think that we have enough problems without having to baby-sit some Yank bird that you're trying to pull? '

This time I hated to admit that he had a point.

John Murray had one almost impenetrable barrier stopping him entering into a meaningful relationship with any member of the female sex, and that barrier was Anne-Marie Greene. John had been besotted with her since college days, and in spite of no indications that the feelings were reciprocated, he still held a torch for her. To me this was nothing more than a cop-out, particularly since John had made no effort to pursue this so-called girl of his dreams since the day that we had all parted company at college and gone our separate ways. He hadn't been in touch with her since that day and still somehow miraculously expected a fairy tale ending. Subtle and less-than-subtle hints dropped by me that maybe he should forget her and move on went unheeded, and if anything his obsession grew stronger. No girl that came into John's life stood any chance of success when she was going to be compared to an ideal that existed only in the rose-tinted peripheries of a fading memory. As John's best mate, I had to do something about this 'fatal attraction'. I decided that the only thing to do was to hunt out Anne-Marie and get this thing resolved face-to-face once and for all.

It took one of the immensely talented researchers on my production team less than five minutes to come up with a telephone number for the current whereabouts of Ms Greene. Apparently a simple call to directory enquires had yielded the information which had eluded both of us for so many years. Thus, a meeting arranged, I turned up with a terribly nervous John at an obscure nightclub in one of the less savoury parts of London to hear Anne-Marie's punk band, Puking Monkey, play, and then to have a drink with her afterwards.

John and I must have seemed weird to the multi-coloured-spiky-haired crowd who were jumping up and down in unison to a tuneless ditty being performed by an obnoxious youth on the stage. The music consisted of one chord, C major, being repetitively hammered out to a rhythm-less accompaniment on a mismatched drum kit. Anne-Marie was playing keyboards. The lyrics, from what I could understand in between all the swear words, were some rant about the poor underclass of Britain being screwed by the government. The air was pungent with a potentially lethal combination of illicit pharmaceuticals which possibly explained the semi-comatose state of a significant proportion of the audience. Towards the end of the band's performance, the lead guitarist stopped playing and, amidst much cheering, dropped his trousers and urinated over the audience. What the hell had Anne-Marie got herself into?

When John's object of desire joined us at the table, she was unrecognisable from the stunning creature who had graced our lives and had had most of Sutton College's male population drooling over her. Gone were the flowing blond locks, replaced by pink and black spikes. Safety pins and other metalwork adorned various piercings around her once flawless face. What had been a picture of perfection now looked violated and abused. Her make-up, like that of most of the people in the club, was only one colour: black. Her top seemed to consist of surgical bandages held together with safety pins making her look like some decaying Egyptian mummy, and the fishnet tights she wore under her short red kilt were ragged and ripped. To be frank, she looked worse than some of the homeless beggars on the streets of London. The twinkle had gone from her eyes and she appeared to be doped up on some drug or other. John's shock and hurt were obvious. I should not have done this to him, it was grossly unfair, but the ghosts of the past had to be laid to rest.

After an hour of stilted conversation which served no purpose other than to make us feel even more uneasy in the surroundings and to reinforce how deep the chasm between us had become, John suddenly grabbed Anne-Marie and, pulling her towards him, started kissing her. For a split second Anne-Marie responded, and then, as gently as she could, she prised herself free from John's embrace. John took *her hand and started to stroke it gently. 'Anne-Marie, I love you more than life itself. You always have been and always will be the only girl for me.'*

Anne-Marie sobered up pretty quickly. For a moment, I saw a flash of the girl with whom we had shared two years of our lives. The third musketeer was back with us again. She gripped John's hand firmly and lowered her eyes, unable to look at him directly. 'John, you are a most wonderful human being and I love you dearly. But, please, you have to let go and move on.'

John interjected, 'But why? Look, we can make it work. Just give me a chance and I'll prove it to you.' John's eyes were beginning to well up and he was fighting back the tears. 'Please.'

Anne-Marie shook her head. 'John, it can never work between us because I am in love with someone else.' Where was she going with this? She turned to look me straight in the eye. 'Haven't you ever twigged that it was always Waseem that I loved?'

KABUL – 14 FEBRUARY 2002

Our second trip to Afghanistan began at Kabul Airport, not Bagram airbase, thus depriving John and me of a white-knuckle drive into town. However, the final approach of the small UN aircraft into Kabul Airport more than compensated for our lust for stomach-churning thrills; flying over the mountains that surround the city, the pilot had to engage a missile avoidance pattern which basically involved putting the aircraft into a tight downward spiral and corkscrewing all the way down to the runway. With the wingtips of the plane skimming the tops of mountains and buildings, combined with the 'G' forces exerted by the fast spinning motion and the usual rough turbulence found over the mountainous terrain, the experience was enough to give any theme-park ride a decent run for its money. As we reached for the sick-bags, John eloquently summed up my feelings, that the landing, however unpleasant, was 'infinitely better than a SAM missile up the arse!'

When our aircraft landed, we found the airport was teeming with pilgrims patiently waiting to board planes to be transported to the holy city of Mecca to perform *Hajj*, the annual pilgrimage prescribed for all Muslims. Thousands of devotees, swathed only in the two sheets of white cotton allowed by their religion, were bravely weathering the freezing conditions. Even in my Marks and Spencer Arctic-grade thermal underwear and goose down ski jacket, I was still shivering, which made my respect for these guys, many of whom I was to learn had been at the airport for several days, increase no end.

As we drove by in the rickety old airport bus in which the newly-appointed Afghan ground staff insisted we traverse the few hundred yards across the apron to the terminal building, a raging crowd of pilgrims suddenly burst through the security cordon that had been holding them back and ran past us onto the airfield. Within seconds, hundreds of them had swarmed round an Ariana Boeing 727 aircraft which was about to taxi across to the runway, forcing the plane to a standstill. A number of the pilgrims actually lay down in front of the nose wheel of the jet to prevent the pilot moving it any further.

Why this ancient remnant of Afghanistan's decaying national airline had become the object of the crowd's obvious wrath was a mystery. However, looking over my shoulder as we were shepherded into the cavernous ruin of a building which was somewhat euphemistically signposted 'International Arrivals Terminal', all I was able to see was that a rather distinguished looking gentleman, dressed in a suave European suit, had appeared at the aircraft's open door. He was trying to address the crowd which had gathered around the aeroplane. But before any of us could make out what was happening, we were herded into the building by an overzealous soldier poking us with an automatic weapon, a greeting that none of us felt the least urge to argue with. The 'Welcome to Afghanistan to our dear foreigners' sign placed by the Afghanistan tourist board had obviously failed to catch the notice of our burly escort who had, it would appear, received his hospitality training at the Taliban School of Tourism. Once we were in the terminal we soon forgot what was happening outside and turned our attention to the exciting, new, even more bureaucratic, entry procedures that had been put in place by the Afghan Immigration Authorities since our last visit.

The gentleman in the suit, I was to later find out from my wife who had seen the event on BBC news, was Afghanistan's Aviation Minister. While we completed the multitude of immigration forms and custom declarations in triplicate to be allowed into the country, the Right Honourable Minister was dragged from the plane by the crowd and lynched, apparently for taking the last remaining aircraft in the national carrier's fleet for a personal jaunt to New Delhi, thus leaving the Hajjis stranded.

We had other problems to contend with. Less than fourteen days remained to our on-air date, of which seven or more working days would be lost due to the festival of Eid which would be celebrated with some vigour this time because, significantly, it would be the first chance to have fun since the Taliban had left.

On the first day we arrived for work, the office had no power, no water, no heat, no furniture – and there was no sign whatsoever of the equipment anywhere on the horizon. The Afghan production team we had employed looked somewhat sceptical as, huddled around one small paraffin heater, we tried to describe to them the show that they were going to be producing in a few days' time.

It was in that room on that cold February morning that the name, 'Good Morning Afghanistan', was coined by Manocher – so named, not as a veiled reference to the Robin Williams' movie about a radio station in Vietnam as I had to explain to every journalist who interviewed me subsequently, but because 'Suba Khair', the Dari for 'good morning', literally translated means 'new dawn', a title that the team felt very appropriate for the time in history in which they found themselves.

I sat in as John and Manocher, seated with twenty local journalists on the floor in the main newsroom, started to explain how to use 'jingles' in a radio programme. This was a concept totally alien to most of the young team who had learnt their skills on Radio Sharia, the Taliban-run station where all music was banned, and none of them had a clue what John was talking about. Without any sort of playback facility to demonstrate what he meant, he was forced to hum the jingles to the team: 'Dum, dum, dum dada daaaa, music fades and then you start, 'Good Morning Afghanistan.''

Manocher, translating, repeated in Dari, 'Dum, dum, dum dada daaaa... Suba Khair, Afghanistan.'

I couldn't take any more; suppressing fits of giggles, I left the room before I did the project and John's reputation irreparable damage.

The bemused looks on the faces of the team said it all; they just sat there looking at one another with quizzical expressions questioning the sanity of the *Kharjees* who had been foisted upon them. Not many, it seemed, were convinced of our ability to launch a daily breakfast show in just over a week's time. Given all the odds, I hate to admit it, but my money was also on an abysmal failure.

With Manocher having taken up his proper assignment, working with John to develop the programme format and translating jingle tunes into Dari, I acquired a new sidekick to assist me with the logistical and political officialdom that still remained to be tackled. Jamshed Latifi was Manocher's best friend. Though not intellectually as adept, Jamshed was, nonetheless, streetwise and smart, exactly the skills needed in post-war Afghanistan. Jamshed's approach was typified by the way he used a case of mistaken identity to his advantage, when the Airport Director and Head of Afghan Customs thought that he was the son of the Minister of Finance who was also called Jamshed. He managed to push through in one day all the clearances needed for the importation of the radio equipment, a feat that would have taken those not related to the Minister several weeks and a fair amount of baksheesh or palm-greasing to achieve. So convincing was the pretence, that even to this day Jamshed gets ushered into the director's office each time he is at the airport, where he is plied with endless cups of tea while the poor man insists on going though the motions of singing endless praises of the Minister of Finance, whom he still believes to be Jamshed's father.

Jamshed looked as if he had stepped right out of a Bollywood movie. This gave John and me such an inferiority complex that we simply refused ever to stand next to him, sit next to him or, perish the thought, be photographed with him, because his smouldering good looks made our mature distinguished features look positively unattractive, not that that was much of an issue in Kabul. Granted that our unshaved 'mission fuzz' and unkempt look did nothing to enhance our image, but being with Jamshed really did highlight our inadequacies. But then, Jamshed could have given not only Bollywood but most of Hollywood's leading men a good run for their money. Having to deal with one handsome hunk in Manocher had been bad enough but now to contend with two was going to be impossible. We didn't stand a chance!

Meanwhile, the saga of the equipment continued, with each passing day sounding more and more like a storyline from a bad daytime soap opera, and regular cliff-hangers that weren't doing much for my blood pressure.

Saturday 16th February. We heard that Soren and our Danish engineer, Joergen, who was coming to Kabul to install the equipment, had secured passage on the cargo plane with the equipment. As long as they brought sleeping bags and their own sandwiches, the Russian flight crew had agreed to carry them. Feeling comfortable that they were on their way, I proceeded to cancel their scheduled flights to Islamabad.

Sunday 17th February. Soren and Joergen found themselves offloaded from the flight when they got there because UN officials refused to allow their aircraft to carry non-UN personnel on what was ostensibly a cargo flight. Unfortunately, in the melee that ensued, the equipment was also offloaded.

Monday 18th February. After a flurry of intense diplomatic activity between New York, Brussels and Copenhagen, in addition to a great deal of praying in Kabul, the equipment or at least part of it was cleared by UN officials to travel on the next available flight. There was no indication of when that flight would be, but at least the equipment was going to be on it. Soren and Joergen, however, were now stranded in Denmark – all flights to Pakistan having been fully booked for several months because of all the Pakistani families returning home for Eid. The airlines' flight manifests were so full that they weren't even accepting stand-by passengers. I bullied Aseem, my travel agent in London, to pull whatever stunt necessary to get the two Danes to Islamabad within the next forty-eight hours.

Tuesday 19th February. No news of the equipment. However, Aseem had managed to pull off a miracle and get Soren and Joergen onto a flight to Islamabad. Admittedly they were now flying via Sri Lanka and a twenty-hour layover in Hong Kong, but to be honest, I didn't care how they travelled. All that mattered was that the dynamic duo got themselves to Kabul before the weekend.

Wednesday 20th February. Still no news of the equipment. Totally exasperated with the situation, unable to progress any further without electricity or studio equipment, John issued me with an ultimatum over dinner; either the equipment arrived and was installed within the next four days or he would leave.

Thursday 21st February. Hallelujah! News arrived from Denmark that the equipment was finally airborne and would be touching down in Kabul the following morning.

Friday 22nd February. The president of customs, a representative of the finance ministry, the technical director of Radio Television Afghanistan, Jamshed and I, together with the customary hangers-on, duly made our way to Kabul airport at six in the morning to await the arrival of the plane from Denmark with our equipment.

By midday, after six hours of biting cold as the first snowfall of the spring covered Kabul, there was still no sign of the Danish flight. There had been three or four arrivals at Kabul airport that morning, but none of them had been from Denmark. More worryingly, when we checked with the ISAF authorities who were in charge of running the airport, we were told that there had never been any flight scheduled to arrive from Denmark that day, nor, according to their flight movement charts, was any such flight plan filed for the next few days.

In spite of this, colleagues in Denmark and the shipping company continued to insist that the flight had not only left Denmark, but had already landed in Kabul. With nobody able to find the phantom flight that was supposedly sitting on the tarmac, we really were entering 'X file' territory and it seemed that it would take nothing short of Fox Mulder and Dana Sculley's intervention to resolve this one. The truth was out there, so was the equipment, but where the hell did we start looking?

The only clue from the Danish shipping company was that our equipment would be transported on a big white aircraft with blue stripes – no flight numbers or registration marks, just that we should be looking out for a white aircraft with blue stripes. The only plane we found on the apron that vaguely resembled that description had, we were told by the Russian crew, flown in from Baku in Azerbaijan and was carrying a shipment of live lobsters, crates of fine wines and Perrier water for the French ISAF contingent. Nowhere amongst these gastronomic delights was, we were informed, anything that remotely resembled radio equipment.

As I stood despondently on the freezing tarmac, the sat-phone unexpectedly rang. In the six weeks since I had acquired it, we had only received one call on the phone. The alignment of the satellites needs to be so precise for that particular cheap model to be able to receive a call that nobody had managed to get through. Nobody, that is, except John's mother who apparently had managed to get through first time to wish him a happy birthday! Alas, this call was not news of the missing equipment but my dear wife, Farah, who had also somehow managed to get through to me first time. Apparently she was experiencing some difficulty in printing out a document on the new Apple computer that I had bought just before coming to Kabul and had thought nothing of calling me in Kabul to tell me.

Jamshed looked on bemused as I spent ten minutes justifying my choice of Apple computer to my wife and then a further ten minutes talking her through how to print the blessed document.

At just over five dollars a minute arguing with Farah and then giving her possibly the most expensive computer after-care service anywhere in the world, even so the call had provided me with a much needed respite from what was happening around me. How I longed at that moment to be at home in Stratford worrying about nothing more mundane than how to print a document on my new computer instead of being where I was, freezing my rocks off, having to watch my every footstep in case I trod on a land mine, looking for a six-ton shipment that had mysteriously vanished off the face of the earth.

Just as Jamshed and I prepared to leave the airport and face John's wrath, a UN jeep pulled up on the tarmac and an officious-looking man emerged carrying a clipboard. On a whim, not that he looked like either Mulder or Sculley, I decided to go and ask him if he knew anything about the missing Danish flight.

He saw me coming towards him. 'Ah! Good Morning Afghanistan! We have had a large consignment of freight for you this morning. We were wondering where you'd got to.'

Apparently the large white plane with blue stripes – the flying French delicatessen – that had been sitting on the tarmac right in front of us for most of the morning had begun its journey in Denmark, but because it had changed crew and re-fuelled at Baku, the flight was shown in the airport logs as having originated in Baku and not, as we were told to be looking for, Billund in Denmark.

Our equipment had arrived that morning right under our noses, and had been spirited away by the officious-looking UN man with clipboard to a UN warehouse for safe-keeping. We immediately headed towards the UN compound and arrived just in time to see other officious-looking UN men with clipboards closing up for the day. It was eventually two more days before the equipment finally arrived at the GMA compound.

When we knew that the equipment was at least in the same city as we were, John and I made our way to the IC hotel to invite all our media friends who had pledged assistance to come to the studios, don their overalls and help us paint the place. However, when we got there we found the hotel totally deserted. All the satellite uplinks in the car park were gone. No longer were we tripping over the snaking wires or bits of camera equipment which had previously turned the reception area into a major obstacle course. The coffee shop where we had had to fight to get a table lay empty, the winter wind howling through the broken windows. Waiters who had been rushed off their feet just a few days ago, now sat despondently at the tables playing cards. They now fought for the pleasure of serving us. Without people the place looked positively dingy, and the Taliban-defaced mosaic murals of birds adorning the walls now dominated the room where they had earlier gone unnoticed. While I nursed a cup of insipid coffee and tried to eat a sponge cake that tasted like soggy cardboard, John and Manocher went up to the roof to see if they could find anyone.

Other than one news agency which was still broadcasting, all the makeshift studios that had been erected by networks on the roof had gone. The media circus had vanished into thin air. Almost overnight they had decamped and moved on. Known in the industry as the 'CNN factor', it is commonly acknowledged amongst media professionals that when the giant American news network moves on, the rest of the networks usually follow suit soon afterwards. The mandarins in Atlanta who had the dubious honour of setting the entire world's news agenda had obviously decided that Afghanistan was no longer newsworthy.

However gutted we were about having lost our entire volunteer workforce, John was nonetheless very excited about the fact that the departing news crews had left behind their generators; excess baggage charges to transport them back to base were more than the actual cost of generators in the first place, so it had made economic sense for the networks to discard them when they left. John had found the roof littered with dozens of them.

Over several more bland coffees, John hatched a plan to liberate one of the generators. He argued, very logically, that any media organisation would be only too pleased to know that we would be giving one of their generators a good home. I had to concede that with our own generator still impounded by the UN, having access to electricity could be useful. Anyway, when John's mind was made up, there was no point arguing with him, and we were going to steal a generator no matter what I said.

Next morning over breakfast, John presented Manocher, Jamshed and me with a meticulously prepared plan for taking a generator from the roof of the IC. This was presented to us in the form of a dossier, complete with maps and diagrams explaining in minute detail what he was calling 'Operation Bright Spark'. The plan called for a six-man team: four for the snatch squad – Team Alpha – which would actually go onto the roof and 'retrieve' the generator, while the other two would act as lookouts ensuring the integrity of the designated escape route. One of them – Team Beta – would be guarding the stairs, while the other – Team Delta – would be in the lobby. The assault was planned for the same evening.

'Mission madness' – a malady affecting aid workers who spend too much time away from civilisation and start losing their minds – had well and truly set in. Someone had told us the story of how young boys would purposely herd goats through minefields and then, when they trod on a mine and exploded, the goats became legitimate food for the boys and would be barbequed right there and then in the middle of the minefield. Somehow John and I had found this very amusing and it only took one of us to say 'exploding goats' and we'd both be rolling about the floor in fits of giggles. Mission madness! Then there was the time during a power cut that we decided that our adventures in Afghanistan should be turned into a major Hollywood film and we set about casting it: De Niro was to play John, Leonardo DiCaprio – who else – would play Manocher, Art Malik Saad, and the unanimous decision of the entire group was that the only actor who could do justice to my character was... Whoopi Goldberg! Mission madness!

So that afternoon, instead of doing other work, we sat in the IC coffee shop, casing the joint and going over last-minute details of the raid with John. At 18.00 hours, on the dot, like a well-oiled machine, 'Operation Bright Spark' began to roll.

The snatch crew, dressed in varying shades of black and looking like extras from a bad spy movie, made their way surreptitiously upstairs while I, as inconspicuously as was possible, walked across to my preordained 'look out' position in the lobby. We were all armed with cheap walkie-talkies which not only picked up messages from each other but also managed to pick up a whole host of other radio devices in the vicinity. Keeping open a clandestine secure channel of communication was not going to be that easy.

Team Alpha made their way to the roof with a stealthy precision that would have amazed the SAS. Team Beta was on the stairs, and Team Delta, which I presume was me, was in the lobby. The walkie-talkies crackled into life.

'Team Alpha in position.'

John, who by this stage had assumed the persona of Tom Cruise, acknowledged confirmation: 'Check.'

'Team Beta in position.'

'Check.'

Silence, then John's disgruntled voice came over the walky-talky. 'Team Delta, can you confirm that you are in position?'

John was taking this gig far too seriously for my liking. Reluctantly, I confirmed my position with a sigh: 'Team Delta in position.'

John's authoritative voice came over the airwaves again. 'All units in position. We are go, go, go! I repeat we are go, go, go!' He had obviously been watching too many cop shows.

Suddenly, there was a flurry of activity on the walkie-talkies. I immediately sensed that something had gone drastically wrong; the plan had been to maintain radio silence during the actual raid on the roof.

I tried to remember the contingency plans in the dossier John had given us earlier and to prepare myself for the correct emergency evacuation procedure. I wished that I had paid more attention because I couldn't remember the location of the agreed alternative RV point; was it the gents' toilet on the first floor, the book shop in the basement, or were we supposed to make our own way back to base and regroup there?

Thankfully, before I had to rack my brains any further, through the crackling and interference I heard John's voice yelling into the walkie-talkie, 'Kermit to Big Bird, Kermit to Big Bird. For Christ's sake come in, Big Bird.' It had, of course, been John's idea that we all have call signs based on Muppet characters – I was Big Bird, Jamshed was Gonzo and Manocher, Fozzie Bear.

'Big Bird to Kermit, I hear you loud and clear. Over.'

'Big Bird, we've been shafted. All the fucking generators are gone; some wanker's beaten us to it. Abort mission. I repeat, abort.'

The morning after the great generator heist had gone so wrong, Gonzo and I found ourselves back at our favourite hangout – the frozen wastes of Kabul Airport. With no escape from the howling freezing wind, six inches of brown sludge on the ground and the ISAF forces blowing up unexploded munitions and land mines every few minutes, Kabul airport was definitely my favourite place. This time we were keeping a vigil, waiting for the appearance of Soren and, more importantly, Joergen, the engineer who was going to assemble all the equipment, which was currently lying packed in numerous flight cases, into some semblance of a radio studio from which we would hopefully be transmitting in less than forty-eight hours. At 11.00 hours, the designated time of arrival, the UN flight appeared, circled the airfield twice, and then, as we watched helplessly, turned back to Islamabad. With no radar at Kabul Airport, the pilot has to land the plane solely on visual, and with a low cloud base and heavy snowfall that morning, the pilot had obviously decided that it was not safe enough to attempt a landing.

We spent most of the day waiting on the tarmac for news of the flight and praying. For some of the time, we took refuge in the Airport director's office, but having to listen to him talking continuously about his time at school with the Minister of Finance, we decided that stepping on a land mine on the apron or freezing our rocks off were both infinitely more preferable than having to hear yet another story about how bad at mathematics 'Jamshed's father' had been in his schooldays.

It was well into the afternoon before we heard that the plane was attempting to land again. A combination of bad weather and the impending Eid celebrations meant that the whole of Afghanistan was planning to close down, so if the pilot did not land this time, it would be several days before he would make another attempt.

Suddenly the heavens parted, and riding down to the ground on the last shafts of the setting sun like some awkward albatross was the UN plane. Much to my relief, Soren and Joergen deplaned shortly afterwards.

The next morning the pieces of the jigsaw thankfully started to fall into place. By lunchtime, the generator, after a number of false starts, was working and electricity had been restored to the building. By teatime, the portable studio from Denmark was operational, and we were all ushered into the studio to hear the first sounds of music to be played in the building since the departure of the Soviets a decade earlier. It was an emotional moment and we stood there lost in our own thoughts as we listened to Abba's 'Dancing Queen', the only tape that Joergen had with him. Soon after that rehearsals began in earnest.

I was hanging precariously from the balcony, arms outstretched helping Joergen align the satellite dish for our wonderful new expensive sat-phone, when I heard a voice saying,

'Salaam, Mr Mahmood.'

The shock of hearing the voice so unexpectedly in Kabul made me stumble backwards, and the satellite dish was knocked from my hands. I tried to dive after it, frantically trying to grab the wires trailing behind as it hurtled towards the ground. I managed to catch one; however, the downward momentum was so great that the wire just slipped through my hands, leaving a somewhat painful wire burn across my palm. The dish bounced twice on the concrete below before bursting into three large, distinctly un-repairable parts. Joergen was on the roof, but his colourful Danish expletives reverberated around the whole building, frightening each and every one of our Afghan staff. An apprehensive shiver shot up my back; even I was slightly scared of what Joergen might do to me for having broken his favourite toy.

I turned to the door and there she was, angelic as ever: Farida.

'Sorry!' her voice was barely audible. She was framed in the doorway, the sunlight behind outlining her shape and giving her slight silhouette an almost heavenly glow. She looked exactly what she was, a miraculous apparition. My God, she was stunning – and somehow so out of place here amongst the ruins of Kabul.

'Oh,' I said, 'don't worry, the sat phone was only going to be our link with the outside world. I guess we'll have to carry on making do with smoke signals to communicate.'

She looked at me quizzically, the humour obviously lost on her. I ushered her into the makeshift office and directed her to the only decent chair we had. 'But forget that. When did you get here? What are you doing here?'

'Manocher got a message to me saying that you were actually going to get this crazy radio programme of yours on air, so I thought that you might need some help.'

At that moment, Joergen closely followed by Soren burst into the room. 'Waseem, you bastard...! You...' Sensing Farida's presence, Joergen managed to stop himself, though I knew that this was just a temporary respite in deference to my pretty guest and that I would have hell to pay as soon as she left.

'Guys, I'd like you to meet Farida... our new presenter!'

Farida looked at me, her eyes twinkling. Things were definitely looking up.

However, it isn't over, as they say, until the fat lady sings. At six o'clock the next morning, thirty minutes before the scheduled transmission time, a flustered Jamshed burst through the door of our guesthouse. Abdullah, the other presenter, whom John had spent an immense amount of time grooming, had gone AWOL; the head of the airport, who was to be a live guest answering questions from the public about airport security after the assassination of the Aviation Minister, had not turned up; some of the team in their eagerness to get to the studio on time had broken curfew and been arrested by ISAF; and to top it all John, at the point when Jamshed had come fetch us, had been engaged in a fist fight with a Radio Afghanistan technician who for some reason was refusing to allow the programme to go on air.

Soren, Jamshed, and I leapt in a taxi and made our way to the house of the airport chief. Explaining to him that he had to be at the studio immediately, we bundled him, still in his pyjamas, into the taxi and raced off.

At 6.30, in the taxi heading towards the studio, we switched on the radio and heard a jingle donated to us by a Scottish radio station going out on air. Great! We had made it. But as soon as the theme music ended there was a deadly silence After what seemed like an eternity, but in reality must only have been a few seconds, we heard Farida's faltering voice saying, 'Good Morning Afghanistan...'

PART 4

'Good Morning Afghanistan'

*Our greatest glory is not in never falling, but in rising
every time we fall.*
Confucius

*Never doubt the power of a small group of committed
people to change the world. That's about the only way it
has ever happened in the past.*
Margaret Mead

KABUL – MARCH 2002

The euphoria at having successfully launched the
programme was short-lived. Even before all the sweets
and cakes which were passed around by the jubilant team
at the post-show celebration party had been consumed,
I had already mentally moved on to my next task, that
of ensuring that the show stayed on air. The short-term
funding arrangement we had secured for the initial phase
of the project would be coming to an end in the next few
weeks, and now that we were on-air, what little money
remained was haemorrhaging at an alarming rate. If a cash
transfusion was not made in the coming days, there was a real
possibility that we would have to close the whole operation
down. While the European Commission had indicated
that support would be continued, there was every chance
that the proposal would spend months languishing in some

bureaucrat's in-tray in Brussels while we were producing reams of reports justifying the number of paperclips we intended to use, a situation not totally unheard of when dealing with bureaucracies such as the EC who seem more fixated on the amount of paperwork that projects would generate than on physical implementation in the field.

I addressed the troops after one of the daily production meetings; I felt that they had the right to know what was going on. They listened in sombre silence as Manocher translated the news. Most of them took the fact that they might be without a job in a matter of days with the resigned feeling of 'being let down again' that most Afghans had become all too accustomed to when dealing with the West. When I had finished, Farida chirped up. Whatever she said had the whole team rolling about the floor with laughter. It was a few moments before Manocher was able to stop laughing enough to translate for me. Farida had apparently suggested a practical solution to our cash-flow problem: the Taliban had been circulating leaflets in Kabul offering 50,000 dollars for any foreigners handed over to them, and Farida was proposing that we 'sold' Mr John to them to tide us over till the EC money came in.

I thanked her for her suggestion and assured her that it would not come to that. I was sure that we could find enough candidates amongst the pen-pushers at the EC mission to 'sell' to the Taliban and spare Mr John who thankfully had not been around to hear his proposed role in Farida's money-making scheme. I must admit, however, that we all viewed Mr John in a different light after Farida's suggestion. Dollar signs lit up in some deep sub-conscious part of my brain whenever I saw him.

While John remained in the cosy surroundings of the studio, most of my work was outside and Jamshed and I spent a great deal of our time on the road. Kabul traffic was manic, a true test of your nerve. Each time you went out, it was like embarking on a kamikaze suicide mission, literally taking your life into your own hands. With fighting now officially over, Afghans needed some way to get rid of their excess testosterone and it seemed that the roads of Kabul were the chosen place to channel aggression. Cars had become weapons of mass destruction in the hands of the ex-militias. Ancient vehicles, held together with nothing more than sticky tape, string and a prayer, hared around the pot-holed roads playing games of high-speed chicken at every junction. Overcrowded taxis, with blue-shrouded women crammed into the open boots together with children and small menageries of domestic animals; hoards of the ubiquitous white UN 4x4s; a great variety of unidentifiable modes of wheeled transport; all raced each other at every roundabout and road junction, the right of way going to the driver with the greatest nerve or, in most cases, the larger vehicle.

When the traffic lights started working, they had obviously been switched on, not for any practical purpose, but to brighten up the drab landscape with their colourful lights. Traffic police, who were being sent their uniforms from Germany piecemeal – first the helmets arrived, then the trousers and finally the jackets – failed miserably in their half-hearted attempts to control drivers by using weird painted paddles which looked like giant lollipops.

One of our office drivers tried to rationalise Kabul traffic for me. As he saw it, Kabul traffic represented the sign of a true democracy, because while drivers in the West had to follow rules made by the government, in Kabul everybody was free to make up their own driving rules. So pleased was he by this political analogy that I didn't have the heart to disillusion the lumbering, six-feet-tall ex-Mujhahid by telling him that the scenario he had described was in fact 'anarchy'. Perhaps the driver's confusion over the definitions of 'democracy' and 'anarchy' could go a long way towards explaining a great deal about the state of Afghan politics over the past twenty-three years.

Driving around with Jamshed provided me with an enlightening insight into the psyche of young Afghan men. One day as we passed over the main bridge in Kabul, Jamshed and the driver became very animated and excited.

Desperately wanting to share a piece of whatever action was going down, I asked Jamshed what was happening. He looked at me quizzically and said, 'Didn't you see that good-looking girl walk past?'

It was reassuring to know that certain masculine behaviour, such as lusting after and leering at the female form, were genetically ingrained male activities that transcended all boundaries of race, culture and creed, even in a sexually-repressed country such as Afghanistan.

I immediately looked around, but all I saw was a sea of anonymous blue shrouds bobbing up and down around the van. Either he was winding me up or I had already missed the girl they had got so worked up about. However, they got more animated, and even without understanding the lingo, I could tell that it was becoming more and more lurid; male gestures were apparently also universal. With my curiosity even more aroused, I yelled, 'Where?' at Jamshed in a voice not really befitting my station or, for that matter, my age.

He looked at me as if I was some sort of 'thicko' or worse still, a perverted 'sicko'. 'Just there – ahead of us,' Jamshed replied pointing at one of the blue shrouds.

Either this was a big time 'let's set the *Kharjee* up' or I had lost my well-honed ability to home in on good-looking members of the female sex, in which case life was no longer worth living.

Jamshed put me out of my misery. He explained that during Taliban days, with all girls hidden under the identical blue burkas, boys learnt to tell which were the good-looking girls by reading simple signals, such as the posture the shrouds adopted or the shoes they were wearing. Jamshed said that this extreme form of 'blind date' had a great success rate and he could consistently pick out the really stunning girls, even though they were covered from head to toe. However, no matter how hard I looked, they still all seemed like indistinguishable blue shrouds to me.

What was not made clear and was never elaborated further, was how Jamshed and his mates ever managed to verify the success or otherwise of their methodology, when they were never ever going to be in a position to see the girls without the burka. I decided they had to have been winding me up, after all.

'Last night a 20 year old student, Hamayat Yaqobi, was shot dead by British ISAF troops near the old bakery in the Kartayi Mamurin area of the city. He was taking his pregnant wife, Sara, to a hospital after curfew when the troops allegedly opened fire.

The incident took place around 2 a.m.. The family were in a neighbour's taxi trying to make their way to a police post in the bakery where they had planned to ask for a police escort to take them to hospital. Witnesses say that as soon as the car switched on its lights, it was mown down in a hail of bullets which were fired from the watchtower in the bakery. Yaqobi was struck by a bullet in the back of the head and died instantly. Sara suffered shrapnel wounds to her neck. Fortunately, her baby was unharmed and she gave birth to a boy around ninety minutes later. Her mother-in-law received a bullet fragment in her right leg and the taxi driver suffered wounds to his face.

Mohammed Ishaq, the elder brother of the dead man, vowed revenge, telling 'Good Morning Afghanistan', 'They should be tried and punished in accordance with Sharia law. We want their blood in retaliation for the blood of our brother.'

British officials insisted that the paratroopers only shot at a taxi containing members of the Ishaq family after gunshots were heard and bullets hit their watchtower, but Afghan officials talking to 'Good Morning Afghanistan' have described this as 'complete nonsense'.

Colonel Zemary Fazil, head of the district police, reported that some of his own men had been stationed in the same building as the British paratroopers. According to Fazil, he was 'absolutely certain that the only shooting had been from the ISAF position'.

'Good Morning Afghanistan' reminds listeners that the city's curfew runs from 10 p.m. to 5 a.m. and should not be violated under any circumstances.

This is Ghafar Saleh reporting for 'Good Morning Afghanistan' from Kartayi Mamurin, Kabul.'

With the security situation easing slightly, Manocher invited us to go on a fishing expedition in the mountains. A trip was scheduled for one of the rare Fridays that we managed to get some time off. John, not such a keen fisherman, feigned a heavy work load and excused himself from the outing, but I guessed that his decision was based more on his reluctance to travel on the Bagram road again than on any real pressing work commitment.

After a few hours, Manocher and I arrived at the picturesque Panshir Valley, about fifty miles to the north of Kabul, just a few miles past Bagram; this place was the stronghold of the revolutionary leader, Massoud. What nobody had bothered to mention to me before our departure was the fact that the last part of the journey from Bagram onwards would be on a bumpy dirt track, a route that was said to have the highest density of land mines per square mile anywhere in the world. Large craters in the road and a multitude of wrecked cars, tanks and other twisted metal paraphernalia bore witness to the veracity of the claim and to the huge numbers who had not survived the journey.

Having breached just about every single security rule for expats living in war zones, I decided to put aside all the irrational fears consuming my consciousness and instead focus my energies on getting in a good day's fishing.

It was an idyllic location, the river flowing blue and with lush green vegetation on the banks, and Manocher and I wandered down to the riverside where a lavish picnic had already been laid out in our honour by the local commander, a friend of Manocher's, who was hosting the trip. Afghan rugs had been spread complete with bolster cushions. There were kebabs, nan bread, soft drinks and a multitude of fruits for our delectation. We could have been a bunch of guys out on a fishing trip anywhere in the world. One thing, however, was conspicuous by its absence – nobody was carrying any fishing tackle.

As we sat there, Manocher told me a story one of his brothers had told him about the heavy fighting that had taken place in this region during the American forces' recent campaign to oust the Taliban. This place was riddled with caves and thus had become one of the coalition's primary targets during the war. Apparently, one of the key ways in which the American bombers had pinpointed targets, particularly in these areas where they suspected that caves were being used by Al-Qaeda or Taliban sympathisers, was by training their missiles on lights in the caves.

Using this device, the mountains across from where we were sitting had been subjected to heavy carpet bombing. However, after each mission, when the planes returned for reconnaissance, the lights were always seen to be on, and as a result the Americans would carpet bomb the area again. This carried on for a number of days. Each day the Americans would rain down cataclysmic death and destruction upon the area, only to return the next day to find the lights were back on.

After this apparent failure of the bombing raids to achieve their objectives, the American commanders sent in a whole battalion of elite ground troops to flush out the insurgents from the caves. However, a full-on assault by a crack unit of Marines found the caves deserted and not one showed any signs of human inhabitation whatsoever. A subsequent sweep of the entire surrounding area merely proved that there were no enemy or resistance forces anywhere. Further investigation established that the lights had been put up each night by a band of little old men living in the neighbouring villages purposely to attract the bombers. After the raids, in the morning they would scramble up the mountain, collect the spent bombs and missiles and sell them across the border in nearby Pakistan as scrap metal.

Several hours after we had feasted, and after the customary communal burping, lots of tea drinking and more amusing anecdotes about the war, there was still no sign of anyone producing any fishing rods. Eventually, curiosity got the better of me, and with darkness fast approaching, I asked Manocher what sort of fishing tackle they were planning to use and what sort of bait they found worked best in Afghanistan. Manocher gave me a blank look. When I mimed a fishing rod on the river's edge, the penny finally dropped. 'No, no, Mr Mahmood, we do not fish like that, very slow and very boring. In Afghanistan we fish with grenade!'

As he spoke, he took the pin out of a grenade that had appeared alarmingly in his hand, stood up and tossed it into the river. The explosion echoed around the rock walls of the deep river valley, and as Manocher had promised, dozens of dead fish appeared, floating on the surface.

'See, Mr Mahmood, much better. Many fishes. You want to fish also?'

With that he handed me a grenade.

'More than 2,000 people are feared dead and more than 4,000 injured after a series of earthquakes struck Afghanistan's remote northern province of Baghlan yesterday.

The Afghan Interior Minister, Yunus Qanuni, who travelled to the area, told 'Good Morning Afghanistan' that up to 20,000 had been left homeless.

Afghanistan's interim government has requested international assistance as President Hamid Karzai called off a scheduled visit to Turkey.

'The interim government does not have the capacity to deal with this tragedy,' Mr Qanuni said in an interview with 'Good Morning Afghanistan'. 'We therefore ask all international agencies and foreign countries to help us deal with this tragedy.' Mr Qanuni went on to say that the bodies of at least 1,800 people had so far been pulled from the rubble.

The quakes began in the Hindu Kush mountains rocking the Nahrin and Burqa districts of Baghlan. The initial quake measured about six on the Richter scale, and was felt as far away as Peshawar and Islamabad in Pakistan.

When 'Good Morning Afghanistan' flew over the area on Tuesday in a helicopter, no homes were seen left standing in the villages around Nahrin.

The impoverished farming community mostly lived in crude mud-brick homes, and had already suffered very much during the civil war. Remat Ullah, a local farmer, was inconsolable as he dug away with his bare hands at the rubble trying to rescue members of his family. 'What have we done to deserve this fate... first the fighting, then the droughts and now this... Allah has really forsaken us.'

This is Safi-Ullah reporting for 'Good Morning Afghanistan' from Nahrin in Baghlan.

The sign outside the first 'international restaurant' to reopen in Kabul proclaimed: 'The Golden Lotus restaurant is once again open to cater for all with delicious external and internal foods.' After two days of virtually living in the studios, co-ordinating non-stop coverage of the earthquake in the north of the country, Manocher, Jamshed, John and I took the opportunity to dine out at this new eatery. The interior of the restaurant was an eclectic mix of Afghan and pseudo-western design which did nothing to enhance the local ethnicity and instead made it look like the interior of one of the cheap Balti houses that clutter the streets of most English towns. The tables had glass tops under which had been placed both the menus and the tablecloths, and old Bollywood music blared out from the hi-fi behind the bar. None of the tableware matched, and the glassware consisted of those funny tumblers that I remember we used to have in primary school and I had not really seen much since. The only giveaway that we were in Afghanistan were the two large Mujahideen guards armed with sub-machine guns standing at the door searching everybody entering the establishment. The huge framed portrait of the benignly smiling face of Ahmed Shah Massoud looking down upon the diners was also another clue that we were in downtown Kabul and not sitting on the Ladypool Road in Birmingham.

The menu was as eclectic as the surroundings; Afghan dishes, mainly consisting of grilled slabs of goat, sat alongside the Afghan chef's approximations of lasagne, pizza and satay chicken. In spite of lacking a clearly defined culinary identity and the even more dubious quality of the fare on offer, The Golden Lotus was teeming with people. Aid workers mingled with journalists and gun-toting military personnel, all only too eager to escape the confines of their restrictive compounds and trying hard to convince themselves that life in Kabul was returning to some semblance of normality. With diners rushing their meals in order to be home by the nine o'clock shoot-on-sight curfew and being surrounded by enough firearms to launch a coup in a small African country, 'normality' was, of course, a relative state.

With so many foreigners congregating in a single public place, The Golden Lotus represented a major security risk. We were only too conscious that by simply being there, we were presenting a soft target for rebel Taliban renegades who were still reputedly in Kabul, hunting *Kharjee* scalps. Eating with the constant fear that a RPG missile might bring the meal to a premature end was another factor distinguishing The Golden Lotus from The Thespian restaurant back home in Stratford upon Avon.

Part way through the meal, just as I was digging into my passable lasagne, John suddenly started to hyperventilate and began to look very ill. In no time he was sweating profusely and gasping for air, his face contorted in a mask of pain and turning a bright shade of blue in the process. Rather alarmingly, he was also clutching at his chest complaining of a sharp stabbing pain between his shoulder blades. As inconspicuously as possible in order not to disturb other diners, Manocher and I manoeuvred John out of the restaurant and took him home, while Jamshed was dispatched in search of a doctor.

At the guesthouse, we lay John down and gave him some aspirins which stabilised his condition while we waited for the doctor to arrive. He was no longer blue and his breathing was much more measured. It is at times like this that you begin to think about your own mortality; in our business you spend so much time saving other people's lives, seeing so much intolerable suffering inflicted on mankind, that you sometimes forget that you, too, are human. As I sat there holding John's hand, comforting him, a whole load of irrational thoughts went through my mind. What if John was to die? How could I face the rest of my life without him? What would I tell his poor mother back in Ireland?

John stirred and murmured, 'Waseem.'

'Yes John. How you feeling? Can I get you anything?'

'Waseem, I was just thinking. Isn't Dolly the sheep a pretty animal? Much prettier than any of the floppy eared goats you find here.'

Did he just ask me if I thought a cloned sheep was pretty? Thankfully, Jamshed turned up with the doctor before I was forced to voice my preference. After a cursory examination, the doctor ruled out any major coronary episode; John was definitely not having a heart attack, but as a precaution and more for our own peace of mind, he insisted that we took John to a hospital for an ECG. The doctor, a family friend of Jamshed's, and a neighbour offered to come with us to the hospital in which the neighbour used to work before he had taken up a job as a driver with an American NGO which, unlike the medical profession in Afghanistan, at least paid him a regular wage.

We drove John to the main Jamahiriya hospital in Kabul. The hospital was in darkness and a smell of stale urine hit us as soon as we entered the grounds. A strange inhuman wailing noise emanated from the crumbling building giving the place a creepy feeling, like some forbidding gothic mansion in an old clichéd horror movie. It became pretty apparent as soon as we entered the building that the Jamahiriya hospital was a place where people came to die. Few who arrived here for treatment, it seemed, left the hospital alive.

As we walked towards the cardiac department, a strong musty smell of rotting building mingled with the smell of rotting humans made me feel positively nauseous. I could feel the bile rising up the back of my throat.

The hallways were littered with hundreds of the undead in whom the only sign of life was the persistent coughing symptomatic of chronic tuberculosis. With the wards stretched beyond capacity, patients had taken up whatever space they could find to wait their turn to die. We had to thread our way carefully, making sure that we didn't tread on the bodies sprawled across the floor, not for fear of disturbing them but of what we ourselves might catch through any contact. Many of the lifeless bundles of rags on the ground appeared to have already given up their fight for life. A big healthy rat scuttled across the hallway in front of us.

Jamshed's doctor friend looked visibly embarrassed by what we were seeing, 'When I worked here, would you believe that I had to share a stethoscope with five doctors? If you get ill in Afghanistan, doctors cannot make you better any more, you just die.'

We walked past what I assumed must have been the emergency room; persistent piercing screams coming from the room sent a cold chill down my spine. Morbid curiosity compelled me to look through the door. A young boy of about thirteen, obviously a landmine victim with his right leg shattered beyond recognition, was lying on a filthy, rusting metal-framed trolley. Two large men were holding him down, while someone who was presumably the surgeon was trying to amputate his damaged leg. With no electricity, this procedure was being carried out under the dim light of gas lanterns. The boy let out another blood-curdling scream that riveted me to the spot.

I looked at Jamshed's friend: 'You don't use anaesthetic?'

'No. We haven't had any for years.'

Other patients waited outside the emergency room for their turn for treatment, desperately trying to stem the flow of blood from missing limbs and what appeared to be gunshot wounds.

We walked down many more dark corridors before we arrived at the 'Cardiac Unit' where most of the hospital's medical and nursing staff had descended, ignoring all their other patients just to make sure that the *Kharjee* was comfortable. John was made to lie on a decaying bed with the remnants of a curtain hanging off a frame pulled around it. The walls were coated with indescribable black grime splattered at various places with most of the bodily fluids produced by man. The chipped marble floor was slippery, covered in a layer of some greasy residue the consistency of motor oil. Hygiene was not, it seemed, high on the list of priorities at the Jamahiriya hospital.

The cardiologist sat at a rickety metal desk on a chair whose uneven legs necessitated a major balancing feat on his part to avoid his falling off. He started by going through John's medical history with him. I noticed that he wasn't making any notes while he was questioning John and realised that this was because he didn't have either a pen or any paper. In fact, his desk was totally devoid of anything that might have attested to his status as a doctor. He was wearing a stained white coat which distinguished him as a doctor, but it was so long since the coat had seen a laundry that if my butcher back home had worn it, he would have been contravening so many health and safety regulations that he would have been closed down instantly by the authorities and put behind bars.

After checking John's medical history, the doctor proceeded to undertake a perfunctory physical examination after which he just sat back at his desk making small talk with us. He hadn't even bothered to take John's blood pressure. By this time I was getting very impatient, I wanted to get out of this place as soon as possible and I couldn't understand, with all the preliminaries done, why the hell the doctor was not proceeding with the ECG test. If I had wanted to arrange a social get-together then I would have done so over insipid coffee at the IC or somewhere else, anywhere but here in death's waiting room. After about ten minutes of idle chit chat, I interrupted the conversation which had ventured onto John's favourite subject of gardening and gestured somewhat dramatically towards my watch, indicating to the doctor that we were in a hurry.

The doctor smiled at me, and said, 'Mr Waseem, to do ECG, I need electricity.'

In the dingy, grubby interior of the hospital, I had failed to notice that there had actually been no electricity for almost all the time we'd been there. The room we were in was lit by gas lanterns.

It was a further hour before the power was restored for long enough to allow the ancient ECG machine to be powered up for the test to be carried out. Then finding a razor blade to shave enough chest hair to be able to attach the electrodes required for the ECG had proved impossible, and it was necessary for our driver to make a trip to the guesthouse to retrieve John's own toilet bag. Thankfully, when the test was finally conducted, it proved that there was nothing wrong with John's heart. But he was still very ill and visibly getting worse by the minute. On his chest a painful lump of some sort had appeared which needed proper medical attention. I took the decision to have John evacuated immediately.

He was airlifted the next day to Dubai and then on to London where he was hospitalised. The lump on the chest turned out to be a benign abscess which was operated on and removed. My decision to evacuate him had proved to be correct. John Murray did not return to Afghanistan.

It is reported that US helicopter gunships today opened fired on an Afghan wedding in the village of Kakarak in Uruzgan province in the south of the country, killing 80 and injuring at least 250 civilians.

One survivor, Abdul Qayyum, told 'Good Morning Afghanistan' that the attack began shortly after midnight and continued for more than two hours until US special forces ground troops moved into the area. 'In one village there was a wedding party... a whole family of twenty-five people were killed. No single person was left alive. Most of the dead and injured were women and children. Tell me why they do this. These infidels are no better than the Taliban.'

Ahmed Jawad, a doctor at Mirwais Hospital, told 'Good Morning Afghanistan', 'We have seen on CNN that the American warplanes can pick out objects as close as four millimetres from the ground. How can they mistake a wedding party full of women and children for fighters?'

A farmer, Abdul Bari, who was comforting his heavily-bandaged six-year-old nephew, Ghulam, said: 'Fifteen people from my home are dead. My wife, my brother, everyone is dead. We don't know why the Americans hate us.'

Ma'amoor Abdul Qayyum, a retired local official, said he saw his eleven-year-old son die in front of him. 'The Americans have destroyed us. We have neither seen Al Qaeda nor Taliban but they bombed us. What did we do wrong?'

This is Ilyas Ghurmati reporting for 'Good Morning Afghanistan' from Khandahar.

HEATHROW AIRPORT – MARCH 2002

'Hi Abi, hope you haven't had long to wait.'

The blonde girl wearing a floppy hat and reading some obscure book by James Joyce while sitting on the edge of her suitcase near the Emirates check-in desk at Heathrow Airport's terminal three seemed astonished that I had recognised her. Certain that none of her luggage had any labels that might have given me a clue to her identity, Abigail Brookes was convinced that I possessed some supernatural power that had drawn me to her and made me locate her so easily amongst the thousands of other passengers! I did nothing to dispel this myth as we walked to the departure gate. However, as we boarded the flight, I felt I had to come clean with the young woman with whom I was about to spend a considerable amount of time in a live conflict zone. 'Err, Abi, I knew what you looked like because you emailed me a copy of your passport last week!'

We hit it off immediately. She was obviously not going to be as big a burden as John had suggested when he first heard that I had invited her to Kabul. All that sulking had been in vain. If anything, Abi was the sort of girl John would have fancied like mad. What a shame that he was stuck in hospital with a huge hole in his chest while I would have the pleasure of the delightful Ms Brooke's company for the next few weeks.

Unfortunately, she was one of those people who feel the need to talk non-stop to the person sitting next to them on a plane, whereas for me flights are sacrosanct, to be used for silent inner reflection, the marshalling of one's thoughts and catching up with movies and reading trashy novels that you never get the chance to do in the real world. Thus, by the time we landed in Dubai, I knew all about her childhood growing up in Utah amongst the Mormons, her stint in South America with the Peace Corps, all the people she worked with at the television station – who she liked and who she didn't like – and her Iranian boyfriend who, having lost his younger brother in the 9-11 attacks, had broken up with Abi because she had insisted on coming to Afghanistan to help 'those fucked-up murderers'.

Abi stayed at the guesthouse, and on the first evening Manocher and Jamshed joined us for dinner. Abi had already met Jamshed at the airport where he had swiftly managed to extricate the poor, helpless, American girl who had somehow managed to turn up at Kabul airport without a valid entry visa. A few packs of American cigarettes and the ongoing matter of Jamshed's mistaken identity got Abi effortlessly through the immigration procedure. The nonchalant manner in which Jamshed quickly resolved the situation, his infectious grin and the floppy Hugh Grant hairstyle managed to undo within a few seconds all the patient groundwork and matchmaking that I had undertaken during the long flights on behalf of my mate, John Murray. Abi was already under the

Jamshed spell, and from that point on, no matter what I said in my friend's favour, John just didn't stand a chance. All the grief that Abi had been expressing so tearfully to me for the past two days over her break-up with Mo, the Iranian boyfriend, was somehow miraculously healed as soon as we met Mr Jamshed Latifi.

During the meal loud thumping noises were heard, not very far away. The shock waves followed a few seconds later and the glass in the window frames shook with a discernible rattle. Abi stopped mid-fork and looked at us. Jamshed answered her unasked question, 'Don't worry, Abi *jaan*. Those are just missiles going off.'

'Incoming RPGs' I added, having become some sort of lay-expert in recognising missile types just from the sounds that they made. 'Can you pass me some chips, please, Abi?'

Abi looked at me, startled. I met her stare and just shrugged my shoulders. Around us, conversation and dinner continued as if nothing had happened. Living in a live conflict zone is a surreal experience which is difficult to describe to those who have not gone through it, and no amount of briefings that I gave Abi could ever have prepared her for the ground realities that you find in theatre. It is as if life begins to physically slow down and you live it in slow motion. The completion of the simplest task becomes the equivalent of having achieved a major accomplishment; getting to the office without incident, returning home in one piece, getting to bed every night having survived the day and then waking up the next morning having survived the night, all take on a monumental significance. War-zones are a funny paradox; sometimes it feels as if you are in some new-age floatation tank suffering acute sensory deprivation, at other times as if you are in a goldfish bowl with the whole world looking in, but like the goldfish, you really cannot do anything more than swim around in what seem like meaningless circles.

Living on the edge, in constant fear that the next moment could be your last, highlights how alone the individual really is. One's loneliness is multiplied a million-fold. As Orson Welles said, 'We're born alone, we live alone, we die alone', and nowhere does that really hit home as much as when you are in a war zone. It gets so lonely that sometimes you don't even know yourself. It is ironic that when you endure it long enough, the loneliness actually adds a certain beauty to life. You begin to value life much more and appreciate the little things that you so often overlook in the real world. Your senses are heightened and you savour each and every sensation. Loneliness made the bland fried chicken we were served every day in the guesthouse taste better than any gourmet meal that I had ever eaten. Loneliness made the musky night air smell better, the stench of rotting trash and human waste replaced by the fragrance of blooms in a mystical meadow. Loneliness made every sunset special and gave every setting sun a different hue.

The next day, together with Manocher and Jamshed, I took Abi for the customary sightseeing trip around Kabul. When we arrived at the King's mausoleum on the Majaran Hill, opposite the Olympic stadium, where we traditionally began the tour, we found the place crawling with military personnel. The King of Afghanistan was due to return to Kabul from exile in Italy in the next few days, and ISAF was obviously not taking any chances and had stepped up their security presence to an unprecedented level. A significant number of troops, armed to the teeth, with sophisticated military hardware back-up, were entrenched at various vantage points on the hill. On talking to these troops we learnt that the missiles we had heard the previous night had been a Taliban attack directed at the American Embassy, a few blocks away from where we lived. And I was right – they had been incoming RPGs!

Walking around the tanks and trying to ignore the armoured personnel carriers and Rapier missile launchers scattered about the grounds, we continued the sightseeing. Leaving the mausoleum, we drove to the other side of the hill passing through a massive graveyard. The green flags fluttering in the gentle breeze and the simple stones marking the graves went on forever. A conservative estimate would suggest that close to a million people were buried there. My feelings on the hill that cool spring day in Kabul reminded me very much of what I had felt when I first visited the Arlington National Cemetery in Virginia. But in reality, beyond the fact that both places honoured fallen warriors and proved the futility of war, this shabby dust bowl where I found myself had nothing in common with the pristine green hills covered with neat little white memorials in DC. What lay stretched out in front of me on these Kabul hills amounted to nothing short of genocide, a whole generation lost to over two decades of conflict.

Manocher was looking out of the car window forlornly. 'My father is buried here somewhere. My father was murdered by terrorists; they mistook him for someone else who they thought was a communist collaborator. My father wasn't – he was just a government official. He was a poet, a thinker. I was four years old when they shot him. I saw it all happen. You know, we don't even know where he is buried. I hope that one day I will be able to find his grave and honour his memory properly.'

At that moment, the car's cassette player, which had been jammed, burst into life when we hit a pot hole. The Spice Girls song 'Wannabee' blared out from the speakers and filled the vehicle.

I'll tell you what I want, what I really really want,
So tell me what you want, what you really really want,
I wanna, I wanna, I wanna, I wanna, I wanna really
really really wanna zigazig ah...'

As much as Jamshed tried, he could do nothing to stop the tape. Surrealism took on a new meaning as we drove through the final resting place of countless unnamed victims of Afghanistan's turbulent heritage to an accompaniment of the best of British banality.

On the way back to the guesthouse we passed the American Embassy. In spite of the sign which said 'No stripping' – obviously written by some dyslexic soldier having mistaken 'o' for 'i' – Abi insisted that we stop to allow her to take some video to show her folks back home. So, against my better judgement, less than twenty-four hours after a rocket attack had been launched on the heavily fortified American Embassy, our motley crew consisting of two young Afghan men, an unshaven middle-aged Paki, and an American girl all but hidden under a colourful Afghan scarf, pulled up in the 'no stopping' zone outside the Embassy – at that moment one of the most sensitive buildings in the world – in an battered old Toyota Hi-ace. As I slowly sank in my seat, I tried in vain to warn her about the concept of friendly fire.

'They wouldn't shoot me, I am an American citizen. Anyway, I am exercising my constitutional right as an American taxpayer. I have every right to be photographing what my taxes are paying for…'

I sank further into my seat, debating whether I should be putting on my flak jacket which was kept under the seat in case of emergencies, because obviously waving the 'Bill of Rights' at the security guards was not going to afford much protection.

With the camera pointing out of the car window in one hand, Abi used her free hand to excitedly wave to the soldiers on the roof. 'Look guys, they're waving back.'

No, they weren't waving back, they were motioning us to move on. I cannot begin to imagine what the camera pointed at them through the half-open side window must have looked like through their binoculars, but suffice to say that within milliseconds every single munitions deployed in the protection of the building, from the missiles to the rapid fire automatic weapons, was pointing at us. From the corner of my eye I could see black-clad special ops snipers falling into place and lining us up in their sights. Above us, I swear that I saw a couple of Apache attack helicopters rising over the horizon, fast approaching our position. It was the Bagram Airbase scene all over again. I did a mental stock-take: on the one side several hundred paranoid American troops, on the other a single white van stopped in a restricted zone full of Afghan-type men with a crazy woman yelling out of the window and pointing something in the direction of the soldiers. This was going to be tricky; driving away now would only raise suspicion and possibly attract fire, but staying put was growing more dangerous by the second.

Oblivious to all of this, Abi carried on shouting to the soldiers on the roof: 'Hi guys. Where you all from?'

At times like this it is the waiting for something to happen that is always the most difficult, the fear of the unexpected as your mind rapidly computes the manifold variations of what could happen. And 'what could happen' is always worse than what eventually does happen.

Thankfully in this case, the 'what could have happened' was infinitely worse than the 'what did happen'. What happened was that within a blink of an eye we were surrounded by dozens of American troops and ordered out of the van. Then, with our innocence quickly established, we were allowed to proceed on our way with nothing more than our collective wrists being slapped for having stopped a vehicle in a restricted zone. However, the tape from Abi's camera was confiscated 'in the interests of national security'. As we boarded the van, I could tell that she was not happy.

'My senator will hear about this. This is a gross violation of my fundamental rights as an American citizen…'

By this time I had had enough. 'Abi, just put a sock in it.'

That night, John's 'told you so' tone and roars of laughter when I narrated the incident to him put it all into perspective. Even though he was no longer with me in Afghanistan, he remained my professional and personal sounding board and we spoke almost every evening whenever we were able to get a line. He was right though, the 'Yank bird' could have got us killed for something as stupid as exercising her God-given-right to be an American.

'Good Morning Afghanistan' was growing from strength to strength and we were soon planning to launch a sister programme in the evening, rather nattily entitled, 'Good Evening, Afghanistan'. It was this programme that I had invited Abi to pull together.

Much to my amazement, the donor extended the funding for the radio station with relatively little fuss, thus negating the need for Farida to sell anyone to the Taliban. To celebrate, Jamshed organised a picnic in the Solang valley.

The entire GMA team packed into three rusting buses, and the atmosphere en-route to the chosen spot, about seventy miles north of Kabul, which Jamshed for most of the preceding week had been referring to as 'paradise', was very jovial. 'Abi, this weekend, I take you to paradise,' had been his mantra every time he had set eyes upon her.

'Please would you take me to paradise as well, Jamshed?' I had asked meekly.

'Yes, why not? Why not? I take you to paradise as well, Mr Waseem.'

I had to bite my lip to suppress my giggles. Without John's sobering influence, mission madness had set in early; I was already exploiting Jamshed's naïveté with sexual innuendoes and cheap laughs and the mission was only a few days old. However, without John there to share the laughs, the joke died a premature death, particularly since I began to receive hostile glares from Abi who refused to see the funny side of anything when it came to Jamshed.

Thus, come the Friday, Jamshed and the rest of the boys were seated in the back row of our minibus singing songs and munching their way through bagfuls of cucumbers, almost as we would eat strawberries at home, all on the way to paradise. Even the girls in the team had joined the trip, and participated wholeheartedly in the singing, the joking and the devouring of cucumbers. There was a real festive mood as we drove through the bleak Afghan landscape past the decaying debris of twenty-three years of war, honking our horn at other equally exuberant day-trippers piled into a variety of vehicles making their way out of Kabul. The poignancy of the moment was not lost on me; what we were doing that day, the innocent fun we were sharing, would have meant certain death for each and every single one of us under Taliban rule less than six months earlier.

Farida was sitting in the back and was wearing white shoes which were the source of much consternation amongst some of the girls. Apparently the wearing of white shoes under the Taliban had been banned, and breaking the rule would have resulted in a severe beating by the *Munkrat*, the Taliban's religious police, or, in rare cases, summary execution.

The other girls, it seemed, had still not come to terms with their new-found freedom and were too scared to break Taliban rules, particularly for dress code, just in case the Taliban came back and singled out for retribution those who had transgressed. Thus, in the schizophrenic state that summed up most of post-Taliban Afghanistan, all the girls who worked for GMA wore the burka on their way to and from work, but spent work-time in the office with just their heads covered by scarves. Until this point, nearly six months after the liberation, the spectre of the Taliban remained so powerful that nobody except Farida had yet gained enough confidence to wear 'offensive' white shoes.

When we arrived at the picnic spot, I found that Jamshed's analogy about paradise wasn't far wrong. In the middle of the barren, monotone sepia landscape scattered with rusting tanks that one was so used to in Afghanistan, the Solang valley was a lush oasis of greenery; bountiful vegetation was surrounded on all sides by snow-topped peaks, pink blossom adorned the cherry trees, and a beautiful turquoise river ran through the valley. Barring the mine-clearing operations that we could hear in the distance, we could very well have been in the Garden of Eden.

As Abi and I sat on a large rock by the river, dangling our feet in the cool flowing waters of the Solang River and eating the freshly barbequed chicken prepared by Jamshed and his cohorts, Farida and another presenter, Sharifa, came over to sit by us. They were very intrigued about our lives and grilled us extensively about our respective families and particularly about relationships.

Farida was very keen to know if my marriage had been arranged or if it had been a love marriage. Deciding that the story of my matrimony was too complicated to try and relate to a young Afghan girl freshly released from the clutches of five years of repressive Taliban rule, I replied simply that it had been arranged. Sharifa asked Farida to ask me if my wife had been expensive to 'buy'. I tried to explain that, unlike Afghanistan where brides have to be bought from the girl's family and can cost up to twenty thousand dollars, we did not have the custom of 'buying' a bride in Pakistan where I came from. This did not preclude the fact that my wife had subsequently proved to be a much more expensive proposition, as my bank manager and credit card bills would readily testify.

'Hi John, I'd like you to meet Farah, my wife.'

'You what?'

John dropped the plastic cup of cappuccino he had been drinking whilst waiting the arrival of my flight, splattering its contents over my shoes and the shoes of half a dozen other passengers as well.

'I'd like you to meet the young lady who has consented to be Mrs Waseem Mahmood.'

'That's what I thought you'd said.' John ignored all the abuse being hurled at him for having parboiled a significant number of toes with his coffee and looked me straight in the eye. If there was ever a 'Kodak moment', I guess this was it. After taking a few deep breaths, John grabbed me by the collar and yanked me away from the 'petite creature' whose trolley I was manoeuvring through the throng of arrivals at Heathrow's Terminal Three. 'What the hell do you mean that you are married? When I dropped you here three weeks ago, you were going to attend a family wedding. No mention whatsoever, I seem to recall, about your own bloody nuptials.'

I flashed a reassuring smile at Farah who by now was a little worried by the welcome afforded by my supposed best friend in the entire world. John also beamed a smile at her and turned his attention back to me, 'Anyway, I thought that you were off Asian girls for life after that fling with that Bollywood starlet, what's her name?'

'Simi,' I interjected. The girl was now a major star and had unceremoniously dumped me a few days before her first film had become a major box office hit. 'And anyway, Farah is Persian.'

'Stop changing the subject. You've a lot of God-damned explaining to do, mate.'

John did have a point. Less than twenty-one days earlier, when he had dropped me off at the airport for my short *trip to Pakistan, we had both sat soulfully in the bar in the departures area, crying on each other's shoulders, lamenting the state of our respective love lives, or in John's case, the lack of one. Both had sworn off women and had decided that a life of celibacy was the only realistic solution to our woes. As the late, great Bob Marley had once lamented, 'No woman, no cry.' That, we decided, was going to be the maxim on which we were going to live our lives from that point on. Women, we had concluded, were an unnecessary distraction and we were both going to focus our energies on our careers; John on his new job as radio reporter, having made the switch from acting to journalism, and me on my relentless campaign to become the BBC's first Asian Director General.*

My vow of chastity lasted for precisely forty-eight hours.

Pakistani weddings are elaborate events spread over many days of festivities. They are also the only time in Pakistani culture that interaction between the sexes is overlooked by even the most conservative families, with culturally sanctioned dancing, singing and merriment.

On the first day one has the Mehndi, the henna celebration, when the groom's family take henna to the bride's house and womenfolk paint intricate patterns on the hands and feet of the bride. Shows of singing and dancing put on by close friends and relatives of the bride and the bridegroom in an attempt to outdo one another have nowadays taken on a level of professionalism that would suggest several months of prior rehearsal. Dance moves copied from Hindi movies are choreographed to bawdy songs which, outside the context of the wedding, would be deemed vulgar and obscene even by the most liberal standards. Weddings in Pakistan, it seems, are a sort of twilight zone, an anomaly where strict Islamic values are suspended and it becomes almost obligatory to let one's hair down. It was at my cousin's Mehndi that I first laid eyes on Farah.

She was the bride's best friend and thus in charge of the reception party awaiting the arrival of the groom's retinue to shower us with scented rose petals as we entered with the precious henna. This diminutive girl, with short blondish hair and the most beautiful hazel eyes that I had ever seen, looked vaguely familiar, and I was totally captivated before the first rose petals had even begun to rain down on us. She looked as ill at ease in the bright yellow shalwar kameez, the traditional Pakistani outfit, as I felt in the baggy pants and long shirt that I had been forced to wear. She was more your 501 and tee-shirt type, more used to hanging out at shopping malls than where she was. The blood pact that I had made with John Murray at Heathrow airport a few days earlier had not factored in this eventuality and was quickly forgotten as I planned my move.

By the Nikaah, the wedding ceremony the next day, a judicious bit of research had established her name, the fact that her father was a director of the national airline and that she herself worked as a model and continuity announcer on television, hence the reason she had looked familiar. She was the face of some shampoo campaign in Pakistan and her photo was plastered across numerous billboards around the city. I had also found out that she was of Persian origin, her family having fled when the Shah's regime had been ousted, and that she had spent most of her life being schooled in Washington DC. She had only moved to Lahore a few months before when her father had been transferred there to head up the airline's operation in the city. My duties as best man forgotten, I forced my cousin to get his new bride to introduce me to her best friend as we all sat there on the dais, and then spent the rest of the evening flirting with her, the best that one could in the circumstances. She was as witty and intelligent as she was pretty. With most of the boxes on my checklist for 'ideal wife' ticked, I decided to play my trump card: the arranged marriage, age-old traditions and cultural mores can be so useful when they can be manipulated to one's own advantage!

On the Walima, the third day of feasting, traditionally the reception thrown by the groom's family as an affirmation of *the consummation of the union, I casually dropped the hint to my mother that if they were thinking of arranging my marriage, I would happily agree as long as it was with the girl in pink sitting next to the bride. Before I knew it, I had set in motion a sequence of events that satisfied both families and, most importantly, Farah herself and culminated in my pushing out the new Mrs Mahmood's luggage on my trolley from the baggage hall at Heathrow less than two weeks later.*

One of the advantages or, some might argue, disadvantages of having Abi on the team was her ability to embrace the flourishing Kabul ex-pat social scene. Within days she had become a regular fixture on the guest list of all the important parties and gatherings. As a rule, I avoided most of these functions because I found them very pretentious: the same people meeting day in, day out, getting drunk and bemoaning their hardship posting while conveniently ignoring the fact that most of them, with their tax-free status and comprehensive allowance package including a hefty wad of danger money, would be banking significant six figure salaries for the short time that they were in Kabul. Rumour was rife in the Kabul NGO circles that the average UN package to keep one person in Kabul for a year amounted to a quarter of a million dollars.

On Abi and Jamshed's persistent bullying, I agreed to attend a fancy dress party being held at one of the UN compounds in the city.

The scene that greeted us as we entered was totally unreal. It was as if we were no longer in Kabul. The lawn in the centre of the courtyard had been transformed into a dance floor complete with imported flashing disco lights. Heavy techno music was pounding away, pumped out by a DJ in the corner, and alcohol was flowing freely. Ironically for an organisation whose main stated aim in Afghanistan was to eradicate the drug trade, the selection of pharmaceutical substances readily available at the party was enough to put most inner-city dealers to shame.

The guest list consisted mostly of ex-pats, aid workers and journalists with a few of the younger local Afghan ministry officials thrown in. Most had made some effort to dress up, though there were an awful lot of Mujahideen fighters complete with cardboard or wooden Kalashnikovs scattered around the dance floor and I believe I even spotted one or two Osama Bin Ladens and a Sadaam Hussein. A female journalist from a British broadsheet and an aid worker from an American NGO had turned up in authentic twenties flapper outfits and created a real stir in the very male-dominated party.

Abi, like the lads and I, had made no attempt to dress up for the evening, and in spite of numerous offers of drinks and dances from virtually all the men at the party, she preferred to stay ensconced in a corner in deep conversation with Jamshed. Such open association with locals was frowned upon by most ex-pat communities and I could see many of the men getting visibly agitated by Abi snubbing them in preference to 'a native'.

Standing with Manocher, I watched all that was going on around me, nursing a soft drink which had proved extremely difficult to get at the bar. While there was a plethora of malts and spirits from around the world, there didn't seem to be any soft drinks other than the mixers. Unsurprisingly, most of the party-goers were well and truly pissed. Their drunken antics proved amusing to the Afghans who were not used to seeing this sort of behaviour from the respected professionals who had come to rebuild their country. Some of the guests were attempting to dance to the music. A prominent journalist working for a Washington newspaper was giving a young female aid worker what appeared to be a very raunchy lap-dance. Our old house-mate whose bed John had stolen the first night we were in Kabul, was holding court, a drink in one hand, regaling some French girl with stories of his brave exploits during his Mujahideen days. A couple had moved away from the main dance floor to find some privacy and, unwittingly in full view of the bemused Afghan guards, had started kissing passionately. Looking at Manocher standing next to me, watching the debauchery around us, I wondered what was going through his mind, whether he really saw this as the freedom that so many had given up their lives for.

I grabbed a plate and helped myself to a burger. At the barbeque I was accosted by an American friend. He had a German girl with him and asked me to help sort out an argument they were having. 'Was George Orwell the first post-modern American novelist or not?' I expounded my theories about post-modern American literature and then, making my excuses, moved on to find Abi and Jamshed.

After less than an hour at the party, I had had enough and was ready to leave. It had already started to wind down so that it could be finished by 8 p.m. to allow the guests time to return home before curfew began. I gathered the gang together and, making our excuses, we left.

I don't know how I felt. Did I hate these people for the way in which they openly flaunted their Western freedoms in the face of local customs and kept themselves apart from the reality outside, or did I respect them for trying to lead as normal a life as possible and making the best of a real hardship posting?

Ex-pats on the whole are a funny breed; a few have a genuine desire to assist the countries they find themselves stationed in, some are in it just for the money they can earn and to enhance their CVs with exotic duty stations, but most seem to be people who are running away from something or someone. In my case, I guess that I fell into the latter category; I already knew that I was running away from myself.

Back at the guesthouse, I left Abi – somebody else who I felt was running away from someone or something –

teaching Jamshed how to dance the Salsa in the candlelit dining room. With the sensual music blaring out from the battery-powered cassette player, teacher and pupil were so absorbed in their lesson that they hardly noticed me leave the room to retire for the night.

Farida had failed to turn up for work after the Friday holiday. She had now been uncharacteristically AWOL for two days, and her cousin and boss, Manocher, was beginning to get worried.

Since there was still no telephone system in Kabul other than the expensive cellular one which was out of the reach of most local Afghans, the only way to find out what was going on was to physically send someone to her house. Manocher decided to go himself after work.

Manocher called us just as we were finishing dinner. He sounded in a state of total shock and told us to be ready as he was coming to pick us up. Farida had had a serious accident and was in hospital. He didn't elaborate further on the phone beyond the fact that his cousin was still alive but was in a serious condition. I felt my knees go weak. 'Please God, do not let anything happen to the poor kid.'

The hours following that call proved to be the worst that I experienced in Afghanistan. The country has an uncanny knack of lulling you into a false sense of security and then, when you're complacent and think that it can't get any worse, it manages to throw a googly at you that catches you totally unaware and knocks you for six.

En route to the hospital, we learnt that Farida had been cooking food on Friday for a family get-together when apparently the butane gas cylinder powering the primitive cooker had exploded in her face burning her badly. She was in a critical condition.

Having been to a Kabul hospital before when John had been taken ill, I was mentally prepared what to expect. The hospital proved to be as bad as the Jamahiriya where we had taken John. There were the same smells of human waste, the same unnerving noises emanating from the dying and the same dingy, overcrowded corridors littered with patients for whom space could not be found in wards which were stretched to capacity. The only real difference I noticed was that in this hospital there seemed to be a bigger, much better fed population of rats who were scurrying all over the place. I tucked my trouser legs into my socks. Abi, for whom this was a first experience of an Afghan hospital, had to be taken outside by Jamshed to get some fresh air and she was promptly sick.

There was no information desk or reception, so the only way to find Farida was for us to search the wards for her. Thankfully, it wasn't too long before we found her. She was lying on the floor in a corner of what was euphemistically called the women's ward. In reality, it was just a small room which might have once been an office and had been turned into a ward as an afterthought to accommodate women patients. Flea-ridden mattresses were strewn across the floor and on them had been dumped the dying women who had dared to come to the hospital for treatment. The blood-stained sheets and the lack of or any other familiar signs of treatment told the story of how realistic the women's chances of survival really were. Noises more akin to the death throes of mortally wounded wild animals filled the room. Relatives of the patients occupied what little floor space that remained, their children's crying and screaming adding to the cacophony. Medical staff, were conspicuous only by their total absence.

Even in this hell-hole, Farida had not been considered important enough to be given a mattress, thus when we found her, she was lying on the cold, hard, dirty, marble floor resting on a single blanket that her parents must have brought from home. Her blue burka scrunched up and put under her head served as a pillow, and her only protection against the biting cold were the clothes that she had been wearing when the accident occurred which had been burnt onto her body. Farida's family, her mother, father and her young brother, were sitting on the floor next to her, crying. It was obvious that nobody had left Farida's side since they had brought her in. The food that Manocher's mother had thoughtfully sent with him for the family was probably the first that they had eaten in days.

Farida's father broke down immediately he saw us and he begged us to do anything we could to save his daughter. He grabbed my feet and beseeched me to help. It seemed that nobody in the hospital was listening to him or doing anything for his child.

I had been avoiding looking at Farida since I had arrived, but I could not escape looking at her now. She had seventy per cent burns, her face was virtually unrecognisable, and the doctors had done nothing to treat her or alleviate her pain. They had simply left her to die. Farida was slipping into and out of consciousness, obviously in great pain. I had to turn away. It was now my turn to be sick.

Gathering our wits, Abi and I decided to play the 'foreigner card'. We went to look for the doctor in charge to find out what the hell was going on with Farida's treatment or rather, lack of it. The doctor we managed to corner claimed that the hospital did not have the medicines to treat her. He then went on to tell us that even if they had had the medicines, they would not have wasted precious supplies on a woman when there were still so many men to treat.

I could not believe what I was hearing, and after landing the doctor one of my finest right hooks and flooring him, Abi and I started making calls to see what we could do to help Farida. A few phone calls to friends in the various ISAF field hospitals, cultivated after the John incident, yielded not only the necessary medicines but also numerous offers of help. The Brits sent an ambulance to the hospital immediately and Farida was taken to the German hospital where we were told that the doctors specialised in dealing with burns.

The German field hospital was amazing. It was as if a whole hospital had been lifted wholesale and dropped into Afghanistan. The contrast with the nightmare we had come from was dramatic. Just being there, surrounded by all the equipment and professionalism in a sterile environment, was enough to make one feel better. The trauma team rushed Farida immediately into the operating theatre the moment we arrived.

Like so many others in Afghanistan, I had begun to lose my faith in God since I had started witnessing the suffering, death and destruction carried out in His name. That night, for Farida's sake, I found myself prostrate outside the operating theatre praying, something that I had not done in a long time. If there was any justice in this world, I begged God to save Farida, she had to live. She had so much more to do, so much more to see.

By the following morning Farida's condition had been stabilised. Her family were elated. Even though she was lying there covered in dressings with drips in both arms and numerous monitors attached, having spoken to the doctors I was convinced that she would pull through. I swear that I saw a small mischievous smile on what remained of her once pretty face as she lay there. My faith in God was almost fully restored, and I promised Him that from that point on I would pray at least twice a day if not the full five times a day prescribed in the religion.

Manocher tried to warn me that I was being too hasty. He was proved right. That was the last time any of us saw her alive. Farida died three days later from an infection. With open burns, no treatment and having spent two days in the filth of the Afghan hospital, I guess that I must have known deep down that Farida's chances of survival were slim.

The news of her death devastated me. What faith I had managed to salvage when she seemed to be on the mend was now totally shattered. I could not really bring myself to believe that the cheeky bubbly kid who had captivated me so much was no more. This was unfair of God. No, it was downright cruel. After so many years of suffering, that this was how it had to end for Farida, a stupid kitchen accident.

Back in the guesthouse I paced up and down. I found myself unable to go to the family to offer my condolences and spent most of the night crying uncontrollably. My feelings fluctuated from desperation one minute to sheer rage the next. The difference between life and death in Afghanistan, it seemed, was only a few dollars. If Farida had been given antibiotics and had her wounds cleaned and dressed, she would be alive today. I spend more on drinks in one night at a restaurant than it would have taken to save her life.

That night I knew that the time for me to prepare to leave Afghanistan and move on had come. My days in Kabul were numbered; Farida's untimely death had made sure of that.

MALDIVES – AUGUST 2002

Farah flew from Stratford to spend a few days with me in the Maldives. She had only come on the strict proviso that the few days we spent together, our first holiday together in many years, would be a 'Kabul free' zone; I was forbidden to talk about my work in Afghanistan and had faithfully promised that my mobile phone would remain locked in the hotel safe.

Unfortunately for Farah, when I was reading the Gulf News on the aircraft, I noticed a small headline tucked away in the corner of the front page about Radio Afghanistan. It seemed that the Director General had been sacked by the government, and instead of taking his dismissal with magnanimous grace, he was now occupying the radio building with armed troops and a tank in the car park.

As soon as I got off the plane at Male, I rushed outside to make a call to Manocher, leaving a very annoyed Farah to retrieve our baggage from the carousel. It was an hour later, on the speedboat pulling into the resort, when I finally managed to get through to Kabul.

Thankfully, the standoff at the radio station was over and some compromise acceptable to the Director General had been reached which meant that he had withdrawn the troops and the tank from the studios, but by the look on Farah's face, irreparable damage had already been done to our short break.

While my wife sunned herself, snorkelled in the turquoise coloured sea and tried to enjoy her holiday on the beautiful white beaches, my thoughts remained firmly rooted in the ruined landscape of Kabul. Holidaying seemed so trivial after what had happened in the past six months. Even though I had complied with Farah's wishes and switched my mobile off and left it in the hotel safe, I had ended up making regular excuses to go to the room and call Manocher for frequent updates.

One of the messages left on my answer phone was from MTV Europe in London. I returned the call out of sheer curiosity as to why the hip music channel wanted to talk to a square old rocker like me. I spoke to a trendy researcher type called Krispen who asked me if I had heard of the MTV Europe awards. With two teenage sons in the house, I was familiar with this event which had become a highlight of the satellite generation's social calendar. Krispen told me that the GMA programme had been nominated for the 'Free Your Mind' award, a prestigious annual humanitarian award. The previous year's winner had been Bono from the band U2 for his work in trying to reduce the third world debt.

Krispen asked if I would be willing to receive the award on behalf of the project. The decision, it seemed, was final because we were apparently the only nominee this year. However, Krispen, still needed to get it ratified by the CEO and would call me back.

O n the last night of the holiday the resort had arranged a dinner for us on a deserted moonlit beach. The situation could not have been more contrived. Farah looked sullen and withdrawn; obviously my phone calls to Kabul had not gone unnoticed. However, after eighteen years of marriage I realised that there was something more to it. We had eaten the freshly grilled seafood in virtual silence, and just before we were served dessert, Farah looked directly at me and said, 'You have to make a choice. It is either your work or the family. Have you ever wondered what it's like for me, sitting at home while you play at being some intellectual Rambo, parachuting into war zones trying to put the world to rights? Did you know that the children and I cannot bear to watch the news any more for fear of what we might see? Hearing of explosions and missiles, knowing that you are out there? Being scared each time the phone rings fearing what news it might bring? Do you know what it's like?'

'Yes, I do. But it is who I am and it is what I do!'

Tears had welled up in her eyes.

'How dare you! Do you have so much contempt for me and the children that you place your work above us...? Is it not enough that our trust and love matter so little to you that you would throw it all away for the sake of these, these people?'

'Three days ago, Farah, a twenty-three-year-old girl who worked for me died a painful death and I could do nothing about it...'

'Don't give me that sentimental crap – it doesn't work anymore. You care about the death of this Afghan girl and yet you cannot see that you are killing our marriage.'

I did not need this. I got up from the table and made my way back to the chalet.

'That's it! Walk away!'

I didn't even bother to look back. It was a long night, and next morning I left the Maldives and returned to the relatively safe haven offered to me by Kabul.

KABUL – SEPTEMBER 2002

When I arrived, Manocher took me straight from the airport to the graveyard. I placed a single red rose on Farida's simple grave and said a small prayer.

At last you have departed and gone to the Unseen.
What marvellous route did you take from this world?
Beating your wings and feathers,
you broke free from this cage.
Rising up to the sky
you attained the world of the soul.
Now the words are over
and the pain they bring is gone.
Now you have gone to rest
in the arms of the Beloved.

There she was, a lovely, lively young woman, now lying under a mound of earth with a rock at the head, no grave stone or anything else to give any clue to the identity of the person that lay interred, not a single hint of the bright girl who had been so cruelly taken from this world before she had even had a chance to properly begin her life. 'All the flowers flee from Autumn', but not Farida – she was a fearless rose seemingly destined to flower in the freezing wind, but alas, it was not to be.

Standing at her graveside, I decided that the world had to know about Farida. I could not allow her death to be in vain. She epitomised and personified Afghanistan – in life all that was good about the country and in death all that was so terribly wrong. I decided to accept the MTV award on behalf of Farida and use the platform to tell the billions around the world her story.

I was sitting in my office at GMA when there was a sharp knock on the door.

'Come in.'

It was Karim, an eleven-year-old I had employed to work as the office boy. He was the son of one of the journalists in the office whom I had met on the trip to 'paradise' with Jamshed. Having just returned from six years in a Peshawar refugee camp, Karim was waiting to be admitted to a school. To keep him occupied, I had suggested that he come into the office with his father and help me with odd jobs around the studios; and as he spoke good English, I could use him as an interpreter whenever I needed.

Karim had been given a three-minute-slot on the new evening show in a programme for children. One day he would be bemoaning the fact that communications were so poor in Afghanistan that he could not speak to or send letters to his cousins in the North; another day he would be telling a story about a magical genie who had brought peace to Afghanistan. Within weeks he had become a little star with his own cult fan following.

'Mr Waseem, we need to talk.'

'Go ahead,' I humoured him. 'Is there a problem?'

'Yes' he replied. 'I want fifty dollars.'

'A ten dollar rise?' I asked. We were paying him forty dollars a month; I assumed that he wanted a ten dollar rise. I assumed wrongly.

'No, no, Mister Waseem,' he went on. 'Fifty dollars a week.'

I nearly choked on my coffee. He then went on to present an impeccable case; how he produced three minutes of airtime every day in two languages and how he always managed to record his programmes in one take. He argued, quite reasonably, that many of the journalists working on the team created far less output than him and earned considerably more.

I listened to his argument and had to grant that he had a very valid point. However, as I tried to explain to Karim, I did not have the budget to give him any more money. Unable to get the concept of budgets through to Karim, I called Manocher in and told him that the time had come for him to resolve his own personnel problems.

Karim gave Manocher an even harder time than he had given me. I watched in amusement. If kids like Karim were going to be the future of Afghanistan, if the skills of reason and negotiation were allowed to take precedence in the next generation over the rule of the gun, then there was just a chance that the country would once again prosper. In the end, after a full morning of negotiation, a compromise was finally agreed with Karim: since there was no more money in the budget, Karim would work for just three days a week for whatever we could pay him.

Karim was soon joined by two other children, an eleven-year-old girl, Shakeela, and a thirteen-year-old boy, Hamid. If Karim had been precocious on his own, then the three together were totally incorrigible and the ring leader more often than not was the girl, Shakeela. She had everybody in the office wrapped around her little finger. Batting and fluttering of the eyelids had never been put to such devastating use as they were by Madam Shakeela.

The rest of the team treated these three like adults, and like everybody else they had to pitch stories to Manocher every morning at the production meeting.

One day they decided to investigate why there weren't any playgrounds in Kabul. Manocher agreed that the story was good and asked how they intended to script the feature and most of all, who they were going to interview. Without hesitation, Shakeela piped up, much to the amusement of the adults, that they wanted to go straight to the top and speak to the President, since in their view he was the only one who had the power to get something done. Manocher, also with his tongue firmly in his cheek, humoured her saying that he would speak to the President's Press Office and see what he could do, in reality dismissing it as nothing more than childish fantasy and hoping that Shakeela and her cohorts would soon forget and move on to some other story. Alas, once Manocher had said he would do it, he was hounded relentlessly by the pint-sized monster until he finally had no option but to call the President's office while Shakeela stood watch making sure that he did so. Miraculously, the President consented to be interviewed.

So, on a bright autumn day, we all trooped along to the President's office with Shakeela and Co to witness them interview him about the lack of playgrounds in Kabul. The interview started well, Karim asking the President about his school days, his favourite subjects and whether he was a naughty boy. The President seemed to be really enjoying himself, in fact so much so that he asked his aides to delay his next appointment with a German TV company. The ten minutes the children had been allocated had stretched to thirty when Shakeela decided the time had come to confront the President with the contentious issue of the lack of playgrounds in Kabul.

'Mr President, why are you not building playgrounds for children? You know that we have nowhere to play.'

The President tried to explain that the priorities of a post-war country are to have education, roads, health and these sorts of things. He knew that playgrounds were important but it would take some time before his government would be able to do something positive.

Shakeela's research had obviously pre-empted this response. 'But Mr President, how many cars do you have? Surely you do not need all of them. Why not sell one and give us a playground!'

Within two weeks, the President had passed an edict that all district councils should look at ways of building children's playgrounds or at least providing safe play areas.

With eleven-year-olds brave enough to give the President a hard time and confront me about their salaries, I felt that I had achieved what I had set out to. My work in Afghanistan had, it seemed, come to a natural end. The team now not only had the journalistic skills to take on the world but had also acquired the self-confidence to face the future without needing me to hold their hands every step of the way. What Farida's death had stirred in me, Karim, Shakeela and Hamid had confirmed – the time to move on had come. Farah would get her wish, not because of her emotional bullying but because my objectives in Kabul had been achieved; I would soon be back at home doing the school run each morning and hosting dinners for her Rotary Club friends at weekends.

A few days later, while I was waiting at Kabul airport for my flight home, Jamshed, who had come to see me off, said that he needed to talk to me about some serious private matter. As soon as I had checked in we found a quiet corner in the departure lounge and sat down. I could see that Jamshed was trembling with anxiety. This had to be something really serious.

He took a deep breath and came straight out and confessed that he had been having an affair with Abi. I must say that his confession didn't come entirely as a shock to me; what with the one-to-one Salsa lessons and the long intimate conversations that they were always having, it wasn't rocket science to work out that something was going on between them. In reality, on a strictly personal level, what they got up to was none of my business, but looking at it objectively, the liaison could have serious professional ramifications not only for them individually but also for the project as a whole. Had they kept a low profile, nobody would have been any the wiser about the relationship, but as snide comments around the office had already shown, discretion had not been one of either Abi or Jamshed's main considerations. Even without Jamshed's confession, the office grapevine had been ablaze with juicy rumours for some time.

Jamshed went on to explain that while their feelings for one another had been simmering in Kabul, the relationship had really came to a head while he was in Pakistan with her just before her return to America a couple of weeks before. They had gone there, ostensibly, to sort out some passport problem that Abi was experiencing which had conveniently necessitated a trip to the American Embassy in Islamabad. Why she had taken him, an Afghan, to help her in Pakistan, had admittedly confounded most of us in the office. Some mischievous elements had rung the Islamabad hotel that Abi and Jamshed were reputedly staying in only to find that no-one under his name was registered... although their investigations did establish that a Ms Brookes was staying there with an unnamed male guest!

Jamshed admitted to me that he saw what he shared with Abi as something very special. However, at the same time he was very confused about the precise nature of his feelings towards her. A part of him felt that he might be in love with her and that she was the only woman for him. But at the same time, he had very clear cultural ideas about the sort of woman he wanted for his wife, and he felt that a Western woman could not fulfil those ideals. Firstly, he would expect his wife to come and live with him in Kabul and to stay at home to look after his ailing parents. He also needed to know that he had full loyalty from the woman he married, and would not be able to tolerate it if she were to speak to any other man, even in a totally innocent context – his Afghan sense of honour would not allow it. He could not and would not expect Abi to fit into what, by his own definition, was a narrow-minded, antiquated concept of marriage.

As the conversation progressed, it became apparent that Jamshed had probably not discussed this with Abi. However, because of Abi's actions, he was getting the distinct impression that she had matrimony on her mind. She had apparently narrated to him a dream that she had had, where she had seen herself living with his parents and helping his mother to cook in the kitchen.

What could I say? I could only suggest that he should do what was best for him. After all, if Abi really loved him, I assured him that she would definitely understand whatever he decided to do.

LOS ANGELES – SEPTEMBER 2002

Fund-raising events were the bane of my life and I hated them with a vengeance. However, I was also a pragmatist and realised that our very survival depended on them. Thus John and I found ourselves in LA, pressing the flesh and generally being nice to some insufferable people in the hope that they would deem it appropriate to donate funds to keep us in business. Soren hated fund-raising soirées even more than we did and had pulled rank to press-gang us both into representing the organisation on this tour of California.

After the rollercoaster ride of the past twelve months, this trip was going to be time-out, and John and I were determined to make the most of it and have some fun.

The gods were obviously smiling upon us when things started looking up from the moment we landed. For once, I was not randomly selected for questioning by the American immigration authorities, and when we went to pick up our hire car at LAX, due to an administrative error the car that had been booked for us was not the sedate sedan which the office had asked for but a mean-looking red convertible. With roof down, stylish shades in place, Beach Boys CD blaring, LA attitude engaged, we drove the short distance to Beverly Hills where we were staying. Even in a town of excess, this garnered us a rather spectacular entrance when we drove onto the forecourt of the Le Meridian hotel and handed the keys to the valet parking attendant, particularly since the sun had gone in and light rain had been falling on and off for the last fifteen minutes of our journey.

On checking in, we realised that the place was crawling with hundreds of Barbie look-alikes. One entered the lift with us.

'So, what brings a nice girl like you into this town?' The words appeared to have come from the mouth of my revered colleague and friend, John Murray – but surely not. He had never initiated communication with a member of the opposite sex in all the years that I had known him and definitely not one who looked as gorgeous as this.

'We're in town for the Playboy Golf tournament,' she replied in her sweetest Southern-accented Barbie voice. 'Are you guys also here for the tournament?'

How we wished at that point that we had never scoffed at those men who wasted their days wearing stupid trousers and chasing small balls around a park.

'No, no. We are here on business,' John managed to stammer, his initial bravado gone, and reverting to the John I knew around good-looking girls.

'What a shame.'

Before the conversation could progress any further, we had arrived at our floor and the lift doors parted. Playboy girl exits. We exit. Playboy girl turns right. We turn right. Playboy girl looks over her shoulder at the two middle-aged men still wearing sunglasses following her. We smile. Playboy girl quickens pace. We subconsciously fall into step and also quicken up. Playboy girl now almost running arrives at her room and fumbles with her key card, dropping it in her haste. John bends down, picks up the card and hands it to the Playboy girl.

'Looks like we are neighbours. Isn't that great?' John really could not contain his excitement at the thought of our room sharing a common wall with a Playboy centrefold.

A look of sheer terror washed across the girl's face as she finally managed to open her door and retreat to the safety of her room.

'I think she liked me!' John sounded as if he really believed the utter rubbish he had just spouted.

The rest of the trip proved uneventful. We managed to pull off all the meetings without offending anyone, managed a trip to Universal Studios, managed to spend every single minute in LA wearing our sunglasses, managed to drive everywhere with the car roof down irrespective of the weather, and managed to work our way through the entire Beach Boys and Monkees CD collection several dozen times.

On our last night together in LA – I was off to San Francisco in the morning and John back to the UK – I was keen that we go down to the bar to have a drink, as who would know when we would be together again. John, however, was riveted to the movie, 'Armageddon', which was playing on HBO. Having just seen it on the flight over, I really could not be bothered to sit through another two hours of Mr Willis and Co saving the planet yet again, so in a huff I changed into my jim-jams and dozed off.

Next morning, as the valet was helping us load up the car, he asked if we had attended the Playboy party the previous evening. We looked at him quizzically. He explained that the young ladies from the fine Playboy publication had thrown a party in the hotel bar to mark the end of the golf tournament.

'You should have been there, guys. It was like a dream. I really thought that I had died and gone to heaven... Hmmm... wall-to-wall babes!'

The bar had been closed for the party and only invitees and hotel guests were allowed entry.

I did not say much to John on the drive to LAX and he definitely must have got the message when I threw his bags out on the sidewalk at the airport and raced off without so much as a goodbye. I felt that I might have been permanently scarred by this episode, and I did not know when I would be able to bring myself to watch a Bruce Willis movie again – the wounds were far too raw.

Abi had finished her sabbatical in Afghanistan and had returned to work in San Francisco where she had re-immersed herself in the whirl of her pre-Kabul existence. Within the first few weeks of getting back, she had been invited to the lavish San Francisco Opera Guild Dinner which was held at one of the most exalted restaurants in the most prestigious hotel of the city – the Westin St. Francis. Abi had asked me to accompany her which is why I was en-route to the city.

The event was a fundraiser which patrons had paid several thousand dollars per table to attend. It was unclear to me whether the people who attended these events did so because of a genuine desire to help those less fortunate than themselves, or because it was just another fixture on the social calendar of San Francisco high society necessitating attendance by anybody who was anybody on the social scene.

The room was stunning, with a view of the entire San Francisco skyline. The opulent décor ironically made me think of what the inside of the IC Hotel in Kabul must have looked like before the war – long, richly-textured drapes, regally high ceilings, opulent pillars, sparkling chandeliers. Everything so clean and orderly!

We had been invited to attend by Miriam, an Afghan American. Beautiful and charming and a very successful businesswoman, she was in the top stratum of the elite of the San Francisco Bay Area.

Her choice of guests for the table exemplified the importance to her of elegance and class. Everyone seated around the table was dressed in the latest fashion, excessively bejewelled, and they could not flatter each other enough.

'Oh, your hair! You must tell me who did it! It looks fabulous!'

'No, darling, you look absolutely stunning! And you must tell me, where did you get that sapphire?'

Although Abi had done her best to dress the part, it did not take much to see that she felt out of place and different. Kabul had changed her. I had seen this happen so many times before. Life becomes a succession of parallel universes where several realities coexist and you live somewhere in between.

In her mind Abi was still in Kabul and I could see her looking with palpable disdain at the women's outfits, I guess calculating how many Afghan children might have been given an opportunity to attend school, or how many Faridas' lives might have been saved with the money it must have cost to make up each woman's ensemble. Kabul does that to you.

Miriam sensed our unease and did her best to integrate us into the group in which we clearly did not belong. We found ourselves the 'novelty show' of the table, as Miriam proudly announced that 'these guys just returned from Kabul last week!'

In some way the polite remarks of 'How fantastic!' and 'How wonderful!' seemed grossly inappropriate, since we had not found our experience of Afghanistan either of those things. Abi caught my eye. We realised that these people, like many Americans, would never be able to connect with our Afghan experiences. We made polite excuses and left as soon as we could.

In the corridor outside, Abi accosted me: 'Waseem, I want to go back to Afghanistan. The six weeks I spent there have changed my life. I just cannot readjust to being back here. Everything I see or do here reminds me of Kabul. I need to get back.'

Get back to Kabul or back to Jamshed, I wondered. But I said, 'And for that you are prepared to give up your job and everything you have here.'

'Yes.'

She was in luck; with my having wound down my presence in Kabul and Alexander still not back at work, we needed someone to manage the project. Abi had fitted in well, being equally at ease with the staff as with the donors and Ministry officials. As far as I was concerned, she was the ideal candidate to take over. However, before I could let her go, there were issues, particularly the Jamshed issue, that I felt needed resolution.

The next day we were in her car driving to Robin Williams' house. Apparently, she had met with the Hollywood star at an ice cream parlour and got him to agree to record the tag line 'Good Morning Afghanistan' for us in the same style as his famous 'Good Morning Vietnam' line.

She had been pursuing him since that meeting without much success, having gone to his house so many times that she had been warned off by his security team for allegedly stalking him. She took me to show me where he lived and pointed out the best vantage points to actually see what was going on in the house. No wonder his security people were getting worried.

In the car, parked where we had a clear unobstructed view into Robin Williams' house, I took the opportunity to have the chat with Abi that we both knew we had to have.

'Abi, I do not wish to get involved or receive any clarifications or explanations, but as a friend I feel it necessary to tell you that I know about Jamshed and that it has to stop.'

I guess that she suspected that I had known what was going on.

'Waseem, firstly it is my private business, and then, Jamshed and I are just good friends!'

'Please understand, Abi, that there is no such thing as 'private business' in Afghanistan. I know about the dream. I know what happened on the trip to Pakistan. And trust me, 'just good friends' is not how Jamshed sees it. Have you spoken to him?' She seemed somehow astounded by how much I knew. 'I want you to go back to Afghanistan to look after the project, but we both know that with this hanging over you, you will have no respect from the team and it will compromise your position. It might even endanger your life.' As dramatic as it sounded, she knew exactly what I was talking about. 'You will have to sort it out.'

It took her a minute to regain her composure. 'Waseem, I promise you that I will resolve it. You have nothing to worry about.'

'Right then, let's go to the Cheesecake Factory.'

As we left, I could hear several police sirens in the distance heading our way. We were leaving the vicinity of Mr Williams' residence just in time.

KABUL – OCTOBER 2002

I returned to Kabul one last time, ostensibly to facilitate the MTV team who were scheduled to shoot a feature on 'Good Morning Afghanistan' to be used at the 'Free

Your Mind' awards ceremony. But I also had to tie up loose ends for the ultimate handover of the project to Abi and the rest of the Afghan team.

To celebrate the MTV award, I decided to sacrifice my principles and do what I loathed the most: throw a party inviting the entire local ex-pat crowd.

For some reason, however, the MTV crew's trip to Kabul kept being delayed. Twice they pulled out just hours before their arrival. It seemed that Krispen's meeting with the CEO to get our award ratified kept being pushed back, apparently for no other reason than the boss's hectic schedule. Though warning bells were beginning to sound somewhere in my subconscious, I was assured that everything was still on target. In Krispen's view, since there were still no other nominees, the meeting with the CEO remained no more than a formality. Krispen had even caught the CEO in the lift and he had been very keen on the idea. Afghanistan was very 'in' and MTV was all about being 'in'.

On the day of the planned party, Krispen's long awaited post-CEO-meeting call came through. We were all in the 'Good Morning Afghanistan' newsroom, huddled around the satellite phone, glasses charged, waiting on tenterhooks for the news that the award to GMA had been formalised.

Alas, it was not to be. 'Good Morning Afghanistan' had not won the 2002 MTV 'Free Your Mind' award. Apparently, at the weekend, some English footballers had been called racist names while playing a match in Slovakia, and the CEO who had been watching the game thought that that was a much more important issue for the MTV audience.

I hit the roof. I walked out of the newsroom and got hold of Krispen on the phone and for nearly an hour I gave him hell. This was not about me or even the achievements of GMA; this was about reassuring the twenty-six million Afghans that the West really cared about them, reassuring them that the West would not turn their backs on them this time. Donor fatigue was already setting in and many of those who pledged money had still not delivered on their promises. The audience of MTV could have been instrumental in bullying their governments and mobilising those funds. The award was a way of keeping the issue of Afghanistan on the world agenda. However, as I informed Krispen, MTV's attitude was indicative of the West's attitude in general towards Afghanistan. At the end of the day, they really did not care a shit.

'Some overpaid footballers' feelings are hurt because they are called names and that is more important than the lives of twenty-six million people.' My tirade continued. I told him that I understood that getting footballers on stage was far sexier than some Afghans...

He interrupted me: 'I wouldn't say that, some of the girls in the office think Karzai is really sexy... MTV really want to support GMA and the CEO is offering to fly two of your journalists to Barcelona to report on the awards.'

I really could not believe what I was hearing and told him exactly what MTV could do with their offer.

I hung up fuming. I now had to break the news to the team who had been ecstatic when I had first told them about the award several weeks ago. It had brought a fresh impetus to the work after Farida's death. Now I had to tell them that calling footballers names and hurting their fragile feelings was more important to Westerners than Afghan lives.

Abi had arrived back in Kabul and, having her own problems to contend with, she was unable to offer me much solace. As she had promised in San Francisco, resolving the Jamshed issue was easy, one intense conversation and it seemed as if it was all hunky dory again. I don't know what she had said and frankly didn't care as long as the situation was defused. Since her return, she had maintained a suitable distance from Jamshed, I presume to reassure the rest of the team that the relationship had returned to a level that was purely professional. Even Jamshed, it seemed, was less tense than he had been. The fixed foppish grin and the permanent smile were once again in evidence.

However, a bigger problem than dealing with the Jamshed issue loomed for Abi; she had promised us Robin Williams, and she was determined to get him to record the 'Good Morning Afghanistan' tag-line no matter what. Having learnt that the Hollywood actor had arrived in Bagram to entertain the American forces, she had made her way to the airbase in an attempt to try to see him and make him deliver on his promise. After failing to gain entry to the base, in spite of bullying the guards that as an American citizen it was her constitutional right to be allowed onto the base and boldly informing the Duty Sergeant that it was her tax dollars that were feeding his family back home, she was promised that the Sergeant would personally deliver a note to Mr Williams on her behalf. I just wish that I could have seen Robin Williams' face when someone handed him the note and informed him that the weird stalker he had been trying to avoid back home in San Francisco had turned up at Bagram Airbase in Afghanistan asking to see him.

The thought of this really cracked me up. A final attack of mission madness suddenly, miraculously, cleared away the haze that had begun to cloud my final days on the project. The original carefree spirit of the endeavour was back. It was almost as if MTV didn't matter any more – what we had achieved didn't need the justification of some music channel for it to be deemed successful. We knew what we had done and the difference that it had made in so many lives. When we ran a competition to mark the first anniversary, 'I like GMA because…', we received 30,000 entries from around the country, a remarkable feat in a place with no postal system. Even more remarkable was the winner, a little old man from somewhere in the

North who answered, 'I like GMA because you tell less lies than the rest!' That for me was a higher accolade than any MTV award; it was the trust of our audience.

Having spent the better part of a year in Kabul, I knew it was going to be difficult not being there any more, but the time had come when Manocher and the team had to take on the responsibility for their own destinies. I did not feel that I was deserting them; Afghanistan would always be with me. I owed that to the little boy I saw crying in the rubble of the Defence Ministry when I first arrived, I owed it to Shakeela, I owed it to the memory of Farida.

I proposed a toast, 'Stuff MTV!'

The shout, 'Stuff MTV', resonated around the room, guests and staff alike.

I went into the garden where we had banished Shakeela and Karim to prevent their witnessing the excesses that our international colleagues were capable of. As I approached, I heard them arguing. Both apparently wanted to be Kofi Annan when they grew up and some truce was being worked out to allow them both to achieve that position. As I watched them, a thought occurred to me that maybe, just maybe, what the world really needed was a Shakeela or Karim to be a Kofi Annan.

PART 5

Epilogue

This blemished light, this dawn by night half-devoured,
Is surely not the dawn for which we were waiting,
This cannot be the dawn in quest of which, hoping
To find it somewhere, friends, we all set out.
Faiz Ahmed Faiz

BIRMINGHAM – JANUARY 2003

Alexander Graziani's body was found in his bathroom. His wrists had been slit and at the side of his bath was a half-drunk glass of fine burgundy. No suicide note was found; however, when the police arrived the television was flickering, and when examined further a VHS tape was found in the video cassette player. I didn't need to be told which tape he had been watching.

The memorial service was a solemn affair. I stepped into the pulpit to address the few family, friends and colleagues gathered.

'It just happens that on this occasion it is our good friend and colleague Alexander Graziani who is in the coffin we see before us. It could well have been any one of us.' I directed a stare toward Farah seated in the front row with whom an uneasy truce had been agreed just before Alexander's death. 'War claims many victims, both combatant and what is now euphemistically known as collateral damage. What most people fail to realise is that war continues to take its toll many months, many years after the last bullet has been fired on the battleground. Alexander's death was one of these, an unfortunate reminder. In our job, we pick up the pieces after other people's battles and try to make right lives devastated by conflict. But who is there to pick up the pieces after we come home? The truth is, nobody.' Farah looked down and fidgeted uncomfortably in her seat. 'Only those in theatre can understand what we go through, and before we even have time to get over the last assignment we move on to the next one. Last year, Kosovo, this year, Afghanistan, and who knows, we might all be in Iraq sooner rather than later. In theatre we accept the risks that go with it, a stray bullet, a missile, a land mine are all part and parcel of the work and an occupational hazard.

What makes Alexander's death unfathomable is the fact that it was at his own hands. We can only begin to imagine the atrocities that would have driven him to take his own life. At the end of the day, Alexander was a consummate professional whose dedication to the job ultimately claimed his life. His cavalier, gung-ho attitude will never be replaced. He always went the extra mile to help those less fortunate than himself.

To finish, I read to you an e-mail sent to me by the young production team which he trained in Kosovo. 'We shall be eternally grateful for the skills that Mr. Graziani gave us. In the chaos of our country after war he gave us a sense of being, a sense of self-respect and the best damn youth show in the world. Thank you. You shall be missed."

As I returned to Farah's side the final prayer began as the coffin began to descend. Then in accordance with his last wish, Guns and Roses' version of 'Knock knocking on heaven's door' blared out. Alexander, a joker to the end.

John caught up with me as we left the crematorium. 'The bastard still owed me fifty quid! I hope he made some provision in his will to repay me!'

GLOSSARY OF TERMS.

Afghanis – Afghan currency.
al-Qaeda – meaning "the Law", "the foundation", or "the base". A militant Sunni Islamist organization with the stated objective of eliminating foreign influence in Muslim countries, eradicating those they deem to be "infidels" and re-establishing the caliphate.
Allah-o-Akbar – God is great.
Angrezi – the English language.
Azan – call to prayer.
Beta – son.
Bodgier – Danish bar.
Chadari or Burka – all encompassing shroud worn by women in Afghanistan.
Charpai – a wooden bed strung with coarse string.
Dhamal – a mystical trance.
Eid – Muslim festival.
Faals – hidden messages in texts.
Fajr – morning prayers.
Hajj – the a pilgrimage to Mecca that a Muslim is required to make at least once in their life.
Hajjis – pilgrims.
Inshallah – God willing. If God wills it.
Jaan – a term of endearment.
Jihad – an Islamic term meaning to strive or struggle in the way of God.
Kafirs – non believers.
Kharjee – foreigner.
Khutba – sermon.
Kismet – fate.

Koran – the holy book of Islam.

Lilatul Qadr – the 27th day of Ramadan, considered to be the holiest day, when The Prophet Muhammed (PBUH) is said to have ascended to the heavens on a winged horse.

Masala – spices.

Mehndi – Henna party held the day before the wedding ceremony.

Memsahib – term used to refer to a married British woman.

Mujahideen –an Islamic-Arabic term for guerrillas.

Munkrat – religious police.

Naan – unleavened bread.

Namaz – prayers.

Nao Roz – Afghan new year.

Nikaah – the wedding ceremony where the vows are exchanged.

Qawwali – traditional Sufi devotional song.

Radio Shariat – the name of the Taliban radio station.

Ramadan – the holy month of fasting.

Shalwar-kameez – a baggy long shirt and trousers worn both by women and men

Shamal – a seasonal wind that blows across Afghanistan.

Sharia Law – the body of Islamic law. The term means "way" or "path". The legal framework within which public and some private aspects of life are regulated for those living under a legal system based on Muslim principles of jurisprudence.

Shawe-shash – the traditiônal celebration held by Afghan families on the sixth day after the birth of a new baby.

Suba Khair – Good morning.

Sunnis, Shias – sects of Islam.

Tajiks, Pashtoons – ethnic groups inhabiting Afghanistan.

Talib – a Taliban.

Taliban – a Sunni Islamist fundamentalist movement which effectively ruled most of Afghanistan from 1996 until 2001.

Tandoor – clay oven.
Thakt ya Thakta –a throne or coffin.
VT – video tape.
Walima – the post wedding feast.
Zohr – lunchtime prayers.

Author's note

The book is based on the true story behind the setting up of 'Good Morning Afghanistan', an EC-funded project which I saw through getting on air and then managed during its first year. All the incidents narrated took place virtually as described; however, I have had to change the names and combine certain characters, in places merging backgrounds and altering minor details. This I have done at the behest of those involved to protect their privacy and in some cases their identities in what remain difficult times in Afghanistan.

I would like to thank all at GMA for the warmth and love with which they accepted me. I would particularly like to thank Barry Salaam, Ramin Ahmedyaar, John Murray, Colleen McLaughlin, Rachel Martin, Bent Nørby Bonde, Ralph McMullen and not least Charles Fletcher. It is difficult for anyone on the outside to appreciate the depth of what we experienced together; living for three years in virtual isolation from our own families, these friends and colleagues became a surrogate family who shared with me all the highs and lows of a hardship posting. This book is a tribute to them and the selfless way in which they put their lives on hold to help rebuild a country which many hadn't even heard of prior to 9-11. I was fortunate to be awarded an OBE and Charles an MBE in recognition of our work, but for me the real heroes will always be the Afghans we worked with.

The time that I spent working in Kabul on GMA and several subsequent projects remains the most professionally rewarding of my life and provided me with the inspiration for this story. The people and their resilience astounded me; in spite of all their suffering they always had smiles on their faces. Their hospitality and generosity was a humbling experience which I will cherish for ever. I pray that they find the peace and security they so desperately need to pull their country back from the edge of oblivion.

'Good Morning Afghanistan' was an unprecedented project and only happened because several visionary individuals at the Rapid Response Mechanism of the EC in Brussels really believed in us and the concept. In particular, Andrea Ricci and Nicolaas Schermers at RRM and Julian Wilson, the first head of the EC delegation in Kabul need to be singled out for their championing of the idea – I only wish there were more like them in the EC.

I would also like to thank Colin Marriott, Simon Whittaker, Kim Hudson, Tjill Dreyer and Imam Chishty who provided me with valuable input throughout the painful process of writing my first book. In that context, I have been fortunate in finding a publisher and editorial team who really believed in what I was trying to say. I must thank Dan Hiscocks at Eye Books who not only believed in the story but also shared my vision of the greater role of media as a positive force; Catriona Scott, my editor, for fulfilling a role that I now see as all too often overlooked in publishing, with authors taking all the credit – trust me, behind every good author is an even better editor; and last but not least Pedro Carvalho at Fnik PR who was charged with the job of making a book about Afghanistan sexy to the general public.

I must also sincerely thank Warren Mountford, Peter Hutchinson, Lindsay Osmond, Shelia Smither, Elizabeth Weaving, Ghazanfar Iqbal and rest of the Emirates gang at Birmingham Airport who moved heaven and earth not only to help me ship an entire studio to Afghanistan but somehow always to find me and my team seats, often at the last minute, on closed manifests, even if it meant sitting on the pilot's lap! Thanks guys – you really don't know what it means to see you all at the gate whenever I return from mission, and yes, buying a second ticket or flying business class is always cheaper than paying your excess baggage charges!

I will be eternally grateful to my wife, Farah, and my two boys, Khurrum and Khaiyyam, who put everything on hold for nine months while Baba wrote his book.

A special word of thanks is due to Catherine Marcus who first inspired me to write the GMA story and to share it with a wider audience.

And lastly, I wish to pay tribute to my father, Sultan Mahmood, who was one of the most respected journalists of his generation and first planted the writing seed in me. The endless hours of teaching me spelling and writing skills were obviously not in vain. *Thank you Dad!*

Waseem Mahmood
Kabul

WASEEM MAHMOOD

Waseem Mahmood is a media development consultant, specialising in post conflict media and public diplomacy. His work is driven by his desire to counter violent extremism and has seen him work directly in regions tackling The Taliban, Al Qaeda, Boko Haram and IS.

An award winning broadcaster, he began his career at the BBC in the General Programmes Department, producing for both television and radio. He left the BBC in 1988 to set up TV Asia, a satellite subscription service for the British Asian community, where he was controller of programmes.

He has been instrumental in several and various development projects in Africa and the Middle East, notably, the launch of a Hausa language TV station in Nigeria and more recently, in his work with Lapis, a strategic communications agency that supports local and global efforts to bring about positive change in frontier markets and challenging environments. Other highlights of his career include running a successful Pashto radio soap for young people, "Da Duniya Zamung Duniya" (Our World) on 4 FM Radio Stations in Peshawar/FATA and the "Yeh Hum Naheen" (This is not us), anti-terrorism foundation in Pakistan aimed at de-radicalising young Muslims. In 2008, "Yeh Hum Naheen" developed and ran a major multimedia campaign which culminated with world record breaking 62.8 million Pakistanis signing a petition condemning terrorism. Other CVE initiatives include the production/distribution of video/audio vignettes featuring personal testimonies of survivors of terrorism from around the world and developing comprehensive social media strategy to engage potential Jihadist recruits.

Waseem was awarded an OBE in 2005 in Her Majesty's New Year's Honours List "for services to the reconstruction of Media in post war countries", and received the KAPPA award "for most outstanding contribution to media".

Married with two children, he divides his time between Stratford-upon-Avon and the Middle East. He is fluent in Urdu, Punjabi, and English.

Eye Books
June 2016

ABOUT EYE BOOKS

www.eye-books.com

Eye Books is a small, independent publisher founded in 1996 with the aim of publishing books about the extraordinary things ordinary people have done: everyday people who decide to stop talking about their life and actually go out and grab it. There is often a strong travel element to these stories.

Lightning Books is a new independent publisher founded in 2015 with the aim of creating a process to allow authors and publishers to work better together and give authors the chance to earn up to 50 percent of their royalties.

Eye Books and Lightning Books have agreed to work in association. Eye Books is offering Lightning Books access to its 20+ year history and infrastructure in return for having exclusive access to Lightning Books' proprietary publishing process. Lightning Books is using its proprietary process in conjunction with access to the Eye Books infrastructure.

Together they aim to publish books that challenge the way we see things, with Eye Books focusing on non-fiction and Lightning Books on fiction.

Like our writers, we passionately believe that the more you put into life, the more you get out of it. We also know that it isn't easy to stop what you know and start what you don't know. Through the books we publish we hope to inform, educate, motive and inspire our readers to be able to let go and do what they think they can't do, however big or small. We believe that by challenging the way we see things, we can evolve and grow and hope our books – both fiction and non-fiction – help readers achieve this.